Defending
the Faith

Also by Richard Abanes

Embraced by the Light and the Bible
Journey into the Light
American Militias

Defending
the Faith

*A Beginner's Guide
to Cults and New Religions*

Richard Abanes

Baker Books

A Division of Baker Book House Co
Grand Rapids, Michigan 49516

Published by Baker Books
a division of Baker Book House Company
P.O. Box 6287, Grand Rapids, MI 49516-6287

Printed in the United States of America

Library of Congress Cataloging-in-Publication Data

Abanes, Richard.
    Defending the faith : a beginner's guide to cults and new religions / Richard Abanes.
        p.   cm.
    Includes bibliographical references (pp. 227–28) and index.
    ISBN 0-8010-5782-5 (pbk.)
    1. Apologetics. 2. Theology, Doctrinal. 3. Cults—Controversial literature.
4. Christian sects—Controversial literature. 5. Sects—Controversial literature. I. Title.
BT1102.A28   1997
239'.93—dc21   97-23941

For current information about all releases from Baker Book House, visit our web site:
http://www.bakerbooks.com

For all Christians who tirelessly and lovingly share the gospel with cultists

> Therefore, my beloved brethren, be steadfast, immovable, always abounding in the work of the Lord, knowing that your toil is not in vain in the Lord.
>
> 1 Corinthians 15:58

Contents

7

Acknowledgments

Thanks must first go to my wife, Bri, for the unending supply of love and encouragement she has given me throughout my many projects. Her worth far exceeds that of the most precious jewels (Prov. 31:10–11).

To all of my friends and family who have diligently kept me in prayer, I am sincerely indebted. I could not have completed this manuscript without their intercession.

A word of gratitude also belongs to the many countercult ministries around the country. Their resources were extremely useful in producing this book. Especially helpful were the materials received from the Christian Research Institute; Answers in Action; Witness, Inc.; Watchman Fellowship; and Personal Freedom Outreach.

Finally, I would like to express my appreciation to the staff of Baker Book House for producing this work in hopes of equipping God's people to "contend earnestly for the faith which was once for all handed down to the saints" (Jude 3).

Introduction

I am a liberal Democrat with a foul mouth and a bad temper. I have spent the last fifteen years as a television writer *(Moon-lighting, Hill Street Blues)* and a creative consultant *(Roseanne, Grace Under Fire)*, promoting the culture of sex and violence corrupting the moral fabric of America. . . . I believe in the theory of evolution; I'd go to war to keep prayer out of public schools; and from what I've observed of American family values, I wouldn't wish them on Jack the Ripper. . . . [Additionally] I don't believe the Bible is the "literal and inerrant Word of God." I think it's a book. . . . Salvation. I don't know what that means. . . . [F]rankly, the word *saved* makes me cringe unless it's being used to describe someone pulled from a burning car. Here's my bottom line on the whole issue: Any god who would send Gandhi (or for that matter George Burns) to hell for not having accepted Jesus as his personal savior is not someone I'd want to spend a day with, much less all of eternity. . . . The point is, I am a pretty average Christian.

Karen Hall
television writer[1]

I became a born-again believer in 1979 at the age of seventeen. I can still remember how fervently I told my friends about Christ, how shocked my parents looked when I began heading out the door on Sunday mornings "all dressed up for church," and how unabashedly I passed out *Jesus Is the Answer* tracts to surprised strangers quietly munching tasty treats at my favorite neighborhood hangout—Mr. Donut. I also can recall how encouraging and exciting it was whenever a new acquaintance said to me, "I'm a Christian too." Simply put, those were the good old days.

I have since made two important discoveries. First, not everyone wants to hear about Jesus Christ. Some individuals, in fact, can be quite adamant when expressing themselves on this point. Second, not everyone who claims to be a Christian really *is* a Christian (Matt. 7:15, 21–23). My latter discovery may be more obvious today than ever before. False believers are so common within our society that the word *Christian* has lost virtually all of its theological specificity.

In previous centuries, of course, things were different. For hundreds of years it was widely understood that a "Christian" was someone who embraced the doctrines outlined and defined by one or more of the church's creeds (statements of belief). Some of the most well known and popular include the Apostles' Creed in its various forms (A.D. 341, 350, 354–430, 390, 570, fifth–sixth century), the Nicene Creed (A.D. 325), the Niceno-Constantinopolitan Creed (A.D. 381), the Chalcedonian Creed (A.D. 451), and the Athanasian Creed (eighth–ninth century).[2] These official affirmations of faith provided a standard by which a person's religious beliefs could be judged as either orthodox or heretical. The declarations gave a clear and concise expression of those doctrines, which, if confessed by an individual, placed him or her within the Christian community.

Until the 1800s such articles of faith served as fairly accurate standards by which one could determine the validity of another person's Christian profession. But the doctrinal significance of all the creeds began to dramatically decrease as newly formed, non-Christian religious groups started using biblical terminology "but in an entirely different sense from that intended by the writers of Scripture."[3]

Consider Mormonism, also known as the Church of Jesus Christ of Latter-day Saints (LDS), which was founded in the 1830s by Joseph Smith. Mormons claim to believe in both God the Father and Jesus Christ. Consequently, their church is often thought of as just another Christian denomination. In reality, however, the LDS view of God the Father and of Jesus Christ differs radically from that of true Christianity. Unlike Christians, Mormons maintain that heavenly Father is a spiritually advanced man who produces spirit children via celestial sex with a heavenly wife. Jesus, according to LDS doctrine, is one of these children. He is also said to be the spirit-brother of Lucifer.[4]

This practice of theological term switching is regularly used by non-Christians to promote their churches, religious communes, and "Bible studies." Some of these groups—usually referred to either as cults or new religious movements—have been able to attract millions of followers. In his landmark book *The Kingdom of the Cults*, Dr. Walter Martin made a very important observation regarding word usage by cults.

> The average non-Christian cult owes its very existence to the fact that it has utilized the terminology of Christianity [e.g., Jesus Christ, God, salvation], has borrowed liberally from the Bible, almost always out of context, and sprinkled its format with evangelical clichés and terms wherever possible or advantageous. . . . [T]his has been a highly successful attempt to represent their respective systems of thought as "Christian."[5]

Unfortunately a growing number of people are starting to view non-Christian cults as legitimate forms of Christianity. Religion scholars at American seminaries and universities, for example, are teaching that it is spiritually naive and intellectually narrow-minded not to recognize as Christian any group claiming to be Christian, even if that group's doctrinal views bear little resemblance to historical Christianity.[6]

Furthermore, several mainstream denominations (Episcopalians, Presbyterians, United Methodists, etc.) are granting membership and ministerial credentials to persons who openly reject key biblical doctrines such as the virgin birth, Christ's deity, Jesus' resurrection, and salvation by grace through faith.[7] No one, it seems, is to be excluded from the Christian category if that is the category in which they wish to be included.

It is not surprising that cults and new religious movements, under the guise of "Christianity," are gaining converts at alarmingly rapid rates. It is also no surprise that a 1996 survey by the Barna Research Group found that eight out of ten (84 percent) persons claiming to be born-again believers held nonbiblical views on at least one of eight statements concerning key doctrines of the Christian faith. Thirty-nine percent of those surveyed agreed that "if a person is generally good, or does enough good things for others during their life, they will earn a place in heaven." Thirty percent stated that "Jesus Christ was a great teacher, but he did not come back to physical life after he was crucified." In many cases, according to this survey, "the beliefs of born-again Christians were not too different from those of non-Christian Americans."[8]

Clearly, the secular community and the Christian church are suffering from a severe lack of understanding when it comes to orthodox Christian beliefs and the way cults and new religious movements distort them. It is my hope that *Defending the Faith* will dispel at least some of this confusion in a concise, easy-to-understand fashion that is both thought-provoking and user-friendly.

Persons unfamiliar with biblical doctrine and/or non-Christian cults should note that this book is not a technical manual on theology, nor is it a scholarly volume meant to foster debate among high-minded academicians. It is a beginner's guide. It should, therefore, provide a relatively easy path on which even the most doctrinally insecure Christian can safely walk while journeying toward an understanding of the essential Christian beliefs that the cults deny.

Unlike most books on cults, *Defending the Faith* does not take a cult-by-cult approach. Instead, the church's creeds will serve as an outline for our text. Each chapter explains one Christian belief, then goes on to show how that one belief is twisted by today's various cults and new religious movements. Before diving into doctrine, however, a few basics about the world of the cults must first be discussed. These cult basics will be the subject of part 1.

People think that . . . it's only the dregs of society who get into cults, but that is simply not true. . . . Almost everybody, at some time, is vulnerable to joining these groups.

Margaret Singer, Ph.D.
University of California, Berkeley

Christians have a worldview that is based on Scripture. Branch Davidians have this same kind of thing. They have a presuppositional base, a worldview set in their minds through which they interpret everything. All the information they receive they put through this interpretational system. . . . When they start to get information that would normally indicate, or should indicate, "Well, wait a minute, this is wrong, this is false, something's funny here," instead they interpret it by running through their processing system and figure a way out of the dilemma. They'd work it out to where they'd think, "No, this is okay. This is God's doing. God works in mysterious ways," and then blah, blah, blah. So, this idea that they were mindless, unthinking people is not true. They thought a lot. They did a lot of thinking, a lot of analyzing, and a lot of data processing, but their entire base, their entire worldview, their presuppositional base was completely crazy. It was false.

David Bunds
former Branch Davidian

Cult Basics

1

A Clear and Present Danger

Those who cannot remember the past are condemned to re-
peat it.

George Santayana (1863–1952)
Spanish philosopher[1]

The 1990s may go down in history as the decade of cults. Consider a
few of the newspaper headlines that appeared during this era: "4 Federal Agents Killed in Shootout with Cult in Texas"; "Swiss Cult's
Bizarre Last Act Leaves 'Wax Museum' of Death"; "Secretive Japanese Cult Linked to Germ Weapons Plan."[2]

Not since the 1978 mass murder-suicide of more than nine hundred people at Jonestown, Guyana, has cult awareness throughout
the world been so high. Concerned individuals everywhere, although
separated by distance, cultural background, and social status, are ask-
ing the same question: How can I protect myself and my loved ones
from the destructive influence of religious cults?

Before answering this question, a review of the most recent cult-
related tragedies is necessary. Only by familiarizing ourselves with
these horrors can we understand the importance of confronting cults
and the Christian's responsibility to bring doctrinal enlightenment
to persons lost in cultic belief systems (2 Tim. 2:24–26). A look back
will be our first step forward into the destructive world of the cults.

17

Korean Devastation

I anxiously waited in my car for B. J. Oropeza, a fellow author with an extensive background in ministering to cultists. It was slightly before 11:00 P.M., and the streets of Pasadena, California, were nearly deserted. I had been there for more than an hour. Just as I was about to call it quits and head home, a battered Yugo turned the corner and pulled up beside me.

"I thought you weren't going to make it," I grumbled, rolling down my window.

B. J.'s reply was surprisingly calm: "It's not even eleven o'clock yet."

Interpreting his unhurried attitude as a mark of experience, I overlooked his tardiness and proceeded to follow him to our destination. A half hour later we were standing outside a Korean church situated on a desolate road in downtown Los Angeles. According to worshipers inside the old building, Jesus' second coming and the departure of all Christians to heaven would take place within thirty minutes. Security guards stationed outside the church facility had been instructed to prevent nonmembers from entering. As a result, B. J. and I were forced to wait in the cold evening air for Jesus' midnight arrival.

But the Lord never came. Only a few relatives of church members showed up to console loved ones who might leave the late-night religious service after realizing that doomsday was not going to materialize. That evening brought to a close nearly two years of misguided hopes and planned deception. It was a tragic tale that first gained national attention through a full-page ad appearing in the October 20, 1991, issue of USA *Today:*

RAPTURE
OCTOBER 28, 1992
JESUS IS COMING IN
THE AIR

This was only one of many warnings distributed by Bible-based groups associated with the Korean *Hyoo-go* ("Rapture") movement. One sect predicted that beginning on October 28, 1992, "50 million people will die in earthquakes, 50 million from collapsed buildings,

1.4 billion from World War III and 1.4 billion from a separate Armageddon."[3]

The instigating force behind the fear-filled movement was Lee Jang Rim's Korean best-seller *Getting Close to the End,* which promoted an October 28, 1992, date for the end of the world. Churches involved in the movement included Rim's Dami Church (known in the United States as Mission for the Coming Days), Taberah World Mission, Shalom Church, and Maranatha Mission Church. The number of followers reportedly fluctuated between twenty thousand and one hundred thousand.[4]

Adherents to the movement appealed to numerous sources in addition to Rim's teachings to support their doomsday deadline. One brochure, produced by Taberah World Missions, borrowed a twisted time calculation made by American prophecy pundit Jack Van Impe.[5] Divine revelations given to a twelve-year-old boy named Bang-ik Ha also were used to confirm the October date.[6]

As "the end" drew nearer, social disruption mounted in South Korea. Believers quit their jobs, sold their homes, abandoned their families, and ran up debts. Several pregnant women reportedly had abortions "so they would not be too heavy to be lifted to heaven" and at least four followers "committed suicide before October 28."[7] Police agencies, fire companies, and ambulances were all placed on alert in an effort to prevent a second Jonestown.

When the predicted date finally arrived, thousands gathered in churches around the world, especially in Korea, to await their glorious departure into the heavens. The South Korean government responded by dispatching fifteen hundred riot police to Mission for the Coming Days, one of Seoul's largest *Hyoo-go* churches. Fifteen minutes after the deadline passed, Rev. Chang Man-Ho—pastor of the Mission for the Coming Days—took the pulpit and simply said, "Nothing has happened. Sorry. Let's go home."[8]

Loyal followers were outraged and brokenhearted. Many began weeping uncontrollably. Some physically attacked the preachers who had misled them. One distraught member tearfully commented, "God lied to us."[9] Months after the disappointment, parents were still searching for children "who were kidnapped and taken to mountain hideouts by some of the more radical rapture sects."[10]

Forty-six-year-old Lee Jang Rim was eventually sentenced by a Korean court to two years in prison for "defrauding believers out of four million dollars and illegally possessing United States currency."[11] His conviction and the movement's failed prophecy left the Korean community shocked and emotionally shattered. But four months later their sufferings were obscured and eclipsed as the attention of the world's media was grabbed by another doomsday cult—the Branch Davidians.

Unforgettable Waco

Hardly any trace remains of what occurred on the outskirts of Waco between February 28 and April 19, 1993. Time, bulldozers, and the dusty winds that blow across the lonely flatlands of East Texas have virtually erased the reminders of the Branch Davidian tragedy. Nevertheless, the fiery image of nearly one hundred cultists dying at the hands of government authorities has been forever seared into American minds.

Few events in this country's recent history have so greatly charged emotions and divided public opinion as has the Waco disaster. Debates about religious freedoms, gun control, government conspiracies, and a host of related issues sprang from the incident like water from a broken dam. The resulting deluge of newspaper stories, magazine articles, and television specials still haunts our nation's collective consciousness.

The bloody saga began in February 1993 when one hundred armed agents of the Bureau of Alcohol, Tobacco, and Firearms (BATF) raided the isolated Davidian compound. Federal authorities stormed the fortress because cult members—led by David Koresh, their "Son of God" prophet—had stockpiled an enormous cache of weapons, many of them illegal.[12] To the Davidians' prophecy-gorged minds, however, the intruders had come to fulfill a different destiny—Armageddon.

When the smoke cleared from the gun battle that followed, four BATF agents were dead and sixteen other agents were wounded. Six Davidians had also been killed. The ensuing fifty-one-day standoff pitted government might against religious fanaticism in a deadly game that had no rules. For example, FBI negotiators with extremely limited religious backgrounds and little biblical knowledge were forced to deal with Koresh, who spoke about nothing but Scripture and prophecy.

Complicating the situation was dissension within the government's own ranks about how to handle the siege.[13] FBI negotiators wanted to end the stalemate through diplomacy. FBI tacticians chose psychological terrorism, which included shining powerful spotlights into the compound at night and blasting the religious group with loud music, Tibetan chants, sirens, and the ear-shattering screams of rabbits being slaughtered.[14] This latter approach only strengthened the Davidians' "us against them" mentality and bolstered their view that the outside world, especially the government, was utterly evil and untrustworthy.

On April 19 the government initiated a plan to force an end to the standoff. Unfortunately Justice Department officials failed to calculate one factor into their decision—religious fervor. Six hours after the introduction of tear gas into the Davidians' domicile, tiny puffs of smoke began to seep through one of its many second-story windows. Minutes later, the entire structure was engulfed in flames. The world watched in disbelief as the Branch Davidian fortress burst into a city-block-sized funeral pyre. Only nine cult members escaped. Coroner reports indicated that although many Davidians perished from smoke inhalation and fire, a significant number of them, including Koresh, died from a single gunshot wound to the head.

Interestingly, several Davidians were well-educated and intelligent individuals. Group members included an attorney, a nurse, an engineer, and a former police officer. Such a collection of respectable citizens destroyed once and for all the false notion that only the ignorant, foolish, or unintelligent get involved in destructive religious cults. This point would be made again in 1994 by the Order of the Solar Temple. Its deadly influence stretched from Canada to Switzerland to France.

Order of the Sun

Gruesome, shocking, and bizarre is how public officials and police referred to the series of cult-related deaths that began just after midnight on Wednesday, October 5, 1994, when "villagers in the tiny Swiss farm community of Cheiry, 45 miles northeast of Geneva, saw the moonless sky lit by flames over the farmhouse of Albert Giacobino, a wealthy retired farmer who had bought the place four years [earlier]."[15] By the time fire engines from nearby Fribourg arrived on the scene, the secluded dwelling was fully engulfed in flames. Three hours later, when firefighters were finally able to enter the burned-out ruins, they found Giacobino lying dead in his bed. A plastic bag tied around his head concealed a bullet wound.[16]

Further exploration of the property by police yielded an underground garage leading to a door. This opened into a meeting room containing, among other things, a trail of blood that stopped at the room's wooden paneling. A secret entranceway in the wall accessed a small, inner sanctuary decorated entirely in red. Investigators who entered it were horrified by the sight of eighteen bodies—men, women, and a boy about ten years old—arranged in a circle, face up, beneath the portrait of a robed Christlike figure holding a rose. Another corpse was eventually found in an adjacent room. Three more bodies were discovered in an adjoining chapel.

Many of the victims wore either red-and-black or white-and-gold ceremonial robes. Some of them had their hands tied behind their backs; ten had plastic bags over their heads. Most of those killed had been drugged with a substance described by Swiss investigating magistrate André Piller as "a powerful violent substance."[17] Twenty of the victims had been shot in the head at close range. According to a forensics expert at the University of Lausanne's Institute for Legal Medicine, some of the victims at Cheiry had as many as eight bullet wounds in the head.[18]

At approximately 3:00 A.M., as police officials were still trying to piece together what had happened in Cheiry, another fire broke out one hundred miles south at three neighboring ski chalets in the small city of Granges-sur-Salvan. Firefighters sifting through the rubble of these chalets uncovered another macabre sight: "25 bodies, all of them badly burned, including the remains of at least five children."[19]

Within twenty-four hours, Canadian authorities halfway around the world were confronted with their own grisly discoveries at Morin Heights, Quebec. Fire had broken out in another remote chalet. Inside this isolated retreat, authorities found the badly burned bodies of a man and a woman wearing red-and-gold medallions engraved with the letters *TS*. In a nearby villa, police found three more bodies: those of Tony and Nikki Dutoit and their three-month-old son, Christopher.[20] The couple in their mid-thirties had been stabbed perhaps fifty times and then rolled in carpet. Christopher had been suffocated and "stuffed behind a water heater with a bag over his head."[21]

All of the persons found dead were members of a highly secretive religious cult known as the Order of the Solar Temple, which blended elements of astrology, freemasonry, New Age spiritualism, occultism, and quasi-Christian beliefs focusing on doomsday. The group was led by forty-six-year-old Luc Jouret and seventy-year-old Joseph di Mambre. Jouret, a Belgian homeopathic doctor, founded the group in 1987 and served as its spiritual leader. Di Mambre, a shadowy figure who had served six months in a French jail in 1972 for posing as a psychologist, was the group's financial director. The bodies of both men were found in the Salvan chalets.[22]

One victim carried a note in her clothing, which she had addressed to surviving relatives. It stated that she had come to Switzerland to die. Three other letters with similar messages were sent by cult members to Jean-Francois Mayer, a Swiss authority. One read: "We leave this Earth in full freedom and lucidity in order to find a dimension of Truth and Absolute, far from the hypocrisies and oppression of this world."[23]

Cassette tapes and documents uncovered near the bodies indicated that the killings were indeed linked to a belief that the end of the world was imminent. Jouret apparently had convinced his followers that the world's destruction would result from humanity's degradation of the environment.[24] "The present world chaos is not just by chance," Jouret taught his followers. "We have arrived at the hour of Apocalypse."[25] According to former members, Jouret also taught that only those who joined him would escape perdition because he, as the "new Christ," had been chosen to save them.[26]

Even after the fifty-three deaths, faithful members of the Temple who had not been part of the suicide-murders remained faithful to Jouret's teachings. Then, fourteen months later, some of these surviving members decided that their time had come to enter the spiritual realm and join their master. The method of departure was a second wave of grisly suicide-murders. Their bodies were discovered after

Swiss and French authorities launched a massive hunt for Solar Temple members in December 1995.

Law enforcement officials began the search when sixteen cultists—half from France and half from Canada—were reported missing.[27] Within days a helicopter spotted burned corpses on a remote forest plateau in the Alps of southeastern France. Fourteen of the sixteen bodies were arranged in a star pattern. The victims had used shooting, poisoning, stabbing, and asphyxiation to complete their elaborate deaths. Most of the corpses had plastic bags over their heads.

The two cultists not found in the star pattern had acted as executioners, methodically shooting fellow believers in the head before killing themselves with bullets delivered under the chin. Among those murdered with a .357 magnum were two sisters aged two and four, daughters of policeman Jean-Pierre Lardanchet, who had acted as one of the executioners.[28] A note retrieved from a victim's apartment read: "Death does not exist, it is pure illusion. May we, by our inner life, find each other forever."[29]

Investigators have since learned that the 1994 ritual "was designed to take sect members through fire to a new world on a planet called 'Sirius.'"[30] Cultists who did not participate in the first ceremony may have believed that their deaths in 1995 would lead them to a similar destination.

This is not to say that all of the victims died willingly. A final Swiss report noted that only fifteen of the dead—a fanatical inner circle known as the "awakened"—committed suicide. Another thirty, called the "immortals," shared the apocalyptic beliefs of their leaders but did not kill themselves voluntarily. The rest of the victims, classified as "traitors," were murdered. As of 1997 French authorities remained apprehensive about surviving Solar Temple believers, fearing that devotees might make new converts and instigate more suicide-murders.[31]

It must be noted that Jouret's followers were not spaced-out losers with a far-off look in their eyes. They were well-respected citizens of the European and Canadian communities, who often dined in expensive restaurants and contributed millions to Jouret's twisted religion. Victims of his deception included two police officers, a psychotherapist, an architect, an official in the Quebec finance ministry, and the mayor of Richelieu, Quebec.

The most notable cultist to die was twenty-seven-year-old Patrick Vuarnet, son of skier Jean Vuarnet, the 1960 Winter Olympics gold medalist who became famous for his line of designer sunglasses. Patrick's woman companion, Ute Vérona, and their six-year-old daughter, Tania, also were among the dead.[32] According to Alain Vuarnet, his brother Patrick had always felt guilty for not being in the first group of Temple members to die. During one confrontation, Alain remembers Patrick saying, "Alain, you are the one deluding yourself. You just don't understand."[33]

Aum: Death in the Far East

On March 20, 1995, the world witnessed yet another deadly episode involving misguided religious zeal. This time cult-related tragedy struck the lives of innocent citizens in Tokyo. Members of Aum Shinrikyo ("Supreme Truth") released sarin—a Nazi-invented nerve gas—into the Japanese subway system. Twelve people died, and close to six thousand commuters were sickened with nausea, blurred vision, and breathing problems symptomatic of exposure to biological weapons.[34]

Police immediately began searching for the cult's leader, forty-year-old Shoko Asahara, who had disappeared the day after the attack. In an effort to locate Asahara, Japanese authorities conducted a series of raids at various Aum sites throughout the country. The raids brought forth evidence that the cult was producing sarin and that its members were definitely involved in the subway attacks.[35]

The terrorist act was linked to the cult's belief concerning doomsday, which Asahara—who called himself today's Christ—said would begin between 1999 and 2003.[36] In his March 1995 book *Rising Sun Country: Disaster Is Getting Close*, Asahara prophesied that nerve gas would be the weapon of choice used during Armageddon. Additionally, the volume detailed the chemical characteristics of sarin, how to mix it, and how to treat symptoms if exposed to it.[37] But Asahara obviously wanted World War III to begin sooner than he had predicted.

> The big show was apparently set for November, when plans called for cult attacks on government buildings . . . to spark what Asahara saw

as a world war. . . . To triumph in that war, the cult built a series of munitions factories . . . Aum researchers were trying to develop germ weapons—including the Ebola virus—and an assembly line was about to produce automatic rifles. Behind one building's false walls was a $700,000 lab able to turn out 132 to 176 lbs. a month of the nerve gas sarin—enough to kill 6 million to 8 million people.[38]

Fifty-seven days after the subway attack, Asahara was finally tracked down. He was found lying face down and meditating inside a coffin-like chamber located between two floors of a building at the cult's Kamikuishiki compound. The ten-foot-long by three-feet-high hiding space also contained a cassette player, some medicine, and the equivalent of about $100,000 in cash. When police officers attempted to climb in and get Asahara, he declared: "I'll come out myself. No one, not even my followers, is allowed to touch me."[39]

This was not Asahara's first run-in with the law. In 1982 he was taken into custody and fined for selling fake cures for rheumatism and other diseases.[40] This minor brush with police authorities did not dissuade Asahara. By 1986 he had started his own religion and was claiming the power of levitation. "Now, the length of time I can levitate is about three seconds, but this period of time is gradually lengthening," Asahara told the occult magazine *Twilight Zone*. "In about a year, I should be able to fly freely through the sky."[41]

By 1987 he was telling devotees that he had received secret teachings from the Dalai Lama and had gained the ability to see through objects and meditate underwater.[42] This same year Asahara changed the name of his cult to Aum Shinrikyo. Less than a decade later, he had solidified a vast empire of "over 40,000 followers in over 30 branches in at least six countries, and a global network which had acquired sophisticated lasers, chemical reactors and a Russian military helicopter."[43]

Asahara cleverly used his new religion to fund numerous businesses "ranging from computer stores to noodle shops, with holdings as high as $1.1 million."[44] Most of Aum's financing came from wealthy members who were instructed to donate all of their monetary resources to the cult if they wanted to obtain salvation. The group's total assets eventually rose to more than $1 billion.[45]

With each passing year, Aum's belief system—a blending of Buddhism, Hinduism, and Christian apocalypticism—grew more bizarre. For approximately $600, members were given the privilege of drinking Asahara's bath water; a glass of his blood to drink cost about $12,000.[46] For $10,000, Aum believers could rent a special battery-operated piece of headgear designed to synchronize their brainwaves with those of their "Venerated Master."[47] Cleansing rituals that followers were forced to endure included drinking five liters of water and then vomiting it back up.[48] A particularly strange initiation rite practiced by the group was examined in a January 1995 issue of *Focus*, a popular news and lifestyle magazine.

> First, one drinks some liquid. For 20 hours they see hallucinations. One who experienced it said he could see colorful objects, or things collapsing, and that he had no hearing. If during this hallucination one gets a fever, they pour ethyl alcohol on the person's body to reduce the fever. After 20 hours, diuretics and purgatives are given to get the substance out of the body. During this initiation, they have to wear diapers.[49]

Unusual forms of physical, mental, and emotional abuse soon became a standard practice in Aum. When police raided its Kamikuishiki compound, they found approximately fifty cultists in a state of malnutrition. Many suffered from dehydration. Some were near starvation. Six members in critical condition had to be hospitalized. A twenty-three-year-old woman found hiding in a toilet stall pleaded with police for protection. She apparently had been confined inside a small container for many days.[50]

Torture and intimidation were commonly used against cult members. Persons trying to leave, for example, were bound with handcuffs and imprisoned inside small cargo containers so they could atone for their sins.[51] Some were even given electric shocks: "During one three-month period beginning in October 1994, Dr. Hayashi [a high-ranking Aum doctor] administered more than 600 electric shocks to 130 followers. Afterward, some of them forgot which cult they were in, what the guru was called, even their own names."[52]

Even Aum children were made to suffer. Authorities reported that some of them "were so dirty with matted hair, lice and fleas that they could not immediately tell which were boys and which were girls. . . .

Their living quarters were cramped and dirty. All of the children wore long-sleeved garments even in the summer because 'there was poison outside.'"[53]

Aum leaders also conducted biological experiments on less important followers.[54] Medical tests done on seven cultists rescued from Aum's Satian No. 10 site revealed highly unusual blood characteristics. One had been poisoned by sarin. Another had blood level readings that registered a particular enzyme at forty times its normal level. This latter patient told police: "Every day I was forced to take water mixed with white powder, and also I was supposed to get injections."[55] The victim's symptoms included memory loss and severe muscle stiffness.

Only after Asahara's arrest did the full extent of Aum's criminal activities come to light. One case involved sixty-eight-year-old Kiyoshi Kariya, who in February 1995 tried to keep his sister from giving her wealth to Aum. The sister disappeared and Kariya was abducted by four men. Mystery surrounded the event until after the subway attack, when a senior cult member who had been arrested confessed that Kariya was murdered at one of Aum's compounds. The body was burned in an incinerator.

Another kidnapping-murder dated back to June 1989, just after attorney Tsutsumi Sakamoto began representing a family trying to locate their child in Aum. On November 4, 1989, Sakamoto, his wife, and their one-year-old infant son disappeared. Although friends found an Aum lapel badge in Sakamoto's disheveled apartment, no substantial evidence linking the cult to the crime scene could be found. However, police suspicions were confirmed in 1996 when Tomomasa Nakagawa—a former Aum leader—pleaded guilty to murdering Sakamoto and his family.

> A six-man Aum hit team . . . had entered the lawyer's apartment shortly before dawn, killed the sleeping family, wrapped their bodies in futons, and removed them under cover of darkness. . . . The team strangled Sakamoto and his wife, and smothered their baby. Nakagawa said that Asahara personally ordered the lawyer killed.[56]

At the outset of Asahara's trial on April 24, 1996, the guru faced seventeen charges, including murder and attempted murder, for which the penalty is death by hanging.[57] Throughout subsequent months of testimony, Asahara frequently interrupted proceedings. During one outburst he declared that "fear of his own death had forced him to plot the nerve gas attack."[58] He became extremely agitated when former aide Yoshihiro Inoue began testifying about Asahara's teachings concerning salvation through terrorism. Inoue also stated that the Aum leader had personally plotted attacks against "anything that challenged (his) teachings." Asahara reacted to these charges by proclaiming that "the gods told him that they did not want Inoue taking the stand."[59]

By early 1997, 100 of the 177 Aum members who had been indicted for crimes they committed on behalf of the cult had been convicted. Aum Shinrikyo itself declared bankruptcy soon after a court seized its assets and ordered it disbanded.[60] What of Asahara? His fate may not be known for ten years due to Japan's legal system, which can be rather slow. Many Japanese have called for his execution.

One of the most mystifying aspects of Aum was its membership, which consisted of some of Japan's most promising minds.[61] Converts included lawyers, doctors, and scientists from Japan's top universities, as well as several policemen and thirty members of the Self-Defense Forces, Japan's army.[62] According to a 1995 *Newsweek* article, Japanese citizens were puzzled that "bright young men with impressive university credentials would join the cult, when they could have had fine careers."[63]

A Constant Threat

One might be tempted to think that these high profile cult cases are the only ones that have taken place in recent years. Nothing could be further from the truth. An endless list of cult-related episodes have occurred in the 1990s. Unfortunately smaller tragedies involving lesser known cults rarely receive widespread public attention.

On March 8, 1995, for instance, twenty-five-year-old Kyong-A Ha was beaten to death in Emeryville, California, during an all-night prayer meeting held to cast demons out of her. Ha's death remained unreported for four days by members of Jesus-Amen Ministries because

they believed her spirit would "return from a journey to heaven."[64]
The exorcism began on March 1, when Ha was pinned down by faithful followers of Eun Kyong Park, a thirty-year-old exorcist. She was
then repeatedly struck with fists. On the night Ha died, she was struck
at least one hundred times over a six-hour period and suffered ten
broken ribs.[65]

In mid-1995, Washington, D.C., police arrested thirty-year-old
Robert Floyd, the leader of a cult known as the Daughters of Yemoja.
Floyd was taken into custody and charged with kidnapping after one
of his female disciples told police that she had been forced against
her will to take part in a bizarre ritual on a Maryland farm. The twenty-
eight-year-old woman had angered other members of the cult by
returning home at 2:00 A.M. after spending time with a male companion. As punishment, she was subsequently prevented from going
to bed, blindfolded, and driven to the Maryland farm. She was beaten,
made to roll in excrement, and forced to smear duck blood on herself. She was then sexually assaulted.[66]

The 1990s also witnessed the unnecessary deaths of nearly a dozen
children at the Pennsylvania-based Faith Tabernacle. Common ail-
ments ranging from stomach tumors to pneumonia to measles went
untreated because of the church's teaching that using *any* form of
medicinal assistance shows a lack of faith. A Faith Tabernacle tract
titled *Death of Self* explains their doctrine:

> The Bible plan is to trust in the living God alone, without the slight-
> est remedy of any kind, not even a cup of hot water for dyspepsia, or
> hot lemonade for a cold, or bathing the feet in mustard water for the
> same. The Bible does not permit the slightest remedy upon which we
> could place the least dependence for help.[67]

Of course, not all cults are as extreme as the aforementioned groups.
Many function well within the law, shun violence, and even promote
a few positive social values. Into this category would fall cults like the
Jehovah's Witnesses and Mormons. An obvious question arises:
Exactly how and why is a group defined as a cult?

2

World of the Cults

We do not intend to be demeaning or derogatory when we use the word *cult*. Members of religious cults are usually no different from our next-door neighbor or our colleagues at work.

Ronald Enroth
sociologist
Westmont College[1]

German theologian Ernst Troeltsch (1865–1923) coined the term *cult* in his classic work *The Social Teaching of the Christian Churches* (1912). He applied the designation to any spiritually oriented group or movement that was neither a church nor a sect.[2] Eventually, however, the word *cult* evolved into a disparaging label for any group advocating "curious and unconventional belief and behavior."[3] The 1978 Jonestown tragedy not only reinforced this definition but added an element of danger to it. Most people today continue to think of a cult as a bizarre and destructive religious body that is under the leadership of a crazed, authoritarian, messiah figure.

As we have seen, some groups should indeed be viewed in this manner. Their practices radically depart from societal norms and are quite harmful. But many cults bear little resemblance to groups such as Aum or the Branch Davidians. Consider the Mormons, Jehovah's Witnesses, and Oneness Pentecostals. Each of these organizations have churches in almost every American city, post a worldwide membership well into the millions, peacefully coexist with their neighbors, and enjoy a widespread positive image. Nevertheless, these same groups are viewed as cultic by vast numbers of people, including many scholars, theologians, journalists, and members of the general public.

Cult Controversies

Is it fair to put groups as dissimilar as Aum and Mormonism into one large cult category? I believe it is, as long as great care is taken when stating exactly why a certain religious body is a cult. Scholars generally examine religious groups from three main perspectives: sociological, psychological, and theological. Each perspective focuses on a different aspect of a group's complex composition and includes numerous "red flags" indicating whether an organization is cultic from that particular perspective. If one or more psychological, sociological, or theological red flags are present, then that group can properly be considered a cult. Some groups might be cultic from only one perspective, while others might be cultic from all three perspectives.

Unfortunately, this tri-faceted way of identifying cults can lead to confusion. For example, someone unfamiliar with the unique structure of religious organizations might conclude that a nonviolent cult such as the Jehovah's Witnesses is as murderous and socially deviant as the Order of the Solar Temple, merely because both groups are referred to as cults. This would be a terrible mistake. Religion professor Irving Hexham believes that it is better to discard the term *cult* altogether in favor of a neutral term like "new religious movement."[4]

Predictably, nontraditional religious bodies not only prefer this less inflammatory language but strongly object to being called a cult. Members claim that the term unfairly places them in an extremist category, damages their reputations, hinders their constitutional right to freedom of religion, and subjects them to religious persecution. The cult label also allegedly frightens away potential converts. Members maintain that the negative description slanders their integrity and that of the organization. A few of these groups have actually brought lawsuits against their critics for using the term *cult* against them.[5]

Many sociologists have all but abandoned using the term *cult* in favor of nonjudgmental descriptions (e.g., *fringe, alternative, uncon-*

ventional). For these scholarly religion-watchers, making an extra effort to show impartiality by avoiding biased language might be acceptable. For Christians, however, vague terminology fails to adequately address whether a group claiming to be Christian really is Christian. Hexham offers a suggestion:

> [T]he academic practice of calling such groups "new religious movements" should be followed. An alternative to this neutral terminology available for Christians who oppose such groups would be to revive the usage of "heretic" or simply call such groups "spiritual counterfeits."[6]

Hexham's comment raises an important issue. In studying cults, a Christian should be primarily concerned with the theological errors of a group. We are clearly commanded by Scripture to confront false doctrines and "contend earnestly for [i.e., defend] the faith which was once for all handed down to the saints" (Jude 3). Here is where born-again believers must depart from secularists, who tend to be more interested in an organization's psychological makeup and sociological structure. At the same time, Christians should be able to recognize at least a few psychological and sociological red flags. Therefore we will now take a look at each of the three perspectives that can be used to identify cults (or new religious movements).

Sociological "Red Flags"

Identifying a religious organization as cultic from a sociological perspective involves determining whether that group's religious practices and day-to-day behavior are normative for the surrounding culture. From a sociological perspective, the primary indicator of a group's cultic nature is complete withdrawal from society into a communal, isolated lifestyle. Secondary sociological marks of a cult, at least in America, that are sometimes present include polygamy, incest, adult-child sexual contact, use of illegal narcotics, physical abuse, murder, and the stockpiling of both legal and illegal weapons.

Obviously, sociological red flags tend to appear more frequently in groups that run afoul of the law.[7] We must be careful, however, not to infringe on constitutionally protected forms of religious expression

simply because they diverge from societal norms. Debate regarding
exactly how much freedom is too much freedom remains a heated
and emotional topic that has sparked several court battles. In 1992,
for instance, the U.S. Supreme Court heard a case centering on the
ritualistic killing of animals in Florida by followers of Santeria, a fusion
of Roman Catholicism and African tribal religions (*Church of the
Lukumi Babalu v. City of Hialeah*). The Court ruled that Santerians
should be allowed to practice their sacrifices, even though such acts
are technically illegal and run contrary to established societal norms.[8]

Another dilemma that presents itself when attempting to identify
a cult from the sociological perspective emerges from a surprising
place: sociologists and their literature. Sociologists provide "such a
great variety of reflections that it is practically impossible to come up
with a short, clear-cut, universally acceptable definition."[9] Furthermore, most sociologists, especially those within the secular community, send an unclear message regarding the destructive nature of cults.
Sociologists do not pass judgment on religious groups but simply study
them objectively—in the same way an entomologist might study a
colony of ants. They are primarily interested in the inner workings,
of a cult and how that cult relates to society as a whole.

> [S]ociologists make no judgment on the truth or falsehood of the cults'
> beliefs (as in the theological approach), or on the good or bad effects
> of cult involvement on individual members (as in the psychological
> approach). . . . Sociologists focus on the existence of these new reli-
> gious entities as marginal subcultures or units that are in conflict with
> society at large. They examine the way diverse religious institutions
> and organizations are formed and maintained; the internal dynamics
> that make them viable social entities; their economic, social, and polit-
> ical structures; the type of charismatic leadership that provides divine
> legitimation for the movements' beliefs and practices; and the levels
> and types of commitment demanded of their devotees. . . . They are
> also interested in the conflicts that exist between the new groups and
> the mainline religious traditions and the effects such conflicts might
> have on both. . . . Sociologists study religion as objectively and impar-
> tially as possible. . . . What is important to them is the exploration of
> how and why new values, beliefs, and lifestyles come into being; how
> new religious concepts become popular; and how experimental com-
> munities are formed.[10]

The manner in which sociologists study cults has brought harsh criticism from many observers of the contemporary religious scene, especially parents of cult members and persons associated with organizations committed to helping victims of cult involvement. From the secular community, sociologists regularly receive condemnation for their refusal to pass judgments on religious behavior no matter how psychologically or physically damaging that behavior may be to group members. Irritation within the Christian community centers around sociologists' inclination to "put all religions on the same level." As religion professor John A. Saliba of the University of Detroit Mercy notes, sociologists "are not interested in establishing which religion is true or false, or in defending any one particular religious tradition."[11]

To make matters worse, many sociologists have gone so far as to lend their support to cults in the form of "expert" testimony during lawsuits against distraught parents of cultists and countercult organizations. For example, in a multimillion dollar lawsuit filed by the Church of Scientology against the Cult Awareness Network (CAN), sociologist Anson Shupe testified in opposition to CAN.

The case centered around the alleged abduction of cultist Jason Scott in hopes of deprogramming him.[12] Several persons were involved in the plan to deprogram Scott, including Shirley Landa, a part-time, unpaid CAN volunteer. The lawsuit contended that CAN shared responsibility for the planning and execution of the abduction because Landa had recommended deprogrammer Rick Ross to Jason Scott's mother, who in turn proceeded with the alleged abduction.

Scientology presented no proof of "any foreknowledge of the plan to abduct Mr. Scott let alone any agreement by CAN or its alleged agent to participate in the conspiracy."[13] Nevertheless, the jury found CAN guilty of conspiring to deprive Scott of his civil rights. The verdict was due in part to Shupe's statements concerning the activities of so-called "anticult" groups including CAN.[14] Shupe admitted in court that he knew about CAN's 1988 policy against illegal deprogrammings involving abduction, yet he accused CAN of all but contradicting their official policy by taking a "wink-wink, nudge-nudge approach" to the controversial subject. He voiced his opinion without offering any supportive evidence or documentation.

In CAN's appeal brief to the court, serious doubts are raised about Shupe's neutrality and his "expert" testimony regarding CAN, an organization he had not had any personal contact with since 1976.[15]

[Dr. Shupe's testimony] is completely devoid of any experience, study, or writing about CAN. . . . Dr. Shupe candidly admitted that his colleague [sociologist David G. Bromley], rather than he, had followed CAN. . . . Dr. Shupe admitted to having had interviews with only two CAN personnel over his twenty years of anti-cult "study." . . . Dr. Shupe admitted that he never tried to talk to anyone at CAN about a referral and has never spoken to anyone who has been referred to a deprogrammer by anyone associated with CAN. . . . Dr. Shupe has no specific knowledge, skill, experience, training, or education with respect to CAN upon which any expert opinion about CAN could be based. . . . Dr. Shupe admitted that by the "mid eighties when CAN was formed," its literature did not explicitly recommend deprogramming. . . . Dr. Shupe further admitted that the two CAN personnel he interviewed stated that CAN had a policy against referring people to illegal deprogrammers. . . . Dr. Shupe was not qualified to give opinions about CAN. He simply had no specific training, background, experience, or knowledge about CAN itself to opine about CAN's internal policies. Moreover, Dr. Shupe testified about matters that were irrelevant to CAN but were highly prejudicial. For example, Dr. Shupe was improperly allowed to testify about several egregious illegal deprogrammings that had no relation to CAN in any way. . . . Dr. Shupe's testimony was inflammatory and in other ways prejudiced the ability of the jury to fairly decide the case on the basis of admissible evidence and should have been excluded.[16]

Fortunately there exist a few sociologists willing to stand against cults and the destructive influence they have on individuals and families. Christian sociologist Dr. Ronald Enroth of Westmont College in Santa Barbara has produced a number of books dealing with the sociological danger of cults.[17] According to Enroth, cult leaders

exploit human weaknesses and seek to manipulate individual life situations to the ultimate benefit of the group. The challenge to our society and our churches is to identify the searching, the hurting, the lonely, the unloved people, and to intervene in their lives—in the name of Christ—before they are seduced by the cults.[18]

The Psychological Perspective

Psychologist Michael D. Langone, executive director of the American Family Foundation, notes that the term "cult" is often associated with thought reform (popularly known as "brainwashing"). According to Langone, this "mind control" model of cult involvement suggests "that cult environments, although certainly not 'robot factories,' are compellingly powerful."[19] They are so psychologically powerful, in fact, that cultists allegedly have their personalities radically altered. Furthermore, their ability to make free-will choices is said to be controlled to a large degree by the group's leadership. Psychologists who have adopted this position usually see cultists as *victims* of the group, rather than active participants responding with a totally free will. Langone offers his definition of a cult from this psychological perspective:

> A cult is a group or movement that, to a significant degree, (a) exhibits great or excessive devotion or dedication to some person, idea, or thing, (b) uses a thought-reform program to persuade, control, and socialize members (i.e., to integrate them into the group's unique pattern of relationships, beliefs, values, and practices), (c) systematically induces states of psychological dependency in members, (d) exploits members to advance the leadership's goals, and (e) causes psychological harm to members, their families, and the community.[20]

Langone has been aggressively studying the psychological dynamics of cults since 1978, serving from 1984 to 1987 on the American Psychological Association Task Force on Deceptive and Indirect Techniques of Persuasion and Control. Through counseling hundreds of former cultists, Langone has discovered several psychological red flags common to cults. Each reveals the psychologically manipulative nature of cults:

- Information is withheld from new converts about the group's ultimate agenda.
- The presence of a dictatorial leadership that tells with "excruciating specificity" exactly how members are to think, feel and act.
- An absence of leader accountability to persons outside the group's power structure.[21]

Other religion experts and psychologists have discovered even more ways that cult leaders try to interrupt the normal thought processes of their followers:

1. Isolation of members—psychologically as well as physically—from individuals outside the group whose ideas and philosophies are contrary to those promoted by the group.

2. "Love-bombing" so intense that persons with deep-seated emotional needs are psychologically thrown off balance. They are faced with an agonizing decision: stay with the group and receive love, or leave the group and lose love.

3. A systematic replacement of the pre-conversion identities of members with a new group-related identity. This sometimes includes the destruction of personal possessions and the destruction of family ties.

4. Rapid-fire teaching techniques that do not allow members to think critically about what is being said, coupled with an environment wherein open discussion of relevant issues and the expression of contrary opinions is discouraged.

5. The use of fear and intimidation against members who desire to leave the group, or former members seeking to break ties with the group.

6. Use of deceptive recruitment techniques that include false information about the group's doctrinal beliefs and cover-ups of negative episodes in the group's history.

7. Total, unquestioning allegiance to a central leader or elite core of leaders.

8. The promotion of an "ends justifies the means" philosophy within the group.

9. An "us vs. them" mentality that stresses the group's unique hold on truth and demonizes anyone who opposes that alleged truth.

10. An inordinate emphasis on submission and obedience to group authority, which effectively guilts a person into submission.

11. Consistent stress on the importance of following the divinely revealed truths being taught by a group's leader or leaders.

12. A siege mentality that dismisses all criticisms of the group from outside sources as unwarranted "persecution."

13. Shunning and harsh criticism of "rebellious" members who question the teachings or practices of the group.

14. An elitist attitude that is drilled into members, which states that those outside the group are spiritually lukewarm, comprising, or entirely lost.

15. Excessive control over personal aspects of members' lives: e.g., where to live, where to work, who to date, who to marry, what literature to read, when vacations can be taken, etc.

16. Rigid restrictions relating to the sleeping habits, food intake, exercise, and leisure time of members.[22]

Of course, not every technique must be used by a group in order for it to be cultic from a psychological perspective. Meeting only a few of these points might be enough to legitimately call a group cultic. According to psychologist Margaret Singer—another advocate of the "mind control" model—a cult is basically a power structure wherein "one person [or persons] has proclaimed himself [or herself, or themselves] to have some special knowledge. And if he [or she, or they] can convince others to let him [or her, or them] be in charge, he [or she, or they] will share that knowledge."[23]

But do these practices amount to "brainwashing"? Do cultists really have their wills rendered almost obsolete? Such thought-provoking questions highlight an extremely controversial area of cult studies. Countless debates between organizations trying to help persons involved in authoritarian groups have arisen over this issue. Many cult researchers disagree with the opinion of Langone and Singer, taking the position that cultists are not "brainwashed" at all, nor are they incapable of making free-will choices.

This alternative view proposes that the psychologically manipulative practices of cults and cult leaders merely disrupt a person's thinking pattern so that their ability to make rational, well-reasoned choices is somewhat hampered, not destroyed (e.g., if a cultist is deprived of sleep and food and encouraged to continue in a Bible study for ten hours straight, then that cultist's ability to make a good choice is certainly hindered, but he or she is still free at any time to simply say, "Look, I'm leaving. I need to get some sleep and food because I can't think clearly").

The fact is that cultists can, and often do, choose to leave a cult. Many cultists, despite being subjected to a vast array of psychologically manipulative techniques, continue processing information and making choices based on what they consciously want to do. During a 1993 interview former Branch Davidian David Bunds explained to me that this was the case within David Koresh's group. Although

Koresh used a number of psychologically manipulative techniques on his followers, each person was still able to reason. Some members left the group. Many others consciously chose to stay:

> [T]his idea that they [Davidians] were mindless, unthinking people is not true. They thought a lot. They did a lot of thinking, a lot of analyzing, and a lot of data processing, but their entire base, their entire worldview, their presuppositional base was completely crazy. It was false.

At this point an especially disturbing observation that has been made by cult researchers must be acknowledged: A surprising number of truly Christian churches, groups, and independent ministries are cultic from a psychological perspective. Although this is a tragic reality in and of itself, there is an even greater danger. Religious groups that are cultic from a psychological and/or sociological perspective are vulnerable to evolving into a cult from a theological perspective. This leads us to the most significant component of a definition of a cult: its theology.[24]

Theological Concerns

Defining a cult from a theological perspective involves judging a group's doctrines against the beliefs of the major religion with which it claims association. This method of cult identification is used not only by Christians but also by members of other major religions. For example, the Nation of Islam (Black Muslims) is a cult of Islam. Aum Shinrikyo is a cult of Buddhism. The International Society for Krishna Consciousness (ISKCON), known as the Hare Krishnas, is a Hindu cult.

Christianity, too, has its share of cults, appropriately termed pseudo-Christian. Several evangelicals have offered definitions for these groups. Although similar, each one adds a slightly different shading to the overall picture of a cult from a theological viewpoint:

- "[A] group of people gathered about a specific person or person's misinterpretation of the Bible. . . . [C]ults contain major deviations from historic Christianity. Yet, paradoxically, they continue to insist that they are entitled to be classified as Christians."[25]

- "[A]ny religious movement which claims the backing of Christ or the Bible, but distorts the central message of Christianity by 1) an additional revelation, and 2) by displacing a fundamental tenet of the faith with a secondary matter."[26]
- "[A group adhering to] . . . doctrines which are pointedly contradictory to orthodox Christianity and which yet claim the distinction of either tracing their origin to orthodox sources or of being in essential harmony with those sources."[27]
- "[A] perversion, a distortion of biblical Christianity and/or a rejection of the historic teachings of the Christian church."[28]
- "A cult of Christianity is a group of people, which claiming to be Christian, embraces a particular doctrinal system taught by an individual, group of leaders, or organization, which (system) denies (either explicitly or implicitly) one or more of the central doctrines of the Christian faith as taught in the sixty-six books of the Bible."[29]
- "[A] group of persons polarized around a heretical interpretation of religious truth. Such groups typically cite the Bible and claim to be in harmony with Christianity, but deny such basic doctrines of the Christian faith as the Trinity, the unique deity of Jesus Christ, salvation by grace alone, and justification by faith."[30]

It is crucial to remember that within legitimate Christian circles there exist several areas of doctrine where honest differences of opinion are acceptable. These peripheral issues include, but are certainly not limited to, one's view of eschatology, baptism, the continuance of gifts of the Holy Spirit, and church government.

Theological cults tend to distort these doctrinal issues as well, often going well beyond the various Christian positions that are biblically feasible, especially concerning eschatology (see chapter 11). More significant, though, are the positions cults take on the "essentials" of the Christian faith. These doctrines would include any beliefs that directly relate to one's identification of and relationship to God (the Trinity, the deity of Christ, salvation by grace alone through faith, the virgin birth, the physical resurrection of Christ, etc.). Divergence from these foundational doctrines of Christianity is a sure sign that a particular organization is a cult, theologically speaking.

A Limited Appraisal

The amount of printed information relating to cults is so vast that all sides of the issue cannot be covered in a volume of this size. Consequently our study will be limited to looking at cults from only one perspective: theological. Moreover, the terms *cult* and *new religious movements* will be used interchangeably. Neither term will refer directly or indirectly to a group's sociological or psychological status. My reason for taking this approach is articulated well in a 1994 article on cults, written by Denver Seminary professor Douglas Groothuis:

> The most important matter for Christian discernment is the ability to treasure Christian truth and to separate truth from error. . . . What we label a particular group is not as vital as comprehending what it teaches, what it practices, how the group stacks up against God's Word, and how we can bring the gospel to those who don't know Christ.[31]

Groothuis goes on to say that if we are to

> know whether a particular religious group conflicts theologically with Christian truth, we must comprehend just what constitutes Christianity. Christians must know basic doctrine regarding the authority of Scripture, the Trinity, the Incarnation, the plan of salvation, heaven and hell. . . . Yet this truth is lost on many evangelical Christians today.[32]

The basic doctrines of Christianity are not difficult to comprehend. Learning how those doctrines are twisted by cults also is not a difficult task. Unfortunately both issues are sometimes presented in ways that make them appear complicated. To avoid these hindrances, the following pages deal with these subjects in a unique fashion. Each chapter presents only one Christian doctrine, which is then compared to the various ways cults diverge from that doctrine.

A religious group's rejection of the doctrines expressed in the church's creeds is inextricably linked to how that group interprets Scripture. So the best way to begin our exploration of the Christian beliefs that cults deny is to take a brief look at the Bible, the source of those beliefs.

3

God's Best-Seller

I am very sorry to know and hear how unreverently that most precious jewel, the Word of God, is disputed, rhymed, sung and jangled in every ale-house and tavern, contrary to the true meaning and doctrine of the same.

King Henry VIII (1491–1547)[1]

The Bible—history's best-selling and most widely distributed book—is enjoying even greater popularity as time passes. Bible sales in 1995 climbed to a record $54 million from $29 million in 1991.[2] Not surprisingly, Bible printing and distribution has become a lucrative industry, with a growing number of publishers and private entrepreneurs entering the business. Even media magnate Ted Turner has released an edition of Scripture: "a gilt-edged, 17-pound, $395 version of the Holy Bible [NRSV]. . . . Printed in Italy on six-colored presses and sparkling with metallic-gold ink, this oversized, boxed masterpiece features rare images from illuminated Renaissance manuscripts locked away for centuries in the Vatican Library."[3]

No one knows exactly how many Bibles have been placed in circulation over the years, but recent statistics are staggering. It is estimated that between 1815 and 1975 approximately 2.5 billion copies of the Bible were sold. By 1994 the Scriptures had been translated into 337 languages, and 2,062 languages had translations of at least one book of the Bible.[4]

Obviously, vast numbers of people look to Scripture for truth, guidance, and comfort. In fact, a recent poll indicates that in a typical month, approximately 100 million adults read the Bible. This same survey found that 80 percent of adults "identified the Bible as the single, most influential book in human history."[5] But as King Henry VIII pointed out long ago, God's Word is not always used properly. Many individuals do not even know what the Bible is or where it came from. Therefore, the origin and nature of the Bible are the first two issues that must be addressed if one is going to delve into the wisdom of Holy Writ.

God's Word to Man

The Protestant Bible, although it is typically thought of as a single book, actually is a compilation of sixty-six books arranged topically and divided into two main sections: the Old Testament, which has thirty-nine books*; and the New Testament, consisting of twenty-seven books. These texts were composed over a period of approximately fifteen hundred years (1400 B.C.–A.D. 100) by some forty different authors of diverse backgrounds (David, a shepherd; Nehemiah, a servant; Peter, a fisherman; Paul, a high-ranking Jew). The books were written in different places (exile, prison, royal court), on three different continents (Africa, Asia, and Europe), using three different languages (Hebrew, Aramaic, and Greek).

The Old Testament was originally composed in Hebrew, except for a few isolated chapters and verses that appear in Aramaic. The New Testament was written in Greek. Although the original manuscripts

---

*The Roman Catholic Bible contains additional books known as the Apocrypha: (1) Tobit; (2) Judith; (3) Book of Wisdom; (4) Ecclesiasticus (also called Sirach); (5) 1 Maccabees; (6) 2 Maccabees; (7) Baruch; (8) Letter of Jeremiah; (9) Additions to Esther; (10) Prayer of Azariah (or The Song of the Three Men); (11) Susanna; and (12) Bel and the Dragon. Although these books total twelve distinct works, they found their way into the Roman Catholic Bible in a slightly different form. The titles numbered 1–6 were inserted as originally written (i.e., as separate books). Numbers 7 and 8 were combined into one book and inserted as Baruch. Number 9 was added to the end of the Book of Esther. Numbers 10–12 were interspersed throughout the Book of Daniel. An excellent explanation of why Protestants reject these books as being part of God's Word can be found in Norman Geisler and William Nix, A General Introduction to the Bible (1968; reprint, Chicago: Moody, 1986), 264–75.

(known as *autographs*) of all sixty-six books no longer exist, ancient copies of them have been located throughout the world. These copies are what scholars use to produce our modern Bible editions.

Despite Scripture's complex origins, its many books miraculously fit together to express a single theme: God's plan of salvation for sinful humanity through the person and work of Jesus Christ. Prominent theologian J. I. Packer comments, "No part of Scripture is without its bearing on these central topics."[6] This unity of thought can be explained "only by assuming, as the book itself claims, that its writers were inspired by the Holy Spirit to give God's message to man."[7]

Scripture itself claims to be divine in origin. Throughout the Old Testament several Hebrew words indicate that God himself is speaking. One such word is *neum*, which comes from a root word meaning "utterance." It is used a total of 366 times to indicate a declaration of God (compare 1 Sam. 2:30; Jer. 31:31–33; Zech. 12:1–2, 4). Another Hebrew word, *amar*, can be translated as either "say," "said," or "says." Out of the several hundred times this word appears in the Old Testament, it, too, is often used to describe an action by God (compare Gen. 32:9, 12; Exod. 4:19, 21; Isa. 54:6, 8). There also is the Hebrew word *dabar* (meaning "speech" or "the spoken word"). It is used 394 times in the Old Testament in reference to how God communicated to his people (compare Isa. 1:18–20; Jer. 10:1–5).[8]

Moreover, the Old Testament writers knew they were recording God's words and thoughts. Jeremiah wrote: "These are the words which the LORD spoke concerning Israel and concerning Judah" (30:4). Isaiah affirmed: "For thus the LORD spoke to me . . . saying" (8:11). David said: "The Spirit of the LORD spoke by me, And His word was on my tongue" (2 Sam. 23:2).

In the New Testament we see numerous confirmations of these Old Testament claims. Paul the apostle called the Old Testament "the very words of God" (Rom. 3:2 NIV). The writer of Hebrews quoted several passages from the Old Testament, referring to them as words spoken by God's Holy Spirit (Heb. 3:7; 10:15). A similar comment by the apostle Peter is recorded in Acts. Theology professor Millard Erickson explains:

> In Acts 1:16 Peter says, "Brethren, the scripture had to be fulfilled, which the Holy Spirit spoke beforehand by the mouth of David . . . ,"

and then proceeds to quote from Psalms 69:25 and 109:8 regarding the fate of Judas. It is notable here that Peter not only regards the words of David as authoritative, but that he actually affirms that God spoke by the mouth of David. David was God's "mouthpiece," so to speak. The same thought, that God spoke by the mouth of the prophets, is found in Acts 3:18, 21, and 4:25.[9]

Jesus himself declared that the entire Old Testament could not "be broken" (John 10:35), not even the smallest part of a Hebrew word or letter (Matt. 5:18–19). He also demonstrated confidence in the Old Testament by quoting and referring to it extensively (Matt. 19:4–5; 21:13, 16; 22:37; Mark 4:12; 7:6; Luke 10:28; 20:17). An especially clear illustration of Jesus' view of the Old Testament can be found in Luke 24:25, where he rebuked his disciples for not believing *all* that the prophets had spoken. Jesus then explained to his followers the things concerning him in the Scriptures, beginning with Moses and all the prophets (v. 27). According to Wayne Grudem, professor of biblical and systematic theology at Trinity Evangelical Divinity School, this episode is highly significant because, for first-century Jews, the Old Testament "included exactly the books of the Protestant Old Testament today."[10]

The authors of the New Testament claimed that they too were writing God's thoughts and words. Paul boldly declared, "This is what we speak, not in words taught us by human wisdom but in words taught by the Spirit, expressing spiritual truths in spiritual words" (1 Cor. 2:13 NIV). Paul also placed the Gospel of Luke on the same level as the Old Testament by calling it "Scripture," which was the Jewish term for the Old Testament (1 Tim. 5:18). Throughout Paul's writings there appear many comments that indicate he knew that God had "revealed" what he was writing (1 Cor. 2:7, 10; Gal. 1:1; Eph. 3:3).

Like Paul, the apostle Peter made statements supporting the holy character of the New Testament. For example, he asserts in 2 Peter 1:20–21 that "Scripture" came from men who spoke as they were moved by the Holy Spirit. Peter then goes on to state that Paul's letters are Scripture (2 Peter 3:15–16).

Other passages indicating that the New Testament is from God include 2 Corinthians 4:2; Ephesians 3:5; and Revelation 1:2; 22:18.

Second Timothy 3:16 is perhaps the most familiar New Testament passage to declare the divine origin of the Bible: "All Scripture is inspired by God [i.e., breathed-out by God] and profitable for teaching, for reproof, for correction, for training in righteousness."

Unfortunately cultists hold several erroneous views of the Bible that invariably lead them into doctrinal error. Their nontraditional ideas relate to what Scripture is, how we received it from God, who can interpret it, and what it says. The remainder of this chapter examines their most common mistakes.

Thy Word Is Truth

Many cults teach that the Bible is a document full of contradictions, mistranslations, and unwarranted additions. Other cults use a slightly different attack on God's Word by categorizing it as a compilation of nonhistorical myths and legends that, at the very best, can offer a few pieces of good advice if read through the interpretive lens of the group's leader. Both positions ultimately communicate the same thought: Scripture is a purely human product and, as such, is not qualified to be an authoritative source of truth. In reality, however, the Bible is one of the most reliable of all ancient documents.

First, the total number of full manuscripts and manuscript fragments of Scripture from ancient times is extraordinary. New Testament documents amount to nearly fifty-four hundred, while Old Testament texts number into the tens of thousands.[11] These copies can be compared to one another in order to get an incredibly accurate picture of how the autographs (originals) must have read. This fact alone separates the Bible from most other ancient pieces of literature, which "have been transmitted to us by only a handful of manuscripts."[12]

Second, some of the Bible's manuscripts and manuscript fragments date back to very near the time of the original autographs. This especially holds true of the New Testament. The following list represents only a small sampling of what has survived the centuries:

- *John Rylands Fragment* (c. A.D. 117–138), portions of John's Gospel (18:31–33, 37–38).

- *Chester Beatty Papyri* (c. A.D. 250), most of the New Testament.
- *Bodmer Papyri* (A.D. second–third century), several portions of the New Testament.
- *Codex Vaticanus* (c. A.D. 325–350), the entire Bible.
- *Codex Sinaiticus* (c. A.D. 340), more than half the Old Testament and nearly all of the New Testament.

It is widely recognized by scholars that the closer a source is to the event it describes, the more likely it is to be reliable. With this in mind, Bible professor F. F. Bruce comments, "If the New Testament were a collection of secular writings, their authenticity would generally be regarded as beyond all doubt."[13] He further notes that the evidence for our New Testament writings "is ever so much greater than the evidence for many writings of classical authors, the authenticity of which no one dreams questioning."[14] In *The New Testament Documents: Are They Reliable?*, Bruce provides a list that clearly supports his point:

- For Caesar's *Gallic Wars* (composed between 58 and 50 B.C.) there are several extant MSS [existing manuscripts], but only nine or ten are good, and the oldest is some 900 years later than Caesar's day.
- Of the 142 books of the Roman History of Livy (59 B.C.–A.D. 17) only thirty-five survive; these are known to us from not more than twenty MSS of any consequence, only one of which, and that containing fragments of Books iii–vi, is as old as the fourth century [A.D.].
- Of the fourteen books of the *Histories* of Tacitus (c. A.D. 100) only four and a half survive; of the sixteen books of his *Annals*, ten survive in full and two in part. The text of these extant portions of his two great historical works depends entirely on two MSS, one of the ninth century and one of the eleventh. The extant MSS of his minor works (*Dialogus de Oratoribus, Agricola, Germania*) all descend from a codex [bound book] of the tenth century.
- The History of Thucydides (c. 460–400 B.C.) is known to us from eight MSS, the earliest belonging to c. A.D. 900, and a few papyrus scraps, belonging to about the beginning of the Christian era. The same is true of the History of Herodotus

(c. 488–428 B.C.). Yet no classical scholar would listen to an argument that the authenticity of Herodotus or Thucydides is in doubt because the earliest MSS which are of any use to us are over 1,300 years later than the originals.[15]

Third, when all of the Bible's manuscripts and manuscript fragments are compared and contrasted, they show only slight variances that are often easily explainable. Apparent conflicts with history and science also tend to fade with time. One example of how an error today can be resolved tomorrow involves Acts 17:6 and 17:8, where Luke uses the Greek word *politarches* for the city rulers (i.e., authorities). This is a word that appears nowhere else in Scripture, and for many years, had never even been seen in Greek literature.

> Earlier critical scholars accused Luke of either ignorance or carelessness. But since then a number of inscriptions have been found, dating from the second and third centuries A.D., several in Thessalonica itself, which have vindicated Luke's use of the title.[16]

Of course, there remains a small number of Bible difficulties that have not yet been resolved. These, however, are limited to secondary, if not tertiary, issues. None of the so-called errors currently found in Scripture deal with major doctrinal points. Additionally, the passage of time continues to resolve textual and critical problems, not multiply them.[17] It would be foolish, as Dr. Walter Martin remarks in *Essential Christianity*, "to abandon faith in the authority of God's initial revelation simply because there remains a relatively small percentage (less than 1/2 of 1% of the New Testament) of questionable material about which we do not yet have enough data to properly evaluate and understand."[18]

Finally, there is the testimony of archaeology, which consistently supports biblical statements relating to history and science. The archaeological evidence affirming Scripture has become so impressive that *Time* ran an extensive news piece on the subject in 1995.[19] Earlier that year, the *Biblical Archaeology Review* published a lengthy article dealing with the same topic. In this latter story, Menachem Mansoor—Hebrew and Semitic Studies professor emeritus at the University of Wisconsin, Madison—stated that biblical archaeology "has

corroborated many historical records in the Bible."[20] Consider the
following discoveries:

- The first archaeological evidence for Pontius Pilate was found
  at Caesarea in 1961 in the form of a plaque. Its inscription read
  PONTIUS PILATE, PREFECT OF JUDEA.[21]
- A tablet recovered at an excavation in Babylon "explicitly confirms 2 Kings 25:27–30, which speaks about the exiled Jehoia-
  chin's rations, a situation previously questioned."[22]
- The discovery of cracked stones and fallen/leaning walls at
  Gezer—an eighth century B.C. site—confirm the words of Amos
  1:1, which speaks of an earthquake that rocked the area "in the
  days of Uzziah king of Judah, and in the days of Jeroboam son
  of Joash, king of Israel."[23]
- An official seal imprinted in a clay figure was identified in 1986
  as having been made by Baruch, Jeremiah's scribe (Jer. 36:4).
  Moreover, Baruch had mistakenly left his fingerprint in the
  upper left-hand corner of the clay artifact.[24]
- The city of Bethsaida, where Jesus performed the miracle of the
  loaves and fishes, was unearthed in 1987.[25]
- A repository for bones was unearthed in 1990 in the Old Jewish
  Quarter of Jerusalem's Old City. Its inscription read JOSEPH
  SON OF CAIAPHAS. "This marked the first archeological
  evidence that the high priest Caiaphas, who according to the
  Gospels presided at the Sanhedrin's trial of Jesus, was a real
  person."[26]
- In 1993, a stone dating to 885 B.C. was found protruding from
  the ground at a site in Galilee (Tel Dan). Its inscription, which
  described a victory in battle by a neighboring king over Israel,
  spoke of King David. Until this find, some scholars had sug-
  gested that David was nothing more than a myth.[27]

Seeds of Doubt

Despite the evidence in favor of the Bible's reliability, cults insist
on attacking it as a severely flawed volume. They do so in both sub-

tle and bold fashions, depending on the image they want to present to the public. For example, the Church of Jesus Christ of Latter-day Saints (LDS) takes the subtle approach, at least publicly. They often quote Scripture during evangelistic campaigns, sell the Bible in their church-owned bookstores, and boast of their reliance on the classic King James Version of Scripture. All of these actions suggest to the unwary onlooker that Mormonism is just another Protestant denomination that upholds the authenticity, reliability, and authority of God's Word. Nothing could be further from the truth. The actual Mormon position on the Bible is found in the LDS Articles of Faith: "ARTICLE 8—We believe the Bible to be the Word of God as far as it is translated correctly."[28]

An obvious question follows: Just how "correctly" translated do Mormons consider the Bible to be? Early LDS apostle Orson Pratt (1811–81) writes: "What shall we say then, concerning the Bible's being a sufficient guide? Can we rely upon it in its present known corrupted state, as being a faithful record of God's Word?"[29] Pratt answered these rhetorical questions himself:

> We all know that but a few of the inspired writings [from the Bible] have descended to our times. . . . What few have come down to our day, have been mutilated, changed, and corrupted, in such a shameful manner that no two manuscripts agree. . . . [W]ho, in his right mind, could, for one moment, suppose the Bible in its present form to be a perfect guide? Who knows that even one verse of the whole Bible has escaped pollution so as to convey the same sense now that it did in the original?[30]

Contemporary Mormons have deviated little from the views of their spiritual ancestors. In his influential 1966 book to fellow Mormons, titled *Mormon Doctrine*, LDS apostle Bruce McConkie (1915–85) stated that "the various versions of the Bible do not accurately record or perfectly preserve the words, thoughts, and intents of the original inspired authors."[31]

The LDS church, however, realizes that the Bible is loved and respected throughout the world. Consequently, they have adopted a twofold evangelistic strategy: (1) present Mormonism to the general public as a Bible-believing, Christian denomination in order to gain the interest of prospective converts; and (2) privately destroy the faith that prospective converts have in the Bible so that LDS doctrines can subsequently be taught with little objection from persons who might see discrepancies between Mormonism and Scripture.

This assertion is easily supported by various documents circulating within the Mormon community. One manual, designed to be used by LDS missionaries, lists the many ways in which the Bible conflicts with Latter-day Saint doctrines.[32] This same volume, titled *Missionary Pal: Reference Guide for Missionaries and Teachers*, also lists so-called "Bible Errors" to be shared with prospective or new converts.[33]

Unlike Mormonism, some cults do *not* try to publicly create the impression that they are great admirers of Scripture. Elizabeth Clare Prophet, leader of the Church Universal and Triumphant, openly declares that "many of Jesus' teachings were altered, deleted, or never recorded."[34] In literature distributed to the general public, she also has remarked that "the Gospels have been edited, interpolated, subjected to scribal errors, garnished by additions and plagued by subtractions."[35]

A few cults make especially harsh comments about the Bible. Consider the words of Roy Masters, founder/director of the Foundation for Human Understanding: "The Bible to me is not holy. . . . I can— if you pardon my expression—take that Bible to the toilet with me and use it the same way as anything else. . . . I wouldn't feel guilty for that."[36]

Of course, not every cult treats the Bible with so little regard. Some groups believe very strongly in the authority and reliability of Scripture. There is, however, a catch. According to these groups, the average person cannot understand Scripture without assistance from the leadership of their particular cult.

Blind Guides

Many cults claim that ordinary people cannot understand the Bible because of its complexity and hidden meanings. These cults also maintain that they alone possess the *real* meaning of Scripture, thanks to the writings or speeches of some uniquely qualified individual or group of individuals. Exactly how rank-and-file cultists receive the proper interpretations of the Bible varies from cult to cult. Some listen to taped messages by their leader(s). Others use a particular study book. Many groups have pamphlets or magazines that are periodically released.

Consider the teachings of a new religious movement known as The Family, which has a lengthy history of advocating pornography, incest, fornication, adultery, adult-child sexual contact, and child-child sexual relations.[37] The Family maintains that the true teachings of the Bible have been buried beneath centuries of men's false interpretations of the text. Only through the writings (Mo Letters) of their deceased founder/prophet—"Moses" David Berg (1919–94)—can Christians rightly uncover the Bible's lost truths.

> [T]he true Plan and Foundation of God as outlined in the Bible has been almost totally <u>buried under the rubble of Churchianity</u> and <u>the traditions of man</u>. . . . <u>WHY WE NEED THE MO LETTERS</u>. . . . If we sweep away all this churchy garbage and get back down and delve underneath to find the foundations, then we can see the Plan. . . . <u>BUT TO REDISCOVER THE TRUE FOUNDATION</u>, it takes an archeologist who comes and clears away the rubble! He digs out the Bible from under all the trash and reveals it to you as it really is and really was. . . . I am your archeologist. <u>WITH EVERY [MO] LETTER I'M CLEARING AWAY THE CHURCH RUBBLE</u>.[38]

The Jehovah's Witnesses (JWs)—ruled by a board of twelve men called the Governing Body[39]—make a similar claim about the Bible being incomprehensible to ordinary people. According to JW publications, those who seek to understand Scripture through a course of personal study will soon find themselves in spiritual darkness[40] and "will not progress along the road of life" no matter how much Bible reading they do.[41] The Bible is not meant to be, and indeed cannot be, understood by individuals.[42] It is an organizational book that can be rightly interpreted only through Jehovah's Organization, "the only organization on earth that understands 'the deep things of God.'"[43]

Witnesses receive spiritual "nourishment" from the innumerable books and magazines that have been published over the years by their parent organization, known as the Watch Tower Bible and Tract Society (WTBTS).[44] According to the WTBTS, the organization's literature is divine in origin: "The resolutions adopted by conventions of God's anointed people, booklets, magazines, and books published by them, contain the message of God's truth and are from Almighty God, Jehovah."[45]

The primary source of JW truth is *The Watchtower,* a WTBTS bimonthly magazine that has been in print since 1879.[46] The text of this magazine is said to contain the only proper interpretations of Scripture. Every word of it is to be believed without question.[47] In fact, any "independent thinking" by members that demonstrates doubt of the organization's doctrinal positions—even if those beliefs contradict earlier views—is labeled as "evidence of pride."[48]

Scripture itself, however, does not promote any such teachings. In 1 Corinthians 12:8–10, a passage about spiritual gifts, there is no mention of spiritually elite individuals or special organizations having authoritative insights concerning Scripture. One would think that if such gifts existed, they would be mentioned as spiritual gifts in the Bible. The importance of such gifts would be tremendous. It can only be assumed that there exists no such thing as a divinely chosen person or group of persons commissioned by God to be his unique channel of biblical understanding to humanity.

Moreover, passages such as 2 Peter 1:3 and Romans 1:16 state that the gospel itself contains what is needed for salvation and that everything necessary for eternal life is given to each believer personally. Acts 17:11 additionally reveals that persons who use the Bible to question the teachings of a religious leader are to be commended for their careful consideration, not condemned for it. Jesus himself gave a sobering message in John 12:47–48 that directly relates to the whole issue of whether Christians need to have the Bible interpreted for them by an organization.

> As for the person who hears my words but does not keep them, I do not judge him. For I did not come to judge the world, but to save it. There is a judge for the one who rejects me and does not accept my words; that very word which I spoke will condemn him at the last day (NIV).

In other words, people will be judged according to the manner in which they followed the words Jesus spoke, not in the way they followed the words of some self-proclaimed "prophet," group, or organization with a supposedly special understanding of Scripture. According to our Lord, we may personally learn of him with the aid of the Holy Spirit, who imparts understanding to our hearts. In fact, Scripture gives us marvelous promises regarding God's desire and willingness to reveal himself to us through his Word: "He leads the humble in justice, And He teaches the humble His way" (Ps. 25:9).

We are also told that when it comes to the Bible, God will help us understand it. First Corinthians 2:12 tells us that the Spirit of God assists us so that we may "understand what God has freely given" (NIV). Jesus assured his disciples that the Holy Spirit would be sent to personally teach and guide God's followers (John 16:13–15). He who wrote Scripture helps us understand it.

This is not to say that the Lord has not called some Christians to be teachers, having gifted them to serve in the church (see Eph. 4:11; 1 Tim. 3:2–10; 2 Tim. 2:2). Such individuals are able to help fellow believers learn about God and grow in Christ. But these teachers are never above Scripture itself (James 3:1), nor are they ever to become mediators between God and his children (1 Tim. 2:5).

Scripture Twisting

Sometimes a cult's false doctrines cannot be attributed to any of the practices thus far discussed. When this is the case, a number of factors may be involved, including: (1) dishonest manipulation of the texts; (2) the use of poor scholarship; or (3) esotericism. A good example of the first type of cult tactic can be seen in the Jehovah's Witnesses' *New World Translation of the Holy Scriptures*.

Greek scholars (both Christian and non-Christian) recognize this Bible version not only as a poor and erroneous translation but as one that belies an intentional manipulation of the texts in order to make it fit the Watchtower's unbiblical doctrines. Julius Mantey, a highly respected and well-known Greek scholar, went so far as to write the Watch Tower Bible and Tract Society after it had quoted him out of context in an attempt to justify their faulty translation:

[I have given] only a few examples of Watchtower mistranslations and perversions of God's Word. . . . In view of the preceding facts, especially because you have been quoting me out of context, I herewith request you not to quote the <u>Manual Grammar of the Greek New Testament</u> again, which you have been doing for 24 years. Also that you not quote it or me in any of your publications from this time on.[49]

If a tailor-made version of the Bible is unavailable, cultists often resort to the use of poor scholarship in an effort to legitimize their beliefs. Passages are taken out of context, texts are changed using uncalled-for deletions or additions, and in some cases, a single verse dealing with a specific topic is used to build an entire doctrine at the exclusion of additional passages dealing with the same issue.

Many cults, on the other hand, rely on an altogether different method of interpreting Scripture known as esotericism. It involves finding hidden or secret messages within biblical passages that appear fairly straightforward. Through esoteric biblical interpretation, words are radically redefined so that they take on completely different meanings than the ones intended. Passages suddenly do not mean what they appear to mean. Christian Science founder Mary Baker Eddy (1821–1910) made the following esoteric reading out of Genesis:

The word *Adam* is from the Hebrew *adamah*. . . . Divide the name *Adam* into two syllables, and it reads, *a dam,* or obstruction. . . . Here *a dam* is not a mere play on words; it stands for obstruction, error, even the supposed separation of man from God.[50]

Elizabeth Clare Prophet uses esotericism when she argues that Jesus' words, "Take my yoke upon you and learn from me" (Matt. 11:29 NIV), really mean "[T]ake my consciousness of my sacred labor, my Christhood bearing the burden of world karma . . . and learn of my Guru, the Ancient of Days."[51] New Age author David Spangler claims that when Jesus said, "Seek first the kingdom of God and His righteousness" (NKJV), he actually was giving instructions to seek "the state of identification with one's true individuality, the source within, the Divine center."[52]

There are several reasons why an esoteric system of reading the Bible is illegitimate. First, nothing in Scripture indicates that it was intended to be read in an esoteric manner. Second, the esoteric approach can be used to make the Bible say virtually anything, which effectively renders it useless as an objective measure for truth. Third, esotericism blatantly cuts across what the authors are plainly saying without offering any evidence that the authors were actually imparting a hidden message. Fourth, Jesus himself declared before the high priests that he had taught "nothing in secret" but spoke "openly to the world" (John 18:20 NIV).

Although esotericism goes against all methods of interpreting a literary work such as the Bible, it is all too often used by nontraditional religious bodies. In fact, it has become a virtual trademark of theological cults. Its sole purpose is to allow for the propagation of so-called hidden teachings, which conveniently support the doctrines of a given group.

"New" Revelations

Undermining Scripture's reliability, teaching that the Bible is a closed book to all but the most spiritually elite, and perverting the clear meaning of biblical texts are not always enough to support various doctrines that are theologically cultic. Consequently, some groups have provided their followers with additional sources of "divine truth." These revelations, whether verbal or written, always contradict and supersede the Bible when it comes to major doctrines of the Christian faith.

Mormons, for instance, look to three "Standard Works" of Scripture in addition to the Bible: the *Book of Mormon*, the *Doctrine and Covenants*, and the *Pearl of Great Price*.[53] The speeches and writings of the *current* LDS presidents are also authoritative. These extrabiblical works cover a wide range of subjects and contain, according to Mormons, the very words of God. Each book allegedly restores truths that were removed from the Bible. The Book of Mormon itself makes this claim, stating that "many plain and precious things" were taken away from the Bible and that because of this "an exceedingly great many do stumble, yea, insomuch that Satan hath great power over them" (1 Nephi 13:28–29).

Although Mormons claim to believe the Bible in its entirety, the truth is that they believe Scripture only where it does not conflict with their extrabiblical books, which were produced by their founder/prophet Joseph Smith. As Bruce McConkie admits: "Acceptance of the Bible is coupled with a reservation that it is true only insofar as translated correctly. . . . The other three, having been revealed in modern times in English, are accepted without qualification."[54]

The place of importance given to Joseph Smith's writings in comparison to the significance given to the Bible is perhaps best seen in a comment made by Ezra Taft Benson (1899–1994), thirteenth president of the LDS Church:

> Men can get nearer to the Lord . . . through the Book of Mormon than through the Bible. . . . [T]here will be more people saved in the Kingdom of God—ten thousand times over—because of the Book of Mormon than there will be because of the Bible.[55]

Many other cults also employ this method of circumventing biblical teachings. Popular New Age groups are especially adept at creating documents that are supposedly new revelations of truth. The Urantia cult, for instance, looks to *The Urantia Book* (UB), a 2,097-page volume of science fiction–sounding "truth" allegedly received during the mid-1920s. According to followers of the UB, several superhuman, angel-like beings known as "the revelators" used thought-dictation to impart the UB to an individual who remains unidentified to this day.[56]

Whether or not God *can* reveal more truths to humanity is not the issue. God can do anything consistent with his nature. The question is: *Has* God revealed more truths? If he has done so, they would certainly line up with what he has already spoken. But the evidence clearly shows that this is not the case. Cult-based revelations regularly contradict the doctrines of Scripture. Each of these beliefs will now be explored using the creeds of Christendom.

Part 2

I believe in GOD THE FATHER Almighty; And in JESUS CHRIST his only begotten Son our Lord; who was born of the Holy Ghost and the Virgin Mary.

Apostles' Creed, Old Roman

I believe in one God, the Father Almighty; Maker of heaven and earth. . . . And in one Lord, Jesus Christ, the only-begotten Son of God . . . begotten not made, being of one substance [essence] with the Father . . . and was incarnate by the Holy Ghost of the Virgin Mary, and was made man. . . . And [I believe] in the Holy Ghost, the Lord and Giver of Life; . . . who with the Father and the Son together is worshiped and glorified; who spake by the Prophets.

Niceno-Constantinopolitan Creed

We worship one God in Trinity, and Trinity in Unity: Neither confounding the Persons: nor dividing the Substance [Essence]. For there is one Person of the Father: another of the Son: and another of the Holy Ghost. But the Godhead of the Father, of the Son, and of the Holy Ghost, is all one: the Glory equal, the Majesty coeternal. . . . The Father uncreate[d]: the Son uncreate[d]: and the Holy Ghost uncreate[d]. . . . The Father eternal: the Son eternal: and the Holy Ghost eternal. . . . So likewise the Father is Almighty: the Son Almighty: and the Holy Ghost Almighty. And yet they are not three Almighties: but one Almighty. So the Father is God: the Son is God: and the Holy Ghost is God. And yet they are not three Gods: but one God.

Athanasian Creed

God in Three Persons

4

Lord of Israel

[God] is incomprehensible, in greatness unfathomable, in height inconceivable, in power incompatible, in wisdom unrivaled, in goodness inimitable, in kindness unutterable. . . . He is Lord, because He rules over the universe; Father, because He is before all things; Fashioner and Maker, because He is creator and maker of the universe; the Highest, because of His being above all; and Almighty, because He himself rules and embraces all.

Theophilus
Bishop of Antioch, late second century[1]

Christianity, like Judaism and Islam, is a monotheistic religion, which means that it teaches the existence of only one God. Unlike Jews and Muslims, however, Christians believe that there is a plurality of persons within the one God. In other words, Christians maintain that the eternal God they worship has revealed himself through Scripture as one divine entity who exists as three distinct persons (or centers of self-consciousness): Father, Son, and Holy Spirit. Each person, however, "cannot be conceived [of] as three separate individuals, but are *in* one another, and form a solidaric unity" (emphasis mine).[2] This concept, hinted at in the Old Testament and fully established in the New, is the doctrine of the Trinity.

Orthodox theologians have explained the Trinity in various ways, but each definition ultimately says the same thing: that there is only

61

one true God, who within his eternal nature exists as three coequal and coeternal persons; namely, the Father, Son, and Holy Spirit. Although these three persons are distinct in function, position, and relationship, they all share the same divine nature (or essence) and, in so doing, exist as one divine being. Each person is in *full* possession of the divine essence. Simply put, the Father, Son, and Holy Spirit *are* the one true God. A.. ...iree persons, therefore, may properly be called God collectively, as well as individually. The Trinitarian belief is often referred to as God's three-in-oneness.[3]

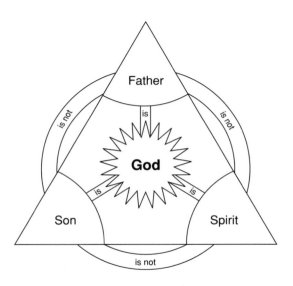

The doctrine of the Trinity is a complex theological view that, although taught in the New Testament, took early Christians several hundred years to crystallize into a *formal* expression (i.e., the Nicene and Niceno-Constantinopolitan Creeds). This does not mean, however, that the doctrine is not true. It also does not mean that Trinitarianism originated with non-Christians. On the contrary, Trinitarian thought can be traced not only to the New Testament (2 Cor. 13:14) but to first- and second-century Christian churches.

Long before the creeds were drafted, there was a substantial amount of discussion among early Christians regarding God's nature. Jesus, after all, had declared himself to be equal with God, which seemingly contradicted Hebrew monotheism. In an effort to understand how Jesus could be God, church leaders of the first, second, and third centuries undertook a thorough examination of both the Old Testament and the recently composed New Testament.[4] An investigation into the nature and function of the Holy Spirit began at approximately the same time.

This quest for spiritual truth resulted in numerous heated debates among various scholars, theologians, and Christian thinkers. Eventually, the Trinity ("tri-unity") doctrine was recognized as the correct and most logical understanding of Scripture. Christian theologian Louis Berkhof rightly comments, "The doctrine of the Trinity is very decidedly a doctrine of revelation. . . . Therefore, it is of the utmost importance that we gather the Scriptural proofs for it."[5]

Blessed Trinity

A good starting point for any study of the Trinity begins with Deuteronomy 6:4, which may be the most important Hebrew passage relating to God's nature: "Hear, O Israel! The LORD [YAHWEH] is our God, the LORD [YAHWEH] is one!" This verse, known as the *Shema*, served as the cornerstone of Old Testament Jewish thought concerning the God of Israel—i.e., there exists only one true God, YAHWEH. By taking such a theological position, the Jews forever separated themselves from the surrounding polytheistic cultures (e.g., Egyptians, Philistines, Babylonians, Canaanites, Moabites).

The reality of the existence of only one true God is stressed again and again throughout the Old Testament (2 Sam. 7:22), especially in the pronouncements of God himself (Isa. 45:21–22; 46:8–9). In fact, one of the main purposes of the Old Testament prophets was to continually call the Jews back from idolatry to the worship of the one true God (1 Kings 18:18ff). The prophets "strengthened monotheistic doctrine by constantly reminding Israel of the vast gulf that separated the Lord from pagan idols and the so-called gods that they represented (Hosea 4:12; Isa. 2:8, 20; 17:8; 31:7; Jer. 10:5, 10)."[6]

Although no Old Testament passages explicitly describe God as a triune being, many Old Testament verses at the very least suggest a plurality within God's nature. For example, in Genesis 1:26 God says, "Let Us [plural] make man in Our [plural] image, according to Our [plural] likeness." The use here of plural pronouns is most interesting. Renowned biblical scholar and linguistic expert Dr. Gleason Archer comments:

> This first person plural can hardly be a mere editorial or royal plural that refers to the speaker alone, for no such usage is demonstrable anywhere else in biblical Hebrew. Therefore we must face the question of who are included in this "us" and "our." It could hardly include the angels in consultation with God, for nowhere is it ever stated that man was created in the image of angels, only of God.[7]

Even more thought-provoking is verse 27: "God created man in His own [singular] image, in the image of God He [singular] created him; male and female He [singular] created them." A striking and deliberate switch to singular pronouns is made here. According to Archer, the verse is implying that "the plural equals the singular. This can only be understood in terms of the Trinitarian nature of God. The one God subsists in three Persons, Persons who are able to confer with one another and carry their plans into action together—without ceasing to be one God."[8]

Some theologians maintain that the use of plural pronouns in Genesis suggests a plurality of majesty, a form of speech a king would use—for example, "We are pleased to grant our request." But this is highly unlikely, according to many other linguistic experts and Bible scholars. Wayne Grudem, professor of biblical and systematic theology at Trinity Evangelical Divinity School, observes that, in Old Testament Hebrew, "there are no other examples of a monarch using plural verbs or plural pronouns of himself . . . so this suggestion has no evidence to support it."[9]

The Old Testament also contains verses wherein one person called God (or Lord) is interacting in some way with another person called God (or Lord). Consider Psalm 45:6–7: "Your throne, O God, is forever and ever. . . . You have loved righteousness and hated wickedness; Therefore God, Your God has anointed You." Consider, too, Genesis 19:24, which refers to Sodom and Gomorrah's fate: "Then the LORD [YAHWEH] rained on Sodom and Gomorrah brimstone and fire from the LORD [YAHWEH] out of heaven." Especially interesting is Isaiah 44:6, "Thus says the LORD [YAHWEH], the King of Israel and his Redeemer, the LORD [YAHWEH] of hosts."

A few verses even mention all three of the persons resident within the nature of the one true God. An outstanding occurrence of this is found in Isaiah 48:12–16. The verse begins with YAHWEH speaking: "Listen to Me, O Jacob, even Israel whom I called; I am He, I am the first, I am also the last" (compare, the Son in Rev. 22:12–13). The passage continues: "Come near to Me, listen to this: From the first I have not spoken in secret, From the time it took place [Israel's deliverance], I was there" (v. 16a). Finally, God declares, "And now the Lord GOD [YAHWEH] has sent Me, and His Spirit."

None of these verses conclusively prove the Trinity. They do, however, serve as a theological doorway through which an understanding of God's triunity can be accessed from the New Testament. Berkhof writes: "The Old Testament does not contain a full revelation of the Trinitarian existence of God, but does contain several indications of it. And this is exactly what might be expected."[10] Robert Lightner, professor of Systematic Theology at Dallas Theological Seminary, remarks: "Throughout the Old Testament there are hints of the Trinity, but God's unity is stressed. The revelation is much clearer and more complete in the New Testament. We need the teaching from both testaments for the full picture."[11]

Like the Old Testament, the New Testament consistently affirms the existence of only one God (Gal. 3:20; 1 Tim. 2:5). Additionally, however, the New Testament presents numerous passages that identify three distinct persons—the Father (1 John 3:1), the Son (1 John 1:3), and the Holy Spirit (John 14:16, 26; 15:26; 16:13–14)—each of whom are referred to as God (*the Father*, John 6:27; Rom. 1:7; 1 Thess. 1:1; *the Son*, John 20:28; Heb. 1:8; *the Holy Spirit*, Acts 5:3–4).

The importance of each of these verses is intensified by the many other New Testament passages that not only designate the Father, Son, and Holy Spirit as God but also ascribe to them the same attributes and divine acts. All three are said to dwell in believers (John 14:17, 20, 23). Each one is said to have been active in the resurrection of Christ (*the Father*, Gal. 1:1; *the Son*, John 2:19–21; 10:17; *the Holy Spirit*, Rom. 8:11), while at the same time we are told that it was God who raised Jesus from the dead (1 Cor. 6:14). All three possess and impart eternal life (*the Father*, John 5:26; *the Son*, John 1:4; 5:21, 26; 10:28; 11:25; *the Holy Spirit*, 2 Cor. 3:6; Gal. 6:8).

The New Testament also presents the Father, Son, and Holy Spirit as having an unusually close union. All are specifically mentioned in the Great Commission (Matt. 28:19), Paul's benediction to the Corinthian church (2 Cor. 13:14), and Peter's salutation to Christians living in Asia Minor (1 Peter 1:2). Jesus' baptism provides an exceptionally vivid illustration of the triune God (Matt 3:16–17). Furthermore, the New Testament applies numerous Old Testament titles and actions reserved for God to Jesus and the Holy Spirit (see chapters 5 and 6 of this book).

Only the Trinity doctrine is able to reconcile these biblical passages with those Scriptures that teach there is only one God. Nevertheless, a number of belief systems deny, compromise, or twist what the Bible teaches regarding the Lord's three-in-one nature: henotheism, polytheism, modalism, and pantheism. Theological cults commonly accept one of these heretical views, each of which will now be examined.

Henotheism: Monotheistic Mask

Many cults feel that Trinitarianism detracts from God's unique status as the only God and, therefore, should be rejected. Such groups frequently state that the Trinity doctrine is false because "God is only one."[12] According to the Jehovah's Witnesses, there has never been "a more deceptive doctrine advanced than that of the trinity. It could have originated only in one mind, and that the mind of Satan the Devil."[13]

Noteworthy is the fact that most cultists spend a great deal of effort condemning what they do not understand. They consistently misrepresent the Trinity, as the following Watchtower quotation shows: "IS THERE A TRINITY? . . . The doctrine, in brief, is that there are three gods in one: 'God the Father, God the Son, and God the Holy Ghost,' all three equal in power, substance and eternity.[14]

Contrary to the above assertion, Christians do not claim that the Trinity is three gods but, rather, that there are three personal self-distinctions (i.e., persons) within the *one* God. The term *persons* does not refer to separate organisms, as when used of people.[15] This clarification has been made again and again by Christian theologians, yet cults continue to charge that the Trinity doctrine leads to belief in more than one God. Ironically, some of these same groups promote the very thing that they claim to stand against—belief in more than one God.

The Jehovah's Witnesses, for instance, teach that YAHWEH (Jehovah) is *Almighty* God. A second god that they recognize is Jesus, whom they designate as a *mighty* god, or a lesser god.[16] In addition to these two gods there exists a spiritually elite class of Witnesses known as the "Little Flock," who supposedly have a divine nature that will fully manifest itself when they are resurrected as gods. Members of the Little Flock represent the Watchtower organization's spiritual cream of the crop. Together with Jesus they constitute "the Christ" of Scripture. Only these specially anointed JWs represent the church. Only they are considered God's children.

- "[T]he saints of this Gospel age are an anointed company—anointed to be kings and priests unto God . . . and together with Jesus, their chief and Lord, they constitute Jehovah's Anointed—the Christ."[17]
- "[T]he titles, Mighty God, and Everlasting Father, are titles which fully understood, are very appropriate to Our Lord Jesus. . . . [T]he same titles are applicable to the Church his body."[18]
- "Our high calling is so great, so much above comprehension of men, that they feel that we are guilty of blasphemy when we speak of being 'new creatures'—not any longer human. . . . [W]e are divine beings—hence all such are Gods. . . . Now we appear like men, and all die naturally like men, but in the resurrection we will rise in our true character as Gods."[19]

Witnesses draw a fine line distinction between all of these gods by worshiping only Jehovah God.[20] This theological position, which reserves worship for just one god while recognizing the existence of more than one god, is known as henotheism. It is pointedly contradicted by every biblical verse that declares there is only one true God.

The Bible leaves no room for the existence of more than one god (Deut. 4:35, 39; 32:39; 2 Kings 19:19; Ps. 86:10; Mark 12:29).

Polytheism: Many Gods, Many Lords

Some cultists go beyond henotheism into polytheism, which entails not only a belief in but also a worship of more than one God. A good example of a modern-day polytheistic cult is the Church of Jesus Christ of Latter-day Saints (LDS), also known as Mormonism. Mormon theology can be traced directly to its founder, Joseph Smith (1805–44), who habitually belittled Christian Trinitarianism.

> Many men say there is one God; the Father, the Son and the Holy Ghost are only one God! I say that is a strange God anyhow—three in one, and one in three! It is a curious organization. . . . All are to be crammed into one God, according to sectarianism. It would make the biggest God in all the world. He would be a wonderfully big God— he would be a giant or a monster.[21]

Mormons tend to stress the biblical verses affirming the plurality of God over those passages demonstrating his unity. The result is a belief in three entirely separate Gods—the Father, Son, and Holy Ghost.[22] As Joseph Smith proudly declared, "[L]o and behold! we have three Gods . . . and who can contradict it?"[23] It is these three gods that Mormons worship.[24]

Latter-day Saints also affirm the existence of other gods, although they do not worship them. LDS apostle Orson Pratt speculated, "If we should take a million of worlds like this and number their particles, we should find that there are more Gods than there are particles of matter in those worlds."[25] Brigham Young (1801–77)—second president of the Mormon church—was much less willing to make estimates. He would only state, "How many Gods there are, I do not know. But there never was a time when there were not Gods."[26]

Mormonism, like many other polytheistic groups, offers its members the reward of godhood if they remain faithful to the tenets of their faith. At a large 1975 gathering of Latter-day Saints, the twelfth president of the LDS church, Spencer W. Kimball (1895–1985), proclaimed: "Brethren, 225,000 of you are here tonight. I suppose 225,000 of you may become gods. There seems to be plenty of space out there in the universe."[27]

God, however, says something altogether different in Isaiah 43:10: "Before me there was no God formed, And there will be none after Me." Another problem faced by polytheists involves passages like Isaiah 42:8 and 48:10–11, which indicate that God will share his glory with no one. Isaiah 44:8 is especially damaging to polytheism. In this passage the all-knowing God of creation declares, "You are My witnesses. Is there any God besides Me. . . ? I know of none." That there is only one God is a clearly presented truth of Scripture. Even demons know there is only one God, and tremble (James 2:19).

But what about verses that seem to suggest that many gods do indeed exist? First Corinthians 8:5, for instance, speaks of "many gods and many lords." In seeking to properly understand such passages, it is important to remember that *anything* can be made into a god: sex, drugs, money, beauty, food. These gods, however, are not true gods. They are false idols of worship. A false god can be a physical idol made by someone's hands (Lev. 19:4; Deut. 27:15), people who think they are gods (Ezek. 28:2, 9; Ps. 82:2–7), or any spiritual entity other than God that someone follows (2 Cor. 4:4). All of these "gods" are not *true* gods or gods by nature (Gal. 4:8). They are "so-called gods" (1 Cor. 8:4–6). There is only one *true* God (2 Chron. 15:3; Jer. 10:10; John 17:3).

Modalism: Spirit of Antichrist

Another anti-Trinitarian theology that has gained popularity among cults is known as modalism. This ancient heresy can be traced back to a man named Sabellius, who in the third century A.D. put forth an unbiblical concept: God is a single divine person who manifests himself in various modes; namely, Father, Son, and Holy Spirit.

Modalists believe that God is *not* three distinct persons but only appears as such in order to reveal different aspects of his character. The analogy used most often to illustrate this heresy is that of a man who is a husband to his wife, a father to his children, and an employee to his boss. Although he is only one person, he holds three different identities that change depending on the individuals with whom he is associating. Sadly, this false doctrine is a perversion of two ortho-dox beliefs: (1) there is only one God; and (2) Jesus is God. Gregory Boyd, a former member of the United Pentecostal Church, explains:

> From these two truths, Oneness groups deduce that Jesus Christ is God in his totality, and therefore that Jesus must himself be the Father, Son, and Holy Spirit. . . . The prolific Oneness writer David Bernard expresses the logic. . . . "If there is only one God and that God is the Father (Mal. 2:10), and if Jesus is God, then it logically follows that Jesus is the Father." . . . So, too, it is customarily argued . . . that if there is only one God and that God is the Holy Spirit, and if Jesus is indeed God, then it must logically follow that Jesus is himself the Holy Spirit.[28]

But to say that the Father *is* the Son ignores the subject-object rela-tionship between them that is demonstrated in Scripture. In other words, the Bible consistently shows interaction taking place between the Father, Son, and Holy Spirit. There *must* be three individual per-sonalities in order for this interaction to take place. This is especially apparent in Gospel passages discussing the Father and the Son:

- "The Father loves the Son" (John 3:35; 5:20).
- The Son was "sent" by the Father (John 3:16; 5:30; 17:8) in the same way that we are sent by Jesus (John 20:21).
- Jesus said that after his resurrection he would return to the Father (John 14:12; 16:27–28).
- The Son speaks to the Father (John 17:1–26) and relates to him as one person relates to another (Matt. 10:32–33; John 10:14–15).

Modalists not only fail to adequately explain these verses but also do not take into account the significance of John 8:17, where Jesus offers a defense of the testimony he made regarding his authority. In this passage, Jesus appeals to the Old Testament standard for judging whether a testimony is true: "Even in your law it has been written that the testimony of *two* men is true" (emphasis mine). Jesus goes on to make a statement that, given his reference to Old Testament law, *must* mean that he and the Father are distinct persons: "I am He who testifies about Myself, and the Father who sent Me testifies about Me" (v. 18).

Jesus' appeal to the Father as an additional witness of his authority plainly expresses the otherness of God the Father from God the Son. If Jesus and the Father were the same person, Jesus could not have appealed to the Old Testament law requiring the presence of at least two witnesses before a testimony could be taken as trustworthy (see Deut. 17:6; 19:15). The modalist interpretation of God's nature would render Jesus' testimony invalid. It would amount to nothing more than him saying: "My testimony is true, and my witnesses are me, myself, and I." Interestingly, Jesus appeals to a third testimony in John 5:30–37. He declares that his *works* also bear witness of his authority. There obviously is a difference between Jesus and his works. So, too, there is a difference between Jesus and the Father, both of whom are mentioned in John 5.

Clear distinctions between Jesus and the Holy Spirit also are made throughout the New Testament. In John 15:26, Jesus promises that he will "send" the Holy Spirit. How can Jesus "send" the Holy Spirit if he *is* the Holy Spirit? A similar verse that is especially troublesome for modalists is 1 Peter 1:12, which mentions "the Holy Spirit sent from heaven." The obvious question is: Who "sent" the Holy Spirit? Demons certainly do not have the authority to command God, neither do angels or deceased Christians. There seems to be no one left to send the Holy Spirit if the Father was really Jesus and Jesus subsequently turned into the Holy Spirit. The biblical answer, of course, is that Jesus sent the Holy Spirit (John 15:26). Consequently, Christ also cannot be the Spirit.

Matthew 3:16–17 provides the most concrete depiction of the Father, Son, and Holy Spirit. The event recounted is Jesus' baptism. After being baptized, Jesus came up out of the water, and the heavens were opened to reveal the Spirit of God descending like a dove, while the Father spoke: "This is My beloved Son, in whom I am well-pleased." Scripture leaves no room for doubt when it comes to whether or not the Father, Jesus, and the Holy Spirit are distinct from each other. For persons who claim that the Father is Jesus, there is a disturbing condemnation given by John: "This is the antichrist, the one who denies the Father *and* the Son" (1 John 2:22, emphasis mine).

Pantheism: All Is God, God Is All

A number of newer cults in America embrace a view of God that
has been directly influenced by Hinduism and other Eastern religions.
Such groups usually are part of the New Age Movement, which cult
expert Elliot Miller defines as "an extremely large, *loosely* structured
network of organizations and individuals bound together by common
values . . . and a common vision (a coming 'new age' of peace and
mass enlightenment, the 'Age of Aquarius')."[29]
Most New Agers espouse a belief about God called pantheistic
monism. This ancient doctrine teaches that everything we see "may
be reduced to a single, unifying principle partaking of the same essence
and reality."[30] It further asserts that all is God and God is all. New
Age spokesperson Benjamin Creme explains:

> [I]n a sense there is no such thing as God, God does not exist. And in
> another sense, there is nothing else but God—only God exists. . . . This
> microphone is God. This table is God. All is God. And because all is
> God, there is no God. . . . God is everything that you have ever known
> or could ever know—and everything beyond your level of knowing.[31]

Is everything ultimately one divine impersonal substance? Is "all
that is" really God? Not according to the Bible. Genesis 1:1 estab-
lishes God as an entity separate and distinct from the universe. Other
passages supporting this are Psalm 33:13–14; Isaiah 40:22; 42:5; 44:24;
and Acts 17:24–25. God, rather than being a *part* of all that exists, is
the *Creator* of all that exists. Moreover, God performs acts that only
a personal being can perform. In Jeremiah 29:11 he declares that he
knows the plans he has made for his people. How could an impersonal force know, think, or have plans?
God is also portrayed in the Bible as a *living* God (Dan. 6:26; 1 Tim.
3:15; 4:10; Heb. 10:31) and is personally distinct from other minds.
He is capable of having interpersonal relationships (Exod. 2:24; Lev.
19:1; Heb. 4:13), is omniscient (1 John 3:20), judges (Ps. 50:6), loves
(Prov. 3:12; Jer. 31:3), and has a will (1 John 2:17). In sharp contrast
to the pantheistic deity connected with the New Age Movement, we
see through Scripture that God is an intelligent, compassionate, and
personal being.

Standard Objections

Many cults object to the doctrine of the Trinity because the word itself does not appear in Scripture.[32] But this objection has no real merit. The term *trinity* simply makes it easier for someone to refer to the Bible's teachings about God's nature. A single word is often used to represent a complex idea. Water, for instance, consists of two parts hydrogen and one part oxygen (H_2O), yet one would never say: "May I please have a glass of two parts hydrogen and one part oxygen?" Instead, "water" is used for the sake of convenience. This is how the term *trinity* is used by Christians. Ironically, the word *Bible* is not in the Bible either, but many anti-Trinitarian cults have no problem using this designation for Scripture.[33]

Another common objection to the Trinity involves the date of its formal appearance in church history. A comment by Victor Paul Wierwille (1942–85), founder of the Way International, typifies this particular charge: "[T]he trinity was not a part of Christian dogma and formal documents of the first three centuries after Christ."[34]

As we have seen, it is true that the doctrine of the Trinity was not *formally* expressed until approximately the fourth century, after the Nicaea and Constantinople Councils. But these gatherings were not convened in order to invent new doctrines. They were convened in order to set forth in a formal manner the doctrines that Christians were *already* believing and to work out a way of accurately communicating these doctrines throughout the world.

In other words, although the Trinity doctrine had not been officially stated until after the Nicaea and Constantinople Creeds, its doctrinal building blocks were already being adhered to by Christians (see chapters 5 and 6). More than one hundred years before the Council of Nicaea, for example, Christians already recognized that God existed in plurality. Note the following quotation from Hippolytus (c. A.D. ?–235):

> There is, brethren, one God. . . . God, subsisting alone, and having nothing contemporaneous [at the same time with Himself], determined to create the world. . . . [T]here was nothing contemporaneous with God. Beside Him there was nothing; but He, while existing alone, *yet existed in plurality* (emphasis mine).[35]

An additional attack on the Trinity focuses on its apparent similarity to ancient pagan deities:

> Long before the founding of Christianity the idea of a triune god or a god-in-three persons was a common belief in ancient religions. Although many of these religions had many minor deities, they distinctly acknowledged that there was one supreme God who consisted of three persons or essences. The Babylonians used an equilateral triangle to represent this three-in-one god. . . . The Hindu trinity was made up of the gods Brahma, Vishnu, and Shiva. The Greek triad was composed of Zeus, Athena, and Apollo. . . . [A]ncient cultures also accepted this idea; cultures such as the Babylonian, Egyptian, Phoenician, Greek, Indian, Chinese, Japanese, Icelandic, Siberian and others.[36]

> [T]he Trinity is not a Bible teaching. . . . [L]ong before Jesus walked the earth gods were worshipped in groups of three, or trinities, in places such as ancient Egypt and Babylon.[37]

> The origin of the trinity doctrine is traced back to the ancient Babylonians and Egyptians and other ancient mythologists.[38]

These arguments are severely flawed, since an apparent similarity between two lines of thought does not necessarily mean that those two lines of thought have the same origin. This is especially true when it comes to religion. Most religions, in fact, have numerous similarities. For example, Buddhism teaches that murder is wrong. So does Christianity. Does this mean to the Buddhist that the Christian stand against murder is "pagan" and, therefore, should be rejected? Consider, too, the fact that some pagans believe in the existence of at least one god. Does this mean that anyone else who believes in one God is actually borrowing from pagan teachings? Of course not.

It also must be remembered that there is a vast difference between the many pagan triads and the Christian Trinity, which is unique in numerous ways. First, pagan triads usually consisted of three *separate* gods. They did not constitute one god. Second, non-Christian trinities were "always or nearly always merely the three gods at the top of the hierarchy of many gods worshipped in polytheistic religions."[39] Third, pagan deities were not thought of as being coequal. One of the deities was always greater than the other. Finally, it cannot be proven historically that Christians borrowed anything from pagan religions to form the Trinity doctrine:

> [T]he concept of God as one in essence but three in centers of consciousness—what the Greek church referred to as three *hypostases* and the Latin church as *personae*—is absolutely unique in the history of human thought. No other culture or philosophical movement ever came up with such an idea of God as this—an idea that remains very difficult for our finite minds to grasp.[40]

Some cults reject the Trinity doctrine because, according to them, it is "contradictory, incomprehensible, and unscriptural."[41] Christian theologians agree that the Trinity is difficult to *fully* comprehend, but it is hardly beyond any degree of understanding. Intellectually grasping a concept, while at the same time not being able to fully comprehend exactly *how* that concept can be true, are compatible states of mind.

I understand that the planet Earth is revolving at a speed of several thousands of miles per hour, but I certainly do not fully comprehend how that can be. I may also understand that the chair on which I am sitting is comprised of millions of molecules moving so fast that they are forming only what looks like a solid object, but I certainly do not fully comprehend how that can be.

If we are willing to accept these physical realities without fully comprehending them, it is only fair that we give the same level of consideration to the doctrine of the Trinity despite our inability to fully comprehend it. God has explicitly told us that certain aspects of his nature are unsearchable (Ps. 145:3; Isa. 40:28; Rom. 11:33). The question to ask, therefore, is not: *How* does the Trinity exist? But simply: *Does* the Trinity exist? According to Scripture, the answer to the latter question is yes. For those whose minds cannot let go of the former question, several analogies for the Trinity may be helpful.

Time, for instance, consists of three distinct things: past, present, and future. These three aspects of "time" correspond well to the Trinity's Father, Son, and Holy Spirit. In both cases, the three aspects are entirely distinct from one another. Moreover, all three aspects of "time," although distinct, share the same nature of that which they comprise. In other words, the past, present, and future can all be referred to individually as "time" in somewhat the same fashion as the Father, Son, and Holy Spirit can each be referred to as God. Also, if any of the three elements of "time" were to be removed, "time" would no longer exist. In this dimension of reality, there is no such thing as "time" without a past, a present, or a future. Similarly, God would not be God without a Father, a Son, or a Holy Spirit. All three persons *are* God, just as all three aspects of "time" *are* "time."

Time is but one of many analogies that have been proposed in an effort to represent the Trinity. Another is the multiplication formula (1 x 1 x 1=1). Unfortunately, no analogy for the Trinity is without serious drawbacks. But this is what one would expect, since we are dealing with a reality that is exalted far beyond our limits of knowledge and reasoning. "My thoughts are not your thoughts, Neither are your ways My ways," says the Lord in Isaiah 55:8. He goes on to explain, "For as the heavens are higher than the earth, So are My ways higher than your ways, And My thoughts than your thoughts" (v. 9).

It should come as no surprise that human analogies would fail to adequately describe a spiritual entity as complex and *non*human as God. Nevertheless, they can still serve as "reminders that the imprint of the triune God may be found in creation."[42] Ultimately the Trinity is a divine mystery with regard to how it could possibly be a reality. That it is a reality, however, has been established by Scripture. In other words, the Trinity may be beyond reason but it certainly is not contrary to reason.

The significance of the Trinity cannot be overstated. It has been described as "the heart of the Christian conception of God . . . central to our faith,"[43] "one of the most important doctrines of the Christian faith,"[44] and a doctrine without which some of the most basic Bible teachings about God would remain "nearly incomprehensible."[45]

In reference to the Trinity, St. Augustine reportedly commented, "In no other subject is error more dangerous or inquiry more laborious, or discovery of truth more profitable."[46] An equally important doctrine, which is closely related to the Trinity, is the deity/humanity of Christ. This will be the subject of chapter 5.

5

Jesus of Nazareth

Now the Word of God is His Son, as we have before said. . . .
The Father of the universe has a Son; who also, being the first-
begotten Word of God, is even God.
                                    Justin Martyr (A.D. 100–65)
                                      early Christian apologist[1]

For thousands of years, extraordinary individuals have periodically
emerged from relative obscurity to change the course of human events.
Such personalities—whether military, religious, or political—have
affected the lifestyles and philosophies of countless millions. Consider
Buddha, Alexander the Great, Julius Caesar, Confucius, Constantine,
Martin Luther, Thomas Jefferson, Abraham Lincoln, Gandhi, Martin Luther King Jr., and Billy Graham. Each has exerted enormous
influence over humanity and will forever be remembered for their
extraordinary accomplishments.

Among the most influential historical figures, one person in particular stands apart from the rest: Jesus of Nazareth. His effect on
humanity cannot be overstated. After two thousand years, Jesus'
teachings continue to spread from culture to culture. His followers,
which at one time numbered only twelve, have steadily increased to
include between 1,674,282,000 to 1,869,752,000 people, as of 1995
(more than one third of the earth's population).[2] He has been the
subject of countless books, magazine articles, movies, public debates,

and private discussions. The entire Western world measures time by his birth and death. Who was Jesus of Nazareth? Was he a man or a myth? Was he a magician or a madman? Or was he, as Christians believe, God in human flesh?

One Person, Two Natures

From the earliest days of Christianity, Jesus' followers believed that he was God incarnate, a unique union of divinity and humanity. Ignatius, Bishop of Antioch (A.D. ?–98/107) called Jesus "God,"[3] as did early Christian apologists Justin Martyr (A.D. 100–65),[4] Irenaeus (A.D. 175–95), and Gaius (A.D. 180–217).[5] Even secular sources attest to the fact that, very early in the history of Christianity, believers looked to Jesus as God. In a letter written to the Roman Emperor Trajan (A.D. 98–117) by Pliny the Younger (A.D. 61–114), who was the Roman governor of Bithynia, Pliny notes that it was the habit of Christians to gather together on a fixed day and recite by turns "a form of words [i.e., a hymn] to Christ as God."[6]

One of the earliest church-sanctioned statements addressing Jesus' identity was drafted by Christians at the Council of Nicaea in A.D. 325 and expanded on at the Council of Constantinople in 381. The resulting Niceno-Constantinopolitan Creed declared that Jesus was "begotten, not made." This assertion was their attempt to make clear the biblical teaching that the Son (Second Person of the Holy Trinity) had always existed and, in becoming a man, simply took on human form as Jesus of Nazareth. The Council also stressed that Jesus' very nature, or essence, was the same as the Father's:

> We believe in ONE GOD THE FATHER ALMIGHTY. . . . And in one Lord JESUS CHRIST, the only-begotten Son of God, Begotten of the Father before all worlds; God of God, Light of Light. Very God of very God, Begotten, not made, Being of one substance with the Father.[7]

Further clarification of Jesus' nature was made in A.D. 451 at the Council of Chalcedon, where Christian leaders reaffirmed that Jesus was truly God and truly man during his incarnation. At this same gathering, it was also agreed that Jesus' two natures—human and divine—were without mixture, confusion, separation, or division.[8] The Chalcedon Creed not only safeguarded Jesus' divinity but also clarified how that divinity existed with humanity.

> [We] teach men to confess one and the same Son, our Lord Jesus Christ, the same perfect in Godhead and also perfect in manhood; truly God and truly man . . . one and the same Christ, Son, Lord, Only-begotten, to be acknowledged in two natures, inconfusedly, inchangeably, indivisibly, inseparably, the distinction of natures being by no means taken away by the union, but rather the property of each nature being preserved, and concurring in one Person and one substance, not parted or divided into two persons, but one and the same Son . . . Jesus Christ.[9]

The true humanity and divinity of Jesus lies at the heart of the gospel message. Having a proper understanding of Jesus' full identity as both God and man is essential to salvation (Rom. 10:9; compare 2 Cor. 11:4). As theologian Robert Lightner comments in his *Handbook of Evangelical Theology*, "To deny either the undiminished deity or the perfect humanity of Christ is to put oneself outside the pale of orthodoxy."[10] Theology professor Millard Erickson agrees: "[O]ur faith rests on Jesus' actually being God in human flesh, and not simply an extraordinary human, albeit the most unusual person who ever lived."[11]

Like the Trinity doctrine, biblical proofs for Christ's humanity and deity can be found in both the Old and New Testaments. Few cults have a problem acknowledging Jesus' human nature. John the apostle plainly states that Jesus actually came "in the flesh" (1 John 4:2–3). Jesus himself said that he was a "man" speaking words of truth (John 8:40). Peter also referred to Jesus' humanity (Acts 2:22). When it comes to Jesus' deity, however, most cults take an altogether different attitude. They condemn belief in Jesus' divine nature as a corrupt and groundless doctrine of the devil. Ironically some of the most impressive statements regarding Jesus' identity as the God-man come from Jesus himself. It is to these texts that we will first turn our attention.

God the Son

Many scholars agree that one of the most revolutionary aspects of Christ's ministry was his emphasis on the unique relationship he had with God:

- "Therefore everyone who confesses Me before men, I will also confess him before My Father who is in heaven" (Matt. 10:32).
- "All things have been handed over to Me by My Father, and no one knows who the Son is except the Father, and who the Father is except the Son, and anyone to whom the Son wills to reveal Him" (Luke 10:22).
- "If I glorify Myself, My glory is nothing; it is My Father who glorifies Me, of whom you say, 'He is our God'" (John 8:54).
- "I and the Father are one" (John 10:30).
- "He who has seen Me has seen the Father. . . . I am in the Father, and the Father is in Me" (John 14:9–10).

To the Jews, such bold pronouncements effectively communicated that Jesus was claiming equality with God (John 10:33). They responded by attempting to stone him for blasphemy: "For this reason therefore the Jews were seeking all the more to kill Him, because He was not only breaking the Sabbath, but also was calling God His own Father, making Himself equal with God" (John 5:18; see also 8:59; 10:33).

Jesus made several other statements that would have been highly "inappropriate if made by someone who was less than God."[12] He said he would send "His angels" (Matt. 13:41), even though they are commonly spoken of as "the angels of God" (Luke 12:8–9; 15:10). He forgave sins (Mark 2:5; Luke 5:20), even though God alone can forgive sins (Luke 5:21; Isa. 43:25). He claimed that he would be the one to judge humanity (Matt. 25:31–34; compare Acts 10:42; 2 Tim. 4:1; Rev. 22:12), even though Scripture teaches that it will be God who judges the world (Ps. 50:6; 98:9; Heb. 12:23; James 4:12).

My Lord and My God

In addition to Jesus' words, there are the remarks of the disciples. John the apostle stated that Jesus existed "in the beginning" as God (John 1:1). Both Paul and Peter call Jesus our "God and Savior" (Titus 2:13; 2 Peter 1:1). Christ is described as the creator of all things (John 1:3; Col. 1:16), even though the Old Testament teaches that God created all things *by himself* (Isa. 42:5; 44:24). We are told that Jesus knew the thoughts of people (Matt. 9:4; Luke 9:47; 11:17; Rev. 2:23), which is an ability that belongs exclusively to God (1 Sam. 16:7; 1 Chron. 28:9). Furthermore, Paul reveals that all those who call upon the name of Jesus will be saved (Rom. 10:9–13), and in doing so quotes Joel 2:32, a verse that applies to calling upon the name of YAHWEH for salvation.

An especially interesting passage supporting Jesus' deity is Hebrews 1:10–12. This passage is a direct quote of Psalm 102:25–27, which is applied to God. In the New Testament, however, it is applied to the Son. Robert Bowman, Christian scholar and author of *Why You Should Believe in the Trinity,* enumerates several other proofs of Christ's deity that appear in the first chapter of Hebrews.

> Hebrews 1:8–12 is one of the most powerful passages in the Bible on the subject of Jesus as God. The opening verses of Hebrews have already declared that the Son was the "heir of all things" (v. 2a; cf. Col. 1:15–17), the one through whom everything was made (v. 2b), the "exact representation" of God's very being (v. 3a), the one who "sustains all things by the word of his power" (v. 3b) and who accomplished our salvation (v. 3c), who is better than all the angels (v. 4), and is worshiped by the angels (v. 6). Thus, the Son has already been described as in essence God, identified as the Creator, Sustainer, Owner, and Savior, and ascribed worship by the inhabitants of heaven. It should come as no surprise, then, that in verse 8 God the Father says "of the Son, 'Your throne, O God, is forever and ever'" (translating literally).[13]

Several Old Testament and New Testament passages also apply exclusively divine titles to Jesus. These verses would not make sense unless Jesus were truly the God of Israel.

DIVINE TITLE	GOD	JESUS
SAVIOR	Isaiah 43:3, 11 (See Luke 1:47; 1 Timothy 1:1; 2:3; Titus 1:3; 3:4; Jude 25)	Luke 2:11; Titus 3:6; 2 Peter 2:20; 3:18; 1 John 4:14
REDEEMER	Psalm 34:22; Isaiah 43:14; 44:24; 49:26; 54:8; 60:16	Galatians 3:13; 4:5; Titus 2:14 (See Isaiah 59:20)
ROCK OF SAFETY	2 Samuel 22:2, 32; Psalm 18:31; 19:14; 62:2, 6; 78:35; Isaiah 44:8	1 Corinthians 10:4
STONE OF STUMBLING	Isaiah 8:14	1 Peter 2:6–8
PLACE OF REFUGE	2 Samuel 22:3; Psalm 62:7–8; 91:4; 94:22; Isaiah 17:10; 57:13	Psalm 2:12

Perhaps the most stunning admission of Jesus' deity comes from Thomas, the disciple who would not believe Jesus had risen from the dead until he saw the Lord's crucifixion wounds. When confronted by Christ, Thomas declared, "My Lord and my God!" (John 20:28). Some cults suggest that Thomas was simply making an exclamation of surprise, such as, "Oh my God!" But this is highly unlikely. First, such an exclamation would have been blasphemous. Second, the Greek text does not read as an exclamation. A literal, word for word translation shows that the phrase is a statement of fact about Jesus: "The Lord of me and the God of me" (*Ho Kurios mou kai ho Theos mou*).

Most cults deny either Jesus' full humanity, his full deity, or both. Some groups say he was nothing more than a man possessing exceptional insight, wisdom, and knowledge. Others maintain that he was a supernaturally enlightened teacher endowed with some kind of cosmic consciousness often called "the Christ" consciousness. A few of the newer cults even have gone so far as to say Jesus was an extraterrestrial astronaut!

The ways in which cults pervert Jesus' identity are many and varied. Paul the apostle warned that there would be "another Jesus" preached to the world (2 Cor. 11:4). It is of the utmost importance, then, to be familiar not only with the real Jesus but also with a few of the more common false ones being promoted in the world of the cults.

The "Good Teacher" Heresy

One of the most widely held beliefs among cults is that Jesus was a mere man sent by God. According to The Way International, Scripture teaches that Jesus Christ was a man[14] but "not God."[15] Jehovah's Witnesses make a similar statement: "[W]hen God sent Jesus to earth as the ransom, he made Jesus to be what would satisfy justice, not an incarnation, not a god-man, but a perfect man."[16]

As we have seen, however, the New Testament presents Christ as God. Jesus, in fact, said that he should receive the same degree of honor as the Father (John 5:23). Assuming that the Bible presents us with an accurate account of Jesus' words and deeds, we are faced with only three options: (1) he was indeed God; (2) he was a liar; (3) he sincerely believed he was God but was not, which means he was a lunatic. Christian apologists Peter Kreeft and Ronald Tacelli elaborate on these well-known propositions.

> Either Jesus believed his own claim to be God or he did not. If he did, he was a lunatic. If he did not, he was a liar. Unless, of course, he was (is) God. Why could he not be either a liar or a lunatic? Because of his character. There are two things everyone admits about Jesus' character: he was wise and he was good. A lunatic is the opposite of wise, and a liar is the opposite of good. There are lunatics in asylums who sincerely believe they are God. The "divinity complex" is a recognized form of psychopathology. Its character traits are well known: egotism, narcissism, inflexibility, dullness, predictability, inability to understand and love others as they really are and creatively relate to others. . . . This is the polar opposite of the personality of Jesus! . . . Jesus had the three essential virtues every human being needs and wants: wisdom, love and creativity. He wisely and cannily saw into people's hearts. . . . He solved insolvable problems. He also gave totally to others. . . . The common verb predicated of those who met Jesus was *thaumazo*, "to wonder." . . . If that were lunacy, lunacy would be more desirable than sanity. If, on the other hand, Jesus was a liar, then he had to

have been the most clever, cunning, Machiavellian, blasphemously
wicked, satanic deceiver the world has ever known, successfully seduc-
ing billions into giving up their eternal souls into his hands. If orthodox Christianity is a lie, it is by far the biggest and baddest lie ever
told, and Jesus is the biggest and baddest liar. But in every way Jesus
was morally impeccable. . . . But if Jesus must be either Lord, liar or
lunatic, and he cannot be either liar or lunatic, then he must be Lord.
He claimed to be God. Either he was, or he wasn't. If he wasn't, he
either knew that he wasn't or he didn't. These are the only possibili-
ties. The first means he is Lord, the second means he is a liar, and the
third means he is a lunatic.[17]

The "lord, liar, lunatic" argument presents a clear difficulty to cults
wishing to maintain a theological position that denies Jesus' full deity.
There is, however, a way in which some groups have been able to cir-
cumvent the plain meaning of those biblical passages that ascribe
deity to Christ—relegate the Gospels to mythology.

The "Once upon a Time" Theory

Another erroneous theory about the historical person of Jesus
and his deity/humanity proposes that Christ never really existed.
Jesus, according to this view, is nothing more than a legend/myth
invented by the Gospel writers. One of the leading proponents of
this theory was the Communist regime of the former Soviet Union.
One of its basic teachings was that Jesus was a second-century myth
designed to "account for an early proletarian [working class] communist movement."[18]

Others have asserted that "Jesus" was a figure invented by Jews to
personify downtrodden Israel, a conquered (crucified) nation of people
who would one day rise up (be resurrected) in victory over Rome.[19]
In 1970 John Allegro, a Manchester University professor, proposed
that the word "Jesus" was not a proper name at all but rather a code
word designating a secret cult based on sacred mushrooms.[20]

The plausibility of these speculations quickly fades when examined in the light of historical documents and careful reflection. Several nonbiblical/secular sources dating to the first and second cen-

turies clearly speak of Jesus as the person from whom Christianity sprang.

- In reference to the death of James (Jesus' half-brother), it was recorded that "Ananus, who, as we have told you already, took the high priesthood. . . . [H]e assembled the Sanhedrin of judges, and brought before them the brother of Jesus, who was called the Christ, whose name was James, and some others; and when he had formed an accusation against them as breakers of the law, he delivered them to be stoned" (Flavius Josephus [Jewish historian, A.D. 37/38–110/120], *Antiquities of the Jews* 20.9.1).[21]
- Immediately after the A.D. 64 burning of Rome, Nero "fastened the guilt and inflicted the most exquisite tortures on a class hated for their abominations, called Christians by the populace. Christus, from whom the name had its origin, suffered the extreme penalty during the reign of Tiberius at the hands of one of our procurators, Pontius Pilatus, and a deadly superstition, thus checked for the moment, again broke out not only in Judaea, the source of the evil, but also in Rome, where all things hideous and shameful from every part of the world meet and become popular" (Tacitus [Roman historian, A.D. 55–120], *Annals* 15.44).[22]
- In a satirical work about the philosopher Proteous Peregrinus, there is a lengthy description of Christians, whose "first lawgiver persuaded them that they are all brothers of one another after they have transgressed once for all by denying the Greek gods and by worshipping that crucified sophist [teacher] himself and living under his laws" (Lucian of Samasota [Greek satirist, c. A.D. 120–180], *On the Death of Peregrinus*, 11–14).[23]
- The emperor Claudius expelled the Jews from Rome in A.D. 49 because "they were indulging in constant riots at the instigation of one Chrestus" (Suetonius [Roman historian, A.D. 69–140], *Life of Claudius* 25.4).[24]

In addition to these historical documents, there is a key aspect to the Jesus accounts that effectively destroys all possibility of them being pure legend: their Jewish setting. Humanities professor Michael Grant comments: "Judaism was a milieu to which doctrines of the deaths and rebirths of mythical gods seems so entirely foreign that the emergence of such a fabrication from its midst is very hard to credit."[25]

Grant also observes:

> If we apply to the New Testament, as we should, the same sort of criteria as we should apply to other ancient writings containing historical material, we can no more reject Jesus' existence than we can reject the existence of a mass of pagan personages whose reality as historical figures is never questioned.[26]

Clearly, only those persons with serious anti-Christian biases would deny the existence of the historical person known as Jesus of Nazareth. In fact, "no serious scholar has ventured to postulate the non-historicity of Jesus—or at any rate very few."[27] Even scholars highly critical of Christianity recognize that Jesus "did exist."[28]

The "Ascended Master" View

The New Age Movement has spawned a number of bizarre concepts about Jesus. One of the most popular views puts him into a category with a host of other religious leaders from the past who have since gone on to become "Ascended Masters" who dwell in higher spiritual planes of the universe. These ethereal entities are said to now be giving guidance and instruction through modern-day human vessels called "channelers," who allow themselves to be periodically possessed by the "Masters."

According to this slant on the biblical accounts, Jesus the Ascended Master was so advanced that he received the "Cosmic Christ," which is variously defined as the Universal Mind, the inner Self that is present in all persons, or the cosmic Source of all knowledge. Denver Seminary professor Doug Groothuis, a New Age expert, explains that this "Christ" is viewed by New Agers as "a universal presence working within all humanity to raise it to a higher level of evolutionary attainment."[29]

Although some New Age cults do not view Jesus as an "Ascended Master," most see him as being entirely separate from "the Christ."

The occult-oriented Rosicrucian Fellowship makes this observation about Jesus: "The Christ spirit which entered the body of Jesus when Jesus himself vacated it, was a ray from the cosmic Christ."[30] Members of the Church Universal and Triumphant embrace this concept as well.

> Churches have changed it all around. They think of Jesus Christ as the only begotten Son of God without understanding that this is the matrix from which we were all made. Christ is the Universal Reality from which we all sprang. . . . For Jesus attained the epitome of that Christhood to which we, therefore, can aspire. We forget that sometimes.[31] Jesus never said that he was the exclusive Son of God. When in John 3:16 he spoke of the "only begotten Son," he was referring to the universal Christ whose Body is individualized (broken) for each of us as our personal inner Teacher.[32]

The Unity School of Christianity, Theosophy, Religious Science, and nearly every other New Age group divides Jesus from "the Christ." According to cult specialist Ron Rhodes, "Fundamental to any discussion of New Age Christology is the recognition that New Agers distinguish between Jesus (a mere human vessel) and the Christ (variously defined, but always divine, and often a cosmic, impersonal entity)."[33]

In contrast to such New Age teachings, Scripture portrays Jesus not as an "Ascended Master" among many but as the "only begotten" Son of God (John 1:18). The Greek word translated "only begotten" is *monogenes*, which literally means "one of a kind." Hence, Jesus is not just one Master among many Masters. Jesus himself warned that there would arise many false Christs (Matt. 24:5).

Furthermore, the Bible does not draw a distinction between Jesus the man and another entity known as "the Christ." Jesus is pictured as being *the* Christ (Greek *Christos*, "anointed one"). Luke 2:11 reads: "For today in the city of David there has been born for you a Savior, who is Christ the Lord." When Jesus asked his disciples, "Who do you say that I am?" Peter resolutely declared, "You are the Christ, the Son of the Living God" (Matt. 16:16). He did not say, "You are Jesus, who has been inhabited by the Cosmic Christ Consciousness."

The "Created God" Concept

Many cults, of course, teach that Jesus is indeed fully divine. Unfortunately they do not identify him as the Second Person of the one Triune God. Such groups make Jesus a second god who at some point in time came into existence. They deny what is called the "eternality" of the Son, also known as the Son's *preexistence*. This is the biblical teaching that the Son has always existed. Theologian Charles Ryrie believes this to be a crucial aspect of Jesus' claims about himself.

> If Christ was not preexistent then He could not be God, because, among other attributes, God is eternal. . . . If Christ was not preexistent then He lied, because He claimed to be [John 8:58]. Then, the question arises, what else did He lie about?[34]

In the New Testament we are consistently reminded that Jesus existed before his birth. The verse most commonly appealed to is John 1:1, which states that Jesus, or "the Word," was "in the beginning" with God. This same Word eventually "became flesh, and dwelt among us" (v. 14). Also in the Gospel of John, we see John the Baptist declare the following in reference to Jesus: "After me comes a Man who has a higher rank than I, for He existed before me" (John 1:30). The Greek in this passage, *protos mou en,* basically means "before I was born, he already was."[35] The comment is significant because according to Luke 1:36, John was conceived six months before Jesus. Only if Jesus had existed prior to his own birth could he be "before" John.

Christ made a number of statements revealing that he actually came from heaven to earth (John 3:13; 6:33, 38, 46, 51, 62; 8:23, 42; 16:27–28). There is additional evidence for Jesus' preexistence in the Old Testament. The prophet Isaiah prophesied that one day the Messiah would come to Israel and would be called the "Everlasting Father" (Isa. 9:6 NIV). At first glance, this title seems to have little to do with Jesus' preexistence. It even sounds a little confusing. But Ron Rhodes, in *Christ before the Manger,* explains the powerful implications behind the phrase.

> "Everlasting Father" in this verse is better translated "Father of eternity." The words "Father of" in this context carry the meaning "pos-

sessor of eternity." Father of eternity is here used "in accordance with
a custom usual in Hebrew and in Arabic, where he who possesses a
thing is called the father of it. Thus, the father of strength means
strong; the father of knowledge, intelligent; the father of glory, glorious [Albert Barnes, *Notes on the Old Testament—Isaiah*, p. 193]." Along
these same lines, "the father of peace" means peaceful; "the father of
compassion" means compassionate; and "the father of goodness" means
good [E. W. Hengstenberg, *Christology of the Old Testament*, p. 196].
According to this common usage, the meaning of "Father of eternity"
in Isaiah 9:6 is "eternal." Christ as the Father of eternity is an eternal
being. John A. Martin thus rightly concludes that the phrase Everlasting Father is simply "an idiom used to describe the Messiah's relationship to time, not His relationship to the other Members of the
Trinity [John Martin, "Isaiah," in *The Bible Knowledge Commentary*,
p. 1053]." Further support for this view is found in "the Targums"—
simplified paraphrases of the Old Testament Scriptures utilized by the
ancient Jews. It is highly revealing that the Targum of Isaiah renders
Isaiah 9:6: "His name has been called from of old, Wonderful Counselor, Mighty God, He who lives forever, the Anointed One (or Messiah), in whose days peace shall increase upon us [Stenning, *The Targums of Isaiah*, p. 32]." Clearly, the ancient Jews considered the phrase
"Father of eternity" as indicating the eternality of the Messiah. There
can be no doubt that this is the meaning Isaiah intended to communicate to his readers.[36]

Although some cults accept the fact that Jesus existed prior to his
birth in Bethlehem, they still insist that at some point in time he was
created by the Father. As the Jehovah's Witnesses put it, "Christ was
the first of God's creations Col. 1:15; Rev. 3:14."[37] Another group,
The Family, approaches Jesus' nature in a similar way:

Here in the 14th verse of the third Chapter of Revelation, Jesus Himself . . . says He is the Beginning of the Creation of God! So what was
Jesus & what is Jesus?—A creation of God. . . . He must've been created before the creation of the Heavens & the Earth.[38]

These two arguments perfectly illustrate the way cults rely on poor
scholarship to justify their beliefs. When one carefully examines the
verses mentioned, it is clear that the biblical authors are communicating a message vastly different than "Jesus is a created being." In

Colossians 1:15–17, the Greek text indicates that Jesus is being referred to as an heir, or the first in rank, who is superior over all creation as Lord. The passage includes the word *prototokos* ("firstborn" or "first-bearer"), rather than *protoktistos* ("first-created"). One example of firstborn being used in this context can be found in Jeremiah 31:9 where Ephraim is called God's "firstborn." Genesis 41:51–52, however, states that Manasseh was *literally* the firstborn, not Ephraim. Ephraim was the preeminent son of the family. Obviously, *firstborn* does not always have to mean the first one born or the first created.

In Revelation 3:14, the Greek word translated "beginning" *(arche)* also does not necessarily refer to a literal beginning. It often connotes the idea of something being "the origin" or the "active cause" of something. In this passage, then, Jesus is being referred to as the source or "origin" of all creation. In other words, Jesus is the one from whom all creation springs. This Greek word *(arche)* is the same one from which we get our English word "architect." Nowhere in the Bible is Jesus spoken of as being a creation of God. He is, in fact, described as the creator of all that exists (John 1:3; Col. 1:16). He also is said to be the same "yesterday and today and forever" (Heb. 13:8). This leads us to another Christian doctrine that is regularly undermined by cults—the virgin birth.

The Virgin Birth Debate

According to orthodox Christianity, Jesus was miraculously conceived inside the womb of the Virgin Mary by the power of the Holy Spirit. Scripture confirms that Mary was indeed a virgin at the time of Jesus' conception and remained so until after he was born (Matt. 1:18–25; Luke 1:26–38). R. C. Sproul observes: "Those who do not believe in the Virgin Birth usually do not believe that Jesus is the true Son of God."[39]

Many, if not all cults, deny this key doctrine. Exactly how, then, do they explain Jesus' conception? A variety of answers have been proposed. Some cults, like the Rosicrucians, are content to simply say that "Jesus, highly advanced as he was . . . had a purely natural birth, with natural parents, Mary and Joseph."[40] Other cults, however, have more inventive theories. Mormons believe that Jesus was conceived through sexual intercourse between Mary and God the Father, whom they believe to be an exalted man.[41] Sun Myung Moon and his Unification Church put forth the notion that Jesus was born as a result of sex between Mary and the aged priest Zacharias, the husband of her cousin Elizabeth.

> As soon as the young girl [Mary] heard that she had been chosen to give birth to the Son of God, she "went with haste and entered the house of Zacharias" (Lk. 1:39). By giving herself to the aged priest, Mary would prove that she was truly a handmaiden of the Lord. Such an act of total surrender, far from being considered immoral in the ancient world, revealed the highest degree of spiritual dedication. By uniting with the priest, Mary "found favor with God" (Lk. 1:30).[42]

Reverend Moon seems to have no problem with the fact that such an act would have made Mary and Zacharias adulterers. According to the Old Testament, the penalty would have been death by stoning for both of them (Lev. 20:10). Moon's theory, however, is not by any means the least tasteful to be found in the world of the cults. The Family's founder "Moses" Berg advanced two teachings about Jesus' conception. He originally taught that Jesus was conceived through sex between Mary and God the Father. This view, however, evolved over the years into The Family's current belief, which is that Jesus was conceived through sex between Mary and the angel Gabriel.[43]

Contrary to what is asserted by cults, there are several good reasons to recognize and accept the orthodox Christian affirmation of the virgin birth. First, the Bible testifies that Jesus was conceived of a virgin (Matt. 1:18–25; Luke 1:26–38). To say that Jesus was not virgin-conceived would go against the authority and reliability of the Bible.

Second, Jesus came into the world not as a newly created being but as a preexistent Person. Consequently, the method used for entering the world would have to be somehow different from the normal means by which a human child is produced.

Third, Jesus had a sinless nature (2 Cor. 5:21; Heb. 4:15; 7:26; 1 Peter 1:19; 2:22; 3:18; 1 John 3:5). If he had been conceived through normal means, he would have inherited our sin nature. This would have disqualified him as Messiah (Isa. 53:9).

Finally, if Jesus had not been miraculously conceived by a virgin, he would not have been able to lay claim to the throne of David. "According to the prophecy of Jeremiah 22:28–30, there could be no king in Israel who was a descendent of King Jeconiah, and Matthew 1:12 relates that Joseph was from the line of Jeconiah."[44]

In Luke 9:18–19, Jesus asked his disciples, "Who do the people say that I am?" He received a number of answers: John the Baptist, Elijah, and "one of the prophets of old" who had been raised from the dead. Today, as in the first century, men and women are still seeking to understand the man called Jesus of Nazareth. But he is not the only member of the triune God that continues to be misunderstood. Cults regularly misrepresent the Third Person of the Trinity as well—the Holy Spirit.

6

Spirit of Truth

"When the Helper comes, whom I will send to you from the Father, that is the Spirit of Truth who proceeds from the Father, He will testify about Me."

Jesus of Nazareth
(John 15:26)

In the previous chapters we have discussed the First Person of the Trinity (the Father) and the Second Person of the Trinity (the Son). But what of the Third Person who exists within the eternal nature of the one true God? According to the celebrated Bible teacher R. A. Torrey, "One of the most characteristic and distinctive doctrines of the Christian faith is that of the personality and deity of the Holy Spirit. The doctrine of the personality of the Holy Spirit is of the highest importance."[1]

Unfortunately there is widespread confusion about the Holy Spirit. Even within Christianity it is not difficult to find unbiblical and occasionally bizarre ideas about the Third Person of the Trinity. All too often I have turned on Christian television only to see an evangelist either throwing the Holy Spirit on believers as if the Spirit were a liquid or shooting the Holy Spirit at Christians as if the Spirit were electricity that could be discharged through the fingertips in a manner similar to the evil emperor's attacks against Luke Skywalker in *The Return of the Jedi*. Such demonstrations clearly indicate that there has not been enough orthodox teaching from American pulpits about the Holy Spirit and how that Spirit works in the hearts and lives of believers.

The problem grows even more theologically unsound in the world of the cults, which presents a wide variety of views ranging from a complete denial of the Holy Spirit's existence to claiming that the Holy Spirit is an impersonal force to acceptance of him as a third god entirely separate from Jesus and the Father. All cults may not agree 100 percent on who, or what, the Holy Spirit is, but most of them have at least three erroneous beliefs in common: the Holy Spirit is not a person of the Trinity, as defined by orthodox Christians; the Holy Spirit is not equal to the Father and/or the Son; and the Holy Spirit is not one in essence with the Father and the Son. Each of these notions is biblically unsound, as we shall now see.

Missing in Action

Some cults, especially those influenced by Eastern philosophy, do not believe in a personal God. To such groups "God" is nothing more than a descriptive term for "all that is" (see chapter 4). Consequently, no personal entity known as the "Holy Spirit" is ever recognized. Although some New Age or Eastern philosophy–based cults may talk about the "One Soul" or "the Spirit," this is merely a reference to the universal consciousness through which all of us are ultimately united as one.

The Rosicrucians believe and have always believed that there is but one soul in the universe, and that is the universal soul or the universal consciousness of God. . . . A segment, or essence, of that universal soul resides in each being that possesses soul. And this essence is never separated from the universal soul or is never an entity in such a sense as to make it independent and individual. The soul expression of each person . . . through the medium of the physical body and through the channel of our education and comprehension of things, may be quite different and thereby give us those characteristics or traits of personality which we interpret as individuality.[2] Yet God, the Initiates and ourselves are all of one Substance, *undivided, indivisible,* but differentiated in vibrational status.[3]

The Bible reveals that there is indeed a person called the Holy
Spirit who is distinct from humanity. Genesis 1:2 tells us that during
creation "the Spirit of God was moving over the surface of the waters."
Other Old Testament passages speak of the "Spirit of God" coming
upon various individuals and enabling them to prophesy and/or render service to the Lord (Num. 11:26; 1 Sam. 10:10; 2 Chron. 24:20).
Several Old Testament verses even speak of the "Holy" Spirit of God
(Ps. 51:11; Isa. 63:10, 11). The New Testament also notes the activ-
ity of a "Holy Spirit" (Acts 19:6; Rom. 15:16; 1 Cor. 12:3; 2 Cor.
13:14; Eph. 1:13; 1 Thess. 4:8).

Obviously the Holy Spirit is not just a "Cosmic All" through which
everything and everyone in the universe is ultimately "One." Some
cults, particularly those originating from within Christianity, recognize this biblical truth. They readily accept Scripture's identification
of a Holy Spirit that is separate from humanity. Sadly, many of these
same groups fail to completely understand the nature of the Holy
Spirit, claiming that the Third Person of the Trinity is not a person
at all.

Power or Person?

Once the personality of the Holy Spirit is denied, cults are free to
apply virtually any label to the Third Person of the Trinity:

- Christian Science: a divine body of knowledge known as
  "Divine Science"[4]
- Christadelphians: "the energy or power of God" used in creation[5]
- Jehovah's Witnesses: "an invisible active force by means of
  which he [God] gets his will done"[6]
- The Way International: "power from on high, spiritual abili-
  ties, enablement"[7]
- Freemasonry: "a Life-Principle of the world"[8]

A few cults use decidedly mystical and highly evocative imagery
to describe the Holy Spirit. Eckankar, for instance, teaches that the
Spirit is God's "Light and Sound. It is the Voice of God speaking to

all creation."[9] According to the Church Universal and Triumphant, the Spirit is the "seventh-ray aspect of the sacred fire, [which] transmutes the cause, effect, record, and memory of negative karma and misqualified energy that result in discord."[10]

In all fairness, it can sometimes be difficult in certain parts of Scripture to uncover the personality of the Holy Spirit. Theologian Louis Berkhof observes that the terms "Spirit of God" or "Holy Spirit" do not "suggest personality as much as the term 'Son' does. Moreover, the person of the Holy Spirit did not appear in a clearly discernible personal form among men, as the person of the Son of God did."[11]

God's Word also draws less overall attention to the Spirit than it does to the Father and Son. This is probably because the primary role of the Spirit is to "bring to completion the work that has been planned by God the Father and begun by God the Son."[12] He gives us new spiritual life through regeneration (John 3:5–8), sanctifies us so we can become more like Christ (Rom. 8:13; 15:16; 1 Peter 1:2), and empowers us for service (Acts 1:8; 1 Cor. 12:7–11).[13]

Although the Holy Spirit is not featured as prominently in the Bible as the Father and the Son, the scriptural proofs for his personality are plentiful. First, numerous Old and New Testament passages ascribe to the Holy Spirit characteristics consistent with personhood: feeling emotion (Isa. 63:10; Rom. 15:30; Eph. 4:30), possessing knowledge (1 Cor. 2:11), and having a mind (Rom. 8:27).

Second, the Holy Spirit acts in ways that only a person can act: He teaches (Neh. 9:20; Luke 12:12; John 14:26), bears witness (John 15:26; Acts 5:32; Rom. 8:16), leads and guides (John 16:13; Rom. 8:14), hears (John 16:13), glorifies Christ (John 16:14), convicts unbelievers' hearts (John 16:8), intercedes for believers (Rom. 8:27), speaks and gives commands (Acts 8:29; 10:19–20; 11:12; Rev. 22:17), calls Christians into service (Acts 13:2), appoints individuals to church offices (Acts 20:28), makes decisions (Acts 15:28), works according to his own will (1 Cor. 12:11), and exhibits self-control by not acting "on His own initiative" when doing so would conflict with the will of the Father and Son (John 16:13).

Ironically the Jehovah's Witnesses, a cult that denies the personhood of the Spirit, printed a story in their December 8, 1973, *Awake!* magazine that is especially relevant to our discussion. The Watchtower article supported the personhood, or personality, of Satan using the following argument: "[C]an an unintelligent force carry on a conversation with a person? Also, the Bible calls Satan a manslayer, a liar, a father . . . and a ruler. Only an intelligent person could fit all those descriptions."[14]

The criteria used by the Watchtower regarding the significance of personal attributes is the same criteria used by Christians to establish the personality of the Holy Spirit. If the Watchtower were to be consistent, it would have to acknowledge the Holy Spirit as a person just as it acknowledges Satan as a person. But this they fail to do.

According to the Greek

The Bible also uses various words and phrases for the Holy Spirit that are properly applied only to a person. For example, three passages in the Gospel of John use the masculine, personal pronoun *he* in reference to the Holy Spirit. This grammatical construction, at the very least, suggests that the Holy Spirit is a person:

"I will ask the Father, and He will give you another Helper *[Parakletos]*, that He may be with you forever."
(John 14:16)

"When the Helper *[Parakletos]* comes, whom I will send to you from the Father, that is the Spirit of truth who proceeds from the Father, He will testify about Me."
(John 15:26)

"If I do not go away, the Helper *[Parakletos]* will not come to you; but if I go, I will send Him to you. And He, when He comes, will convict the world of sin and righteousness and judgment."
(John 16:7b–8)

Some cults have argued that the use of the personal, masculine pronoun *he* (Greek *ekeinos*) in these passages has little to do with the Holy Spirit being a person. They base their position on the fact that the Greek word for "Helper"—*parakletos*—is itself a masculine descriptive term; therefore, a masculine pronoun *must* be used in order to match the masculine noun. In other words, use of the word *he* is simply a matter of good grammar and has nothing to do with the personhood of the Holy Spirit.

Although this argument may sound plausible, it is rendered irrelevant by John 14:26 and 15:26. In these two verses the term *parakletos* is immediately followed by the Greek word for spirit (*pneuma*), which is a neuter expression. The apostle then refers back to *pneuma*, and in so doing, could have used a neuter pronoun (i.e., it). Instead, John continues using the personal pronoun *he* (*ekeinos*), which can also be translated as *him*. John did not have to make this grammatical choice. In fact, he had a perfect opportunity to use a neuter pronoun and clearly indicate that the *Parakletos*—the *pneuma*—was an "it" rather than a person. He chose, however, to deliberately continue using the personal pronoun. According to many theologians (e.g., J. I. Packer, R. C. Sproul, Charles Ryrie) John's word usage clearly indicates that the Spirit is indeed a person. In John 16:13–14, the apostle uses *ekeinos* in the same manner.

> "But the Helper [*parakletos*], the Holy Spirit [*pneuma*], whom the Father will send in My name, He [*ekeinos*] will teach you all things, and bring to your remembrance all that I said to you."
> (John 14:26)

> "When the Helper [*parakletos*] comes, whom I will send to you from the Father, that is the Spirit [*pneuma*] of truth who proceeds from the Father, He [*ekeinos*] will testify about Me."
> (John 15:26)

> "But when He [*ekeinos*], the Spirit [*pneuma*] of truth, comes, He will guide you into all the truth; for He will not speak on His own initiative, but whatever He hears, He will speak; and He will disclose to you what is to come. He will glorify Me; for He will take of Mine and will disclose it to you."
> (John 16:13–14)

Another indication in the Greek text that the Holy Spirit is a person can be seen in Jesus' promise to send "another" Helper to believers (John 14:16). There are two words for "another" that could have

SPIRIT OF TRUTH   99

been used in this verse: *heteros* and *allos*. Both have significantly different meanings. *Heteros* "expresses a qualitative difference and denotes 'another of a different sort.'" *Allos*, on the other hand, "expresses a numerical difference and denotes 'another of the same sort.'"[15]

John records Christ's words using the term *allos*. Jesus, being our first Helper (1 John 2:1), was promising to send another Helper like himself. Bluntly put, if cults want to maintain that the Holy Spirit is not a real person, they will also have to believe that Jesus is not a real person. Christ's use of the term *allos* is also important because it indicates that the Holy Spirit is God (is "another" like Jesus).

God the Holy Spirit

Although some cults go so far as to identify the Holy Spirit as a personal being, most of these same groups deny that he is God. Scripture, however, declares that the Spirit is nothing less than full deity. In Acts 5, Ananias and his wife, Sapphira, sold their property but were dishonest about how much they had received from the purchase. Peter confronted Ananias: "Ananias, why has Satan filled your heart to lie to the Holy Spirit and to keep back some of the price of the land?" (v. 3). Peter goes on to tell Ananias that in lying to the Holy Spirit, he had actually lied "to God" (v. 4). It should also be mentioned here that a person can only lie to another person. This passage, therefore, also gives further proof that the Spirit is not an "inactive force" or an impersonal power.

In addition to this powerful passage, a number of verses attribute divine characteristics and actions to the Holy Spirit. For example, Luke 1:68–70 records Zacharias declaring, "Blessed be the Lord God of Israel. . . . He spoke by the mouth of His holy prophets from of old." Compare this statement with the words of Paul the apostle: "The Holy Spirit rightly spoke through Isaiah the prophet to your fathers" (Acts 28:25). Consider, too, 1 Corinthians 3:16 and 6:19, which state, "The Spirit of God dwells in you. . . . Your body is a temple of the Holy Spirit." Compare these two verses with 2 Corinthians 6:16: "We are the temple of the living God; just as God said, 'I will dwell in them.'" Finally, God is eternal (Ps. 90:2), as is the Spirit (Heb. 9:14).

A few groups that accept both the personality *and* divinity of the
Holy Spirit still manage to miss the orthodox view of the Trinity's
Third Person. Although The Family believes that the Holy Spirit is a
divine person, their Holy Spirit is quite different from the biblical one:

I ALWAYS DID THINK OF GOD AS OUR HEAVENLY FATHER
AND HIS SPIRIT OF LOVE AS OUR HEAVENLY MOTHER. . . .
His beautiful Holy Spirit, God's Spirit-Queen of Love. . . . The Heav-
enly Lover and Mother-God, the Queen of Love. . . . AND SHE'S
DRESSED SO APPROPRIATELY!—Pearls for purity, hearts for
Love—and nudity for Truth![16]

A correct understanding of the Holy Spirit is just as crucial to good
theology as a correct understanding of the Father or Jesus Christ. All
three are the one God with whom we must have a relationship. R. C.
Sproul comments that the response of a Christian to the biblical
teachings concerning the Holy Spirit "is not mere affirmation that
such a being exists, but rather, to obey, love, and adore the Holy Spirit,
the Third Person of the Trinity."[17]

"Spirit" versus "Ghost"

A final comment must be made about various unwarranted distinctions that are made between "Holy Spirit" and "Holy Ghost."
The term *Holy Spirit* appears consistently in most modern translations, whereas the latter term is used in the King James Version of
the Bible (KJV). The variant readings in the KJV have led to a number of confused ideas.

The Mormons, for example, who accept the KJV as their primary
translation of the Bible, believe that there are three gods—Father,
Son, and Holy Ghost. At the same time, they believe that there is
something called the "Holy Spirit," which is said to be a "divine
essence" used by these three gods:

The Holy Ghost is an individual personage, the third member of the
Godhead; the Holy Spirit, in a distinctive sense, is the "divine essence"
by means of which the Godhead operates upon man and in nature.[18]

Mormon doctrine fails to recognize that the same Greek word (*pneuma*) is translated as both Spirit and Ghost in the KJV. The only difference between them is the occurrence of the word *holy (hagion)* as a prefix to *pneuma*. In the KJV, the word *Ghost* is used when *holy* is present. Translators of the KJV tended to use the term *Spirit* if *holy* did not appear before *pneuma*. Because only one Greek word is used, making a distinction between "Spirit" and "Ghost" is erroneous.

Yet another cult, The Way International, makes an equally serious mistake about the Holy Spirit based on their founder's ignorance of proper biblical exegesis (interpretation). In his controversial book *Jesus Christ Is Not God*, Victor Paul Wierwille stated:

> God is Holy and God is Spirit. The gift that He gives is holy spirit. . . . [I]n the Greek manuscripts and texts the word *pneuma*, "spirit," is never capitalized. Therefore, when the word *pneuma* is translated "Spirit" with a capital "S" or "spirit" with a small "s," it is an interpretation. . . . [I]t is understandable why so many people confuse the Giver, Holy Spirit, with the gift, holy spirit. The Giver is God who is Spirit, *pneuma*, and Holy, *hagion*. . . . Luke 11:13. . . . how much more shall your heavenly Father give the Holy Spirit *[pneuma hagion]* to them that ask him? This verse clearly shows that *pneuma hagion* is the gift from God the Father, therefore, should be translated with a small "h" and a small "s."[19]

What Wierwille is saying is that the "Holy Spirit" actually refers only to the Father (the only person Wierwille recognizes as "God"). "Holy Spirit" is just another name for God. He then asserts that there is another "holy spirit," which is an impersonal gift of power from God. This identification of a Holy Spirit/holy spirit is entirely without grammatical or linguistic support. Only one Holy Spirit is mentioned in the Bible and he is not God the Father. In Isaiah 48:16, God the Father is mentioned separately from the Holy Spirit. Isaiah 63:9–10 mentions the Holy Spirit along with God the Father who put the Spirit in the midst of the people. These passages show the two distinct personalities of God the Father and the Holy Spirit. No passages mention a "holy spirit."

The various ways in which cults misunderstand the doctrines relating to the Father, Son, and Holy Spirit are numerous. This is not surprising since God's nature has been perverted by people since the earliest days of history (Rom. 1:18–23). Why? The answer to this question involves what is perhaps the greatest hindrance to a proper understanding of the one true God: sin. Humanity's primary spiritual problem, and God's solution for it, is examined in part 3.

Part 3

[I believe] in one Lord JESUS CHRIST . . . who, for us men and for our salvation, came down from heaven . . . and was made man; and was crucified also for us under Pontius Pilate; he suffered and was buried; and the third day he rose again, according to the Scriptures.

Niceno-Constantinopolitan Creed

Furthermore it is necessary to everlasting salvation: that he also believe rightly [faithfully] the Incarnation of our Lord Jesus Christ. . . . Who although he be [is] God and Man; yet he is not two, but one Christ. . . . Who suffered for our salvation . . . rose again the third day from the dead.

Athanasian Creed

Amazing Grace

7

Natural Born Sinners

We all deal daily with annoyances. . . . Deeper than annoyance lies an array of regrets. . . . But even further toward the alarm end of the trouble spectrum lie certain distresses that theologians call miseries. People feel walled in by loneliness, for example. . . . The whole range of human miseries, from restlessness and estrangement through shame and guilt to the agonies of daytime television—all of them tell us that things in human life are not as they ought to be.

Cornelius Plantinga Jr.
theology professor
Calvin Theological Seminary[1]

On May 23, 1994, in Columbia University's Low Memorial Library, photojournalist Kevin Carter accepted the most prestigious award his profession could offer—the Pulitzer Prize. Shortly after receiving this honor, Carter wrote to his parents: "I swear I got the most applause of anybody. I can't wait to show you the trophy. It is the most precious thing, and the highest acknowledgment of my work I could receive."[2]

Carter won the award for a photo he took of a child dying of starvation under the watchful eye of a hungry vulture standing only a few feet away. The macabre scene epitomized the devastating 1993 famine in Sudan. Carter did not enjoy taking the photo, nor did he celebrate for very long the recognition it brought him. The Pulitzer could not alleviate the inner torment he had been battling for years.

On the evening of July 27, 1994, thirty-three-year-old Kevin Carter drove his pickup truck to a secluded spot where he had often played as a boy. He then "used silver gaffer tape to attach a garden hose to the exhaust pipe and run it to the passenger-side. . . . He got in and switched on the engine."[3] As he listened to music playing on his Walkman, Carter closed his eyes and used his knapsack as a pillow on which to rest his weary head for the last time. The suicide note he left behind echoes the sentiments of many people:

> The pain of life overrides the joy to the point that joy does not exist. . . . I am haunted by the vivid memories of killings & corpses & anger & pain . . . of starving or wounded children, of trigger-happy mad-men, often police, of killer executioners.[4]

These tragic words ring all too true for many people. The world is full of evil and suffering. Crime is on the rise. Wars refuse to cease. Various countries continue perpetrating human rights violations. Man's inhumanity to man thrives unabated. Where does the hatred and violence come from? Why does so much suffering exist? Scripture tells us that the pain and tragedy we see around us is traceable to sin, and that sin is the result of something everyone possesses from the moment of birth—the sin nature. This chapter covers human nature, sin, and salvation; in other words, humanity's main spiritual problem and God's solution for it.

The Fall

The origin of our relationship to sin, the consequences of that relationship, and our inherent propensity toward sinning date back to the very beginning of the human race. The Bible records that Adam and Eve, the first human beings, were perfect and without sin when they were created by God. Both Adam and Eve received life directly from God himself (Gen. 1:27). Adam was made from the dust of the earth (2:7), and Eve was fashioned by God from a portion of bone taken from Adam's side (vv. 21–22). God provided Adam and Eve with great blessings—a beautiful world in which to live (1:29), all the food they could enjoy (vv. 29–31), and, of course, they received the loving companionship of one another (2:21–25).

Adam and Eve also were given free will, a necessary component of a loving relationship between individuals. For a time Adam and Eve enjoyed an unhindered rapport with each other and with God through their free will. But to test their hearts, God commanded that they should not eat of the tree of knowledge of good and evil, which was located in the center of the Garden of Eden, where God had placed them to live (2:8). Unfortunately they chose to disobey God's directive.

The Lord's test was designed to give Adam and Eve a knowledge of good and evil through *obedience*. In the end, however, they came to understand the difference between good and evil in a reverse manner—through *disobedience*.[5] Their actions were the first sins committed on earth. With their deeds came God's judgment on them, as well as on their descendants, the entire human race (3:16–19).

A Deadly Inheritance

The consequences of Adam and Eve's disobedience were disastrous. Earth was cursed and rendered incapable of spontaneously bringing forth adequate amounts of food (Gen. 3:17–19). Human beings, also cursed, could no longer live forever as they were originally designed to do (2:16–17). Physical, emotional, and psychological suffering also began to affect humanity.

> Sin brought disturbance in the entire life of man. His physical life fell a prey to weaknesses and diseases, which result in discomforts and often in agonizing pains; and his mental life became subject to distressing disturbances, which often rob him of the joy of life, disqualify him for his daily task, and sometimes entirely destroy his mental equilibrium. His very soul has become a battle-field of conflicting thoughts, passions, and desires. The will refuses to follow the judgement of the intellect, and the passions run riot without the control of an intelligent will.[6]

As the human race continued on its course of development, the tendency to disobey God increased exponentially. At one point,

the wickedness of society grew so great that the intent of everyone's heart was continually evil (6:5). Throughout Genesis, humanity's estrangement from God can be seen working itself out through
sins that are still common today: murder (4:8), drunkenness (9:21),
lying (12:13), adultery (16:4), homosexuality (19:5), and incest
(19:32–36). In his *Moody Handbook of Theology*, Dr. Paul Enns
insightfully explains that all sin actually falls in two distinct cate-
gories—wrongful acts toward God and wrongful acts toward other
human beings:

> Romans 1:18 refers to "ungodliness and unrighteousness of men."
> Ungodliness refers to man's failure to obey God and keep command-
> ments related to Him (Exod. 20:1–11); unrighteousness is seen in man's
> failure to live righteously toward his fellow man (Exod. 20:12–17).[7]

According to J. I. Packer, sin "may be comprehensively defined as
lack of conformity to the law of God in act, habit, attitude, outlook,
disposition, motivation, and mode of existence."[8] More specifically,
sin may be defined in four distinct, yet related ways:

1. Breaking God's law or standards of right conduct (Rom. 4:15;
   compare Rom. 2:23; 5:14; Gal. 3:19)
2. Nonconformity to what one knows to be the right course of
   action (Rom. 14:23; James 4:12)
3. A principle within man known as the sin nature, often called
   the flesh (Rom. 7:14, 17–25)
4. A state of mind that not only tolerates but actively pursues law-
   lessness (1 John 3:4)[9]

The effects of Adam's choice to disobey God have traveled down
through successive generations as a hideous moral cancer. Scripture
teaches that everyone is born with a sinful nature (Ps. 14:1–3; Rom.
3:23). Packer observes that sinfulness "marks everyone from birth,
and is there in the form of a motivationally twisted heart, prior to
any actual sins; . . . is the root and source of all actual sins; . . . [and]
derives to us in a real though mysterious way from Adam. . . . [W]e
are not sinners because we sin, but rather we sin because we are sin-

ners, born with a nature enslaved to sin."[10] Recent statistics support
Packer. Even someone's age is no barrier to sin's insidious influence:

- In 1991, juveniles were responsible for one in five violent
  crimes, including 1,600 homicides.[11]
- A 1994 survey found that school violence in the previous five
  years had increased in 38 percent of U.S. schools.[12]
- By 1995, 25 percent of all murdered children were being killed
  by other children.[13]
- 1996 crime statistics found 342 children being arrested every
  day for violent crimes.[14]

As disturbing as these figures are, they are overshadowed by the
many heinous crimes now being committed by children across the
country; crimes that at one time only the most hardened and cold-
blooded adult criminals would dare perpetrate. These young law-
breakers have been labeled by Princeton professor John J. DiIulio Jr.
as a new breed of "juvenile superpredators" who "have no sense of
right or wrong and no remorse over violent assaults on others."[15]

- In 1994, fourteen-year-old Eric Smith was sentenced to nine
  years to life for the 1993 stoning and strangulation of four-year-
  old Derrick Robie, who lived near Smith in Savona, New
  York.[16]
- Seventeen-year-old Joseph Cheadle of Milwaukie, Oregon, was
  convicted and sentenced in 1994 for beating to death a 103-
  year-old man and ransacking his home.[17]
- In Chicago, Illinois, 1994 also saw the sentencing of an eleven-
  year-old boy who, when he was only ten, broke into eighty-
  three-year-old Anna Gilvas's house, beat her with her own cane,
  and slit her throat with a ten-inch knife.[18]
- Three Florida youths—aged thirteen, fourteen, and fifteen—
  were sentenced to state prison in 1996 for the 1994 shooting
  of a store clerk during an attempted robbery.[19]
- In 1996, a fourteen-year-old Southern California youth shot
  and killed his mother, then confessed to the murder "with a
  smirk on his face." The teenager had told neighborhood friends
  that he was looking for someone to gun down.[20]

- A twelve-year-old Texas girl was sentenced in 1996 to twenty years in state custody for beating to death a two-and-a-half-year-old child.[21]

It is painfully obvious that Adam's disobedience set in motion a host of problems affecting relationships between human beings. Worst of all, however, the fall separated humanity from God (Isa. 59:2). So devastating were the consequences of Adam's rebellion against God that it not only produced physical death (Gen. 2:17; Rom. 5:12–21; 6:23; Eph. 2:1, 5) but also spiritual death. In the classic work *The Fundamentals* (1917), Rev. Thomas Whitelaw outlined with great clarity the extent to which all of us have been influenced by sin.

It is not a malady which has affected only one part of man's complex constitution: every part thereof has felt its baleful influence. It has darkened his understanding and made him unable, without supernatural illumination, to apprehend and appreciate spiritual things. "The natural man receiveth not the things of the Spirit of God, neither can he know them, because they are spiritually discerned" (1 Cor. 2:14); and again, "The Gentiles walk in the vanity of their minds, having the understanding darkened, being alienated from the life of God through the ignorance that is in them, because of the blindness of their hearts" (Eph. 4:17, 18). It defiles the heart, so that if left to itself, it becomes "deceitful above all things and desperately wicked" (Jer. 17:9), so "full of evil" (Eccl. 9:3) and "only evil continually" (Gen. 6:5), that out of it proceed "evil thoughts, murders, adulteries, fornications and such like" (Matt. 15:19), thus proving it to be a veritable cage of unclean birds. It paralyzes the will, if not wholly, at least partially, in every case, so that even regenerated souls have often to complain like Paul that when they would do good evil is present with them, that they are carnal sold under sin, that what they would they do not, and what they hate they do, that in their flesh, i.e., their sin-polluted natures, dwelleth no good thing, and that while to will is present with them, how to perform that which is good they know not (Rom. 7:14–25). It dulls the conscience . . . renders it less quick to detect the approach of evil, less prompt to sound a warning against it and sometimes so dead as to be past feeling about it (Eph. 4:19). In short there is not a faculty of the soul that is not injured by it. "Sin when it is finished bringeth forth death" (James 1:5).[22]

Even a cursory reading of the daily newspaper supports Scripture's presentation of humanity as being innately sinful. Nevertheless, cults often deny our condition as creations estranged from their Creator. The following sections discuss but a few ways that cults misunderstand the sinful predisposition of all human beings. A few groups, as we shall see, utterly dismiss the entire concept of sin and its effects.

Sin: The Illusion

The doctrinal views of numerous Mind Science groups are built on a foundational belief that everything we see is a mere illusion. Sin, evil, suffering, and even death are relegated to the realm of deceptive fantasy.

[T]he cardinal point in Christian Science, [is] that matter and evil (including all inharmony [sic], sin, disease, death) are *unreal*.[23]

"[E]vil is but an illusion, and it has no real basis. Evil is a false belief."[24]

"There is no evil. . . . [T]he apparent absence of good (evil) is unreal. It is only an *appearance* of evil, just as the moving sun was an appearance."[25]

"Pain, sickness, poverty, old age, death, cannot master me, for they are not real. . . . There is no evil (or devil). . . . Pain, sickness, poverty, old age and death are not real, and they have no power over me."[26]

Many New Agers fit into a similar category. For some of them, anything is permissible because sin is unreal. Satan too is viewed as a false concept. Evil in this belief system is merely "the manifestation of a force that is out of place or out of timing, inappropriate to the needs and realities of the situation."[27] In other words, evil is just a misdirected thought, a glitch in perspective, or a deceptive image originating in the mind of the person perceiving something as evil/sin. The logical conclusion of such a view is that people actually create the tragic events that take place in their lives.

It is difficult for someone living in some kind of intolerable situation, experiencing the throes of terrible physical illness or financial ruin, to think of it all as a game, but that is what it is, nonetheless. Not only are they playing a game, but they are playing their own game. The game that they created for themselves to play.[28]

YOU are the only thing that is real. Everything else is your imagination, movie stuff you've brought into your screenplay to help you see who you really are. . . . There are no victims in this life or any other. No mistakes. No wrong paths. No winners. No losers. Accept that and then take responsibility for making your life what you want it to be.[29]

Obviously it is difficult to effectively communicate biblical truth to persons involved in the Mind Sciences and the New Age Movement. Their nebulous definitions of truth itself, including what is right and wrong, leave almost no place for appeals to the Bible. Fortunately, their worldview has a major weakness. Its practicality often breaks down in the course of daily living, which results in inconsistent behavior.

New Agers, for example, often say that there is no good or evil, yet they simultaneously contend that some things are inherently "good" (ecology, natural health, brotherhood, holistic medicine, etc.) and some things are bad (being intellectually intolerant, passing theological judgments on others, standing against abortion, etc.). Taking a stand on what is right or wrong is irreconcilable with their position that there is no right and wrong or good and evil.

Their inconsistent worldview tends to be brought out even more if they themselves are threatened with something that is "wrong." For example, I have often asked New Agers or Mind Science practitioners what they would do if I stole their wallet or punched them in the face. They immediately responded by saying they would unhesitatingly call for the police. I then ask: "Why?" I have received a variety of answers, each one ultimately breaking down to: "Because it's wrong."

It is here that a Christian can try to demonstrate how everyone uses some criteria for judging right from wrong. New Agers and Mind Science practitioners use their own limited perspective, while

Christians use a guide to life that has been proven throughout the centuries to be a reliable source of truth—the Bible. At this point, Scripture can be used to show that Satan, sin, and evil are all very real.

Jesus, who is revered as a great teacher even by New Agers and Mind Science practitioners, often mentioned Satan (Matt. 13:3–39; Luke 10:18; 13:16). Jesus never said Satan was merely an illusory product of the mind. Instead, he called the devil a "murderer" and "a liar" in whom there is no truth whatsoever (John 8:44). Jesus' temptation in the desert (Matt. 4:1–11) would have been a perfect opportunity to destroy the illusion of Satan by simply showing that the adversary was unreal. Instead, he spoke with the devil, was tempted by him, and overcame him.

Regarding sin, the prophet Jeremiah observed that the heart of man is *desperately* sick (Jer. 17:9, emphasis mine). All have sinned and fallen short of the glory of God (Rom. 3:9–12, 23). Everyone stands justly condemned as sinners before the righteous God of the universe (Rom. 5:18–19), who judges according to his eternal law (Rom. 7:7; James 2:10–11; 1 John 3:4), which is holy, just, and good (Rom. 7:12).

Stumbling toward Immortality

Some cultists actually view the fall as a blessing. Mormons, for instance, who believe that they can eventually become gods, assert that Adam and Eve did not really "fall" but instead stumbled upwards, so to speak. Adam and Eve's disobedience was all part of God's wonderful plan to get his "spirit children" moving toward godhood.

> According to the foreordained plan, Adam was to fall . . . so that the opportunity for eternal progression and perfection might be offered to all the spirit children of the Father.[30]

> When Adam was driven out of the Garden of Eden, the Lord passed a sentence upon him. Some people have looked upon that sentence as being a dreadful thing. It was not; it was a blessing.[31]

To Mormons, then, the events that transpired in the Garden of Eden were not really tragic because they changed Adam and Eve from immortal beings into mortal beings, thereby enabling us (their descendants) to obtain mortality, which is an indispensable prerequisite to godhood. Tenth Mormon President Joseph Fielding Smith explains:

> I never speak of the part Eve took in this fall as a sin, nor do I accuse Adam of a sin. . . . When he ate, he became subject to death, and therefore he became mortal. . . . [N]either Adam nor Eve looked upon it as a sin. . . . [The fall] brought to pass all of the vicissitudes [changes] of mortality. . . . It brought death; but we must not lose sight of the fact that it brought blessings.[32]

Closely tied to this view is another idea promoted by many cults, that man is essentially good. Mormon apostle Boyd Packer writes: "It is critically important that you understand that you already know right from wrong, that you're innately, inherently, and intuitively good."[33] A similar position is taken by the fraternal order known as Freemasonry, a theological cult commonly referred to as the Masonic Lodge. According to well-known Christian apologists John Ankerberg and John Weldon, "Masonic ritual teaches through its symbols and emblems that man is not sinful in the biblical sense; he is merely 'flawed' in a minor and temporary sense."[34]

Scripture, however, does not indicate that humanity is basically good, nor does it state that our character is only in a "rude and imperfect state," which is what Freemasonry asserts.[35] According to the Bible, human beings are fundamentally evil (Ps. 58:3–5; Eccles. 9:3; Jer. 17:9). We continually shun God and seek only to do wrong (Gen. 6:5; Ps. 14:3; Isa. 53:6; John 3:19; Rom. 3:11–12). No one is righteous (Eccles. 7:20; Isa. 64:6; Rom 3:23). In fact, the apostle Paul called unbelievers slaves to sin (Rom. 6:6, 17, 20). John further declared that those who say they have no sin are merely deceiving themselves, and the truth is not in them (1 John 1:8, 10).

Adam and Eve's disobedience was a tragically poor choice that spread physical and spiritual death to all people (Rom. 5:12; 6:23; 8:10). Eve was deceived and Adam deliberately disobeyed God (Gen. 3:13; 1 Tim. 2:14). Only through the person and work of Jesus Christ

can we escape the effect that sin has on us in this life and in the afterlife. Jesus willingly tasted death for everyone (Heb. 2:9), the just for
the unjust, so that we might be brought to God (1 Peter 3:18). Jesus
paid the price for all of our personal sins (1 Cor. 15:3; 1 Peter 3:18).
Paul declares that Jesus gave himself "for our sins" (Gal. 1:4; Heb.
9:28; 10:12). He "bore our sins in His body" (1 Peter 2:24). Through
faith in Christ (Rom. 5:1–2; 10:9; Eph. 2:1–10), we appropriate for
ourselves the work he accomplished on the cross. This results in
receiving the gift God offers—eternal life in his loving presence (John
3:16; Rom. 6:23).

Earning Eternity

Closely associated with the Christian conviction that belief in
Christ delivers us from the power of death (both physical and spiritual) is the Christian view that salvation is obtained solely by God's
grace through faith. Good works do not earn us the salvation God
offers through his Son. Salvation is not of ourselves. It is a gift of
God, "not as a result of works, so that no one may boast" (Eph.
2:8–9).

This concept is usually denied in some way by cults, which invariably insist that before salvation can be obtained, good works or special rituals must be accomplished and added to faith. Mormonism,
for instance, teaches that "individual salvation or rescue from the
effects of personal sins is to be acquired by each for himself, by faith
and good works." Forgiveness for personal sins "can only be obtained
through obedience to the requirements of the gospel, and a life of
good works."[36]

The Christadelphians, another modern-day cult, hold a similar position: "What else is necessary for salvation besides faith?
'Works'—that is obedience to God's commands as taught by
Jesus."[37] Some cults, such as the Jehovah's Witnesses, go to great
lengths to outline the importance of works and the order in which
they must occur.

> It is for the reward of eternal life that every last person on earth should
> now be working. Are you?[38]

To get one's name written in that book of life will depend upon one's works, whether they are in fulfillment of God's will and approved by his Judge and King.[39]

Jesus Christ identified a first requirement when he said in prayer . . . "This means everlasting life, their *taking in knowledge* of you." . . . Many have found the second requirement more difficult. It is to *obey God's laws.* . . . A third requirement is that we *be associated with God's channel*, his organization [the Watchtower]. . . . To receive everlasting life in the earthly Paradise we must identify that organization and serve God as part of it. The fourth requirement . . . requires that prospective subjects of his Kingdom support his government by *loyally advocating his Kingdom rule to others* [i.e., preaching door-to-door].[40]

Jehovah God will justify, declare righteous, on the basis of their own merit all perfected humans who have withstood that final, decisive test of mankind [the release of Satan from bondage after the 1000-year reign of Christ].[41]

Many cults attempt to legitimize the blending of faith and works for salvation by citing James 2:14–17, which tells us that faith without works is dead. But in declaring that a professed faith without works is a dead faith, James is simply saying that those who have a genuine faith will produce good works as a natural consequence of the supernatural working of the Holy Spirit in their life. If no good works are being done by an individual, then the faith which that person says he or she possesses is not a genuine faith. It is a false (or dead) faith. Anyone who has truly obtained salvation by faith will naturally manifest the kind of good works that are consistent with salvation.

Two analogies at this point may be helpful. Consider an apple tree. It does not bear apples in order to become an apple tree. It bears apples because it is already an apple tree. Likewise, a dog does not bark in order to become a dog. A dog barks because it is already a dog. Similarly, a Christian does not do good works in order to become a Christian. A Christian does good works because he or she is already a Christian. Christians do good works *because* of salvation, not *for* salvation (Rom. 4:5).

It is a grave mistake to think that salvation is a reward for which someone must work. Equally erroneous, however, is the opposite doctrinal extreme asserting that the only thing someone has to do to receive forgiveness and subsequent salvation is to mentally assent to (intellectually accept) the identity of Christ. According to this notion, good works are meaningless. No change whatsoever should be expected in a person's life after "accepting the Lord" by faith.

Cultists who hold this position contend that Abraham was justified by faith apart from works (Rom. 4:2–3). But their argument is undone by verses such as Matthew 8:29 and James 2:19, which indicate that even demons recognize truths about God and Christ. Are demons saved? Of course not. Scripture consistently presents saving faith as being inextricably linked with repentance and a changed life (Mark 1:15; Acts 26:20).

As James says, real faith will produce a changed life. This is not to say that every Christian changes in the exact same way or at the exact same speed. God deals with each person individually. For one Christian, a changed life may mean no longer getting drunk and taking illicit drugs. Such changes are easily recognizable. The changes in another Christian, however, may not be as drastic to the observer. Perhaps God wants him or her to simply rise each day with a new attitude about life, and the more visible signs of salvation will come with time. In both cases, lives have changed indeed.

Justified by Faith or Works?

Another issue that must be mentioned involves an entirely different problem that arises when cultists compare Romans 4:2 with James 2:22–24. The former passage, as we have seen, says Abraham was justified by faith. The latter passage declares Abraham was justified by works. Some cultists charge that these verses contradict one another. But this apparent contradiction between Paul and James is easily resolved.

When both passages are carefully read, it becomes apparent that James is speaking of justification before men: "I will show *you* my faith by my works" (James 2:18, emphasis mine). In the Romans passage, justification "before God" is being discussed. In context, then, our justification before God is by grace alone through faith, while justification before others must be *demonstrated* by good works, because others cannot know our heart. Put another way, once a person is saved, that person will produce good works by which he or she will be justified before other people. However, those who try to justify themselves before God in this manner will have their good works counted against them as debt (Rom. 4:4).

A final point must be made about God's law. It is often maintained by cults that we must obey the entire law of God. This is only half true. We are indeed told in Scripture to keep Jesus' commandments (John 14:15, 21; 15:10; 1 John 2:3; 3:22–24; 2 John 6). At the same time, we know that because of sin and the weakness of our flesh, no one can keep the whole law (James 2:10). Consequently, although God's law is itself holy (Rom. 7:12; 1 Tim. 1:8), it is also a curse because it points out our sin (Gal. 3:13). Fortunately for us, Christ kept the law perfectly (Matt. 5:17). Through faith in him, his righteousness is imputed to us apart from the law (Rom. 3:28). In this way, the law is fulfilled in us (Rom. 8:3–4), even though we are not able to keep it.

This does not mean that we are justified by the law. No one is justified by the law (Rom. 3:20; Gal. 2:16; 3:11), and any who seek justification through the law will be cut off from Christ (Gal. 5:3–4). Jesus, according to the Bible, is the end of the law for Christians (Rom. 10:4). Because of him, we are now under grace (Rom. 6:14). Of course, God's grace does not give us a license to sin (Rom. 6:1–2). We are to live, as best we can, in obedience to God through dependence on the Holy Spirit, who empowers us to obey God, knowing that when we fail to meet the Lord's righteousness, Jesus' blood is present to cleanse us from all sin (1 John 1:9). This brings us to the miracle of the atonement, which will be explained in the next chapter.

8

At the Cross

When I survey the wondrous cross,
On which the Prince of glory died,
My richest gain I count but loss,
And pour contempt on all my pride.
Isaac Watts (1674–1748)

Jesus taught many truths that were difficult for his followers to accept and comprehend (John 6:60). In fact, he often had to restate his messages in more understandable terms (Matt. 13:36; 15:15; compare Mark 4:13). Some of Jesus' comments were so foreign to ingrained Jewish notions about God that critics would often use his words against him: "A division occurred again among the Jews because of these words. Many of them were saying, 'He has a demon and is insane. Why do you listen to Him?'" (John 10:19–20).

Among Jesus' most disturbing statements were those focusing on his earthly destiny—to die a violent death. In Mark 10:33–34, he said, "The Son of Man will be delivered to the chief priests and the scribes; and they will condemn Him to death and will hand Him over to the Gentiles. They will mock Him and spit on Him, and scourge Him and kill Him, and three days later He will rise again" (compare Mark 10:45; 12:1–11; Luke 13:33; John 12:24, 27). On one occasion, Peter sternly rebuked Christ for voicing such predictions. "God forbid it, Lord!" said Peter. "This shall never happen to You" (Matt.

16:21–22). Jesus gave a forceful reply: "Get behind Me, Satan! You are a stumbling block to Me; for you are not setting your mind on God's interests, but man's" (v. 23).

Peter did not understand that our Lord's mission was far broader in scope and infinitely more valuable in purpose than merely preaching throughout the Galilean countryside or leading a Jewish revolt against Rome. Christ came to save sinners (1 Tim. 1:15) via his death on the cross (Matt. 20:28; 26:28; Gal. 1:3–4). His life signaled the fulfillment of Old Testament prophecies concerning Israel's suffering servant (Isa. 52:13–53:12; compare Luke 2:25–32; 24:25–32; 1 Cor. 15:3) through whom Jew and Gentile alike would be able to obtain spiritual fellowship with God (1 Cor. 12:13; Gal. 3:28).

Today, as in the first century, Jesus' death is intellectually repugnant and emotionally offensive to many individuals (1 Peter 2:6–8). For Christians, however, the crucifixion is the power of God by which there has been made an entranceway into the kingdom of heaven (1 Cor. 1:18, 22–23). The teaching that Jesus died for sinners so that they may have eternal life in the loving presence of God is known as the doctrine of the atonement. It is one of the most significant theological concepts of the Christian faith.

Our At-One-Ment

The importance of Christ's death on the cross cannot be overstated. It has been called the "heart of the gospel," "center of gravity in Christian life and thought," "crucial point of Christian faith," and "distinguishing mark of the Christian religion."[1] In *The Great Doctrines of the Bible* (1912), theologian William Evans (1870–1950) wrote: "The atonement is the scarlet cord running through every page in the entire Bible. Cut the Bible anywhere and it bleeds; it is red with redemption truth."[2]

But what exactly does the English word *atonement* mean? It has no inherent theological definition. The term merely describes a bringing together of estranged persons. It is an expression that derives from Anglo-Saxon words meaning "making at one," hence "at-one-ment."[3] When used by Christians in a theological sense, however, *atonement* refers to Christ's death on the cross, which healed God's estrangement from humanity that resulted from Adam's disobedience.

The doctrine of atonement can be traced to the Old Testament Hebrew verb *kaphar*. Its root meaning is "to cover over," as in Genesis 6:14, where Noah covered over the ark's woodwork with pitch.[4] Related to *kaphar* is the Hebrew noun *kopher*, which is translated in Genesis 6:14 as "pitch" (i.e., a covering). *Kopher* also is used in the Old Testament to describe a "ransom price that 'covers' an offense— not by sweeping it out of sight but by making an equivalent payment so that the offense has been actually and exactly paid for"[5] (Exod. 30:12, "ransom"; Num. 35:31; Ps. 49:7; Isa. 43:3).

Eventually, these two words (*kaphar* and *kopher*) gave rise to two other words (*kipper* and *kuppar*) that were "set aside to express only the idea of removing offense by equivalent payment and so bringing the offender and the offended together."[6] These two terms are normally translated in the Old Testament as atonement and are used in reference to the animal sacrifices God chose as the method whereby his people could be brought back into a right relationship with him after sinning.

Leviticus 4 deals with unintentional sins. The means of atonement was the same for everyone regardless of their position in the community. Everyone had to participate in the ceremony if they were to be restored to a harmonious relationship with God: "In each case the formula is repeated: the one who sins unintentionally, 'he is guilty.' The guilty sinner then brings the animal to the priests, who offer it in sacrifice. 'In this way he [the priest] will make atonement for man's sin, and he will be forgiven' (4:26)."[7]

Forgiveness for intentional sins is discussed in Leviticus 16, where instructions are given "for a special sacrifice to be offered just once a year, on the tenth day of the seventh month, Tishri."[8] This day was known as the Day of Atonement (Yom Kippur). The entire community gathered together on that day and, through a unique ritual, were corporately forgiven for their sins.

The high priest, following carefully the prescribed steps, brought the blood of the sacrifice into the inner room of the tabernacle and there sprinkled the blood on the cover of the ark [of the covenant]. . . . The sacrificed animal was a "sin offering for the people" (Lev. 16:15) and is specifically said to have been "because of the uncleanness and rebellion of the Israelites, whatever their sins have been" (16:16; cf. 16:21). That annual sacrifice, made before the Lord, was an "atonement . . . to be made once a year for all the sins of the Israelites" (16:34). Following it, Israel was told, "You will be clean from all your sins" (16:30).[9]

Perhaps the most important aspect of the Old Testament sacrificial system rests in its foreshadowing of Christ's actions on behalf of sinners (Hebrews 9). The apostle Paul reveals that although God recognized the Old Testament's yearly sacrifices as sufficient for the "covering" of sins, they served only as a temporary solution to the entire sin problem (Rom. 3:25). Jesus had to die for an eternal atonement to be made. In the New Testament we finally see a full explanation of the Old Testament sacrifices.

> God was willing [in the Old Testament] to accept a person's faith in the place of righteousness, and, admittedly, this seems unfair. Paul's answer is that we can understand the fairness of it now that Jesus has been presented as "a sacrifice of atonement." It is on the basis of the atonement Jesus accomplished that God is shown to have been just and fair in forgiving those who have faith. Heb 2:17 argues that Jesus must have become a true human being to serve both as the High Priest who offered the atoning sacrifice to God and as the sacrifice itself.[10]

The doctrine of the atonement is further expanded on by several key terms relating to Christ's death: substitution, propitiation, reconciliation, forgiveness, redemption, and justification. To fully understand and appreciate the atonement, each of these terms must be discussed.

Substitution

Christ's death is sometimes referred to as a "vicarious" atonement, meaning that it was of a substitutionary nature. Jesus actually died *in the place of* sinners. This idea is expressed in many biblical passages (2 Cor. 5:21; Gal. 3:13; Heb. 9:28; 1 Peter 2:24), especially in Isaiah 53:6: "All of us like sheep have gone astray, Each of us has turned to his own way; But the LORD has caused the iniquity of us all To fall on Him" (see also vv. 4–5). The substitutionary nature of Christ's death is indispensable to a correct understanding of the atonement. Theologian George Eldon Ladd comments:

> In the death of Christ I died; I experienced the doom of sin; everything that the guilt of sin merits from the wrath of God was fulfilled in the death I died in Christ. It is this objective fact which is the supreme manifestation of God's love and which is to be the controlling center of my life, and the quality of this love is derived from the fact that Christ's death was not his own; it was mine. He died not only as my representative; he died in my stead, for it is because of his death that I shall be spared that death. He has died my death in my behalf and in my place.[11]

Many individuals have voiced strong objection to the substitutionary view of the atonement. Some critics of Christianity, for instance, feel that it "smacks of unfairness and injustice. To use a courtroom analogy: Suppose that a judge, on finding a defendant guilty, proceeds to punish not the defendant, but an innocent party. Would this not be improper?"[12] This may at first seem like a reasonable objection. In reality, however, it shows a lack of knowledge concerning a rarely used legal procedure wherein a court can actually punish an innocent person for someone else's crime.

In his *Systematic Theology*, Louis Berkhof explains that this legal procedure is possible only if the innocent person offers himself or herself to bear the penalty and the lawgiver (whether it be a sovereign king or a government) accepts the offer. Of course, there are a number of conditions that must be met:

> (1) that the guilty party himself is not in a position to bear the penalty through to the end, so that a righteous relation results; (2) that the transfer does not encroach upon the rights and privileges of innocent third parties, nor cause them to suffer hardships and privations; (3) that the person enduring the penalty is not himself already indebted to justice, and does not owe all his services to the government; and (4) that the guilty party retains the consciousness of his guilt and of the fact that the substitute is suffering for him. In view of all this it will be understood that the transfer of penal debt is well-nigh, if not entirely, impossible among men. But in the case of Christ, which is altogether

unique . . . all the conditions named were met. There was no injustice of any kind.[13]

By dying in our place, Jesus took the place of sinners, "their guilt
was imputed, and their punishment, transferred to Him."[14] He rep-
resentatively bore the punishment we rightly deserved (Eph. 5:2).
Closely associated with the substitutionary nature of Christ's death
is the propitiatory aspect of his sacrifice.

Propitiation

The word *propitiation* is best understood as an appeasement, or a
pacification, of negative feelings. In Scripture, it is God's wrath against
sinners that we see being propitiated through the death of Christ.
Because Jesus endured for us God's wrath against sin, we are now able
to enjoy God's favor. Jesus fully satisfied "all the righteous demands
of God toward the sinner."[15] The sins of humanity were judged, and
punishment was exacted through Christ's death on the cross. Consequently, God can now "show mercy to the believing sinner in the
removal of his guilt [and sins]."[16] This concept is further explained in
The Moody Handbook of Theology:

> Because God is holy and righteous He cannot overlook sin; through
> the work of Jesus Christ God is fully satisfied that His righteous stan-
> dard has been met. Through union with Christ the believer can now
> be accepted by God and be spared from the wrath of God.[17]

The punishment that Christ bore for us was necessary since God's
just and holy character demands that sin be punished. God could not
have simply dismissed the sins of humanity. To do so would have been
contrary to his perfectly just nature. In fact, because sin was punished
through Christ's death, God's righteousness was demonstrated to the
world (Rom. 3:25–26). We have been reconciled to God.

Reconciliation

As noted earlier, sin created a wall of separation between God and
humanity (Isa. 59:1–2; Col. 1:21–22; James 4:4), and only through
Christ's substitutionary death could that wall be removed (Rom. 5:10;

2 Cor. 5:19). We now have free access to God. Nothing stands in our way. Such is the meaning behind the popular Christmas carol lyrics, "Peace on earth and mercy mild, God and sinners reconciled."

The Bible teaches that all of us were reconciled to God while we were yet sinners (Rom. 5:8). This means that reconciliation is not something we ourselves have accomplished. It is all God's doing. Essentially, he has thrown open his arms and said, "Everything standing between us has been removed. We are reconciled in my eyes. Now it is up to you to either receive or reject the reconciliation that is available."

Even before a person hears the gospel, he or she has been reconciled to God. It is an action that God has done entirely outside of us. Whether or not we choose to receive that reconciliation and enjoy its benefits is another matter. For those who do choose to accept God's graciousness, there awaits complete forgiveness for their sins.

Forgiveness

Forgiveness occurs when God actually applies the work of Christ to us, thereby canceling the debt we owed for our sins (i.e., eternal death or eternal separation from his loving presence and divine favor). This forgiveness comes directly from God (Exod. 34:7; Ps. 130:4; Luke 23:34; 1 John 1:9) and can only be obtained through personal faith in Jesus Christ (Matt. 26:28; Acts 5:31–32; 10:43; 13:39; Eph. 4:32; 1 John 2:12).

Those who reject God's forgiveness will receive judgment (Rom. 2:5; Eph. 5:6; Col. 3:6; 2 Thess. 1:7–10), which is consistent with God's holiness (Rom. 2:2–16; Heb. 13:4). Only persons in Christ will escape God's wrath (John 5:24; Rom. 8:1). Jesus himself taught in Matthew 26:28 that his blood would be shed for the forgiveness of sins.

This is not to say that there was some kind of magical power in Christ's blood that washed away our sins.[18] As R. C. Sproul remarks, "If Jesus had cut His finger in Joseph's carpentry workshop, it would have had no redemptive significance."[19] It must be recognized that in Scripture the phrase "shedding of blood" simply refers to death. "It is the death of Christ, not His physical blood, that has reconciled the world."[20] Consequently, all of the New Testament allusions to Christ's blood are primarily speaking of his death for humanity rather than a mere spilling of blood. At the same time, however, it must be noted that if he had died on the cross *without* spilling any of his blood, no atonement would have been made (Heb. 9:22).

Redemption

The concept of redemption is central to the idea of atonement for sins. Again, we must look to the Old Testament for a foundation on which the teachings of the New Testament may be built. Two Hebrew words translated as either *redeem* or *ransom* are especially important: *padah,* and *ga'al.*

"*Padah* was originally used commercially to indicate a transfer of ownership (e.g., Lev. 19:20). The transfer came through payment of some equivalent transaction."[21] It is commonly used in the Old Testament to illustrate God's ownership of his people whom he rescued from Egypt: "Remember that you were a slave in the land of Egypt, and the LORD your God redeemed you" (Deut. 15:15).

Ga'al, which has a similar background to *padah,* means to "play the part of a kinsman, that is, to act on behalf of a relative in trouble or danger."[22] Both *ga'al* and *padah* speak of persons or objects, which although owned by a particular individual are in the power/control of another. The terms also indicate that the owner of the property is unable to secure the release of his possessions until a third party intervenes:

> Then a third party appears, and this person is able to effect release. *Ga'al* places the emphasis on the relationship between redeemer and redeemed. Because of his close kinship, the redeemer had the privilege and the duty of coming to the relative's aid.[23]

In the New Testament, several words relate to the idea of redemption. Each one refers in some way to how Christ redeemed sinners through payment of a debt. For example, *agorazo* (1 Cor. 6:19–20; 7:22–23) was used in Greek culture to describe one's purchase in the marketplace, often in reference to the purchase of slaves. Its biblical use connotes "the believer being purchased out of the slavemarket of sin and set free from sin's bondage through the death of Jesus Christ" (Rev. 5:9; 14:3–4).[24]

Another Greek word, *exagorazo,* is a strengthened form of *agorazo* and denotes "to buy out," especially of purchasing a slave with a view to his freedom. However, rather than stressing the act of buying, *exago-razo* focuses on the price paid.[25] It is used by Paul in reference to Christ's deliverance of Jews from the law and its curse (Gal. 3:13; 4:5).

A third term that involves the idea of redemption is *lutroo*, which means "to obtain release by the payment of a price."[26] It conveys the notion of being set free through a paid ransom (Luke 24:21). In the case of Christians, we have been purchased by the blood of Jesus Christ (1 Peter 1:18–19). *Lutroo*, unlike the other two Greek words, stresses the actual event of deliverance itself or the act of setting at liberty.[27]

All of these words work together in the Bible to paint a picture of Jesus' substitutionary death, which not only propitiated God's wrath but also made a payment of our sinner's debt so that we could be redeemed from death.

Justification

Justification is the act whereby God declares righteous those who are unrighteous (Rom. 4:5–8; 5:9). This occurs as a direct result of God's grace, or unmerited favor, toward individuals who accept by faith the saving power of Christ's death and resurrection (Rom. 10:9). Through justification, Christ's righteousness is credited to us so thoroughly that we can actually claim his righteousness as our own.[28]

Without justification we would not be able to gain entrance into heaven even though we had been forgiven for our past sins. With forgiveness alone, we would simply be sinners who had been forgiven but who still did not possess the absolute righteousness (moral perfection) necessary to enter God's kingdom. Consequently, forgiveness has been termed the "negative" side of salvation, with justification being the "positive" side.[29] Forgiveness entails the *removal* of something (sin and its penalty), while justification *imparts* something (a person's righteous standing before God).

The most important aspect of justification is understanding that it is appropriated by the believer through faith alone. Nothing we do can contribute to our obtaining a righteous standing before God. We are unrighteous, plain and simple, and always will be in and of ourselves. But God, by his grace, shows us mercy and chooses to impute Christ's righteousness to us as we come to him in faith. The great reformer John Calvin made the following comments:

A man will be *justified by faith* when, excluded from the righteousness of works, he by faith lays hold of the righteousness of Christ, and clothed in it appears in the sight of God not as a sinner, but as righteous. Thus we simply interpret justification, as the acceptance with which God receives us into his favour as if we were righteous; and we say that this justification consists in the forgiveness of sins and the imputation of the righteousness of Christ.[30]

Scripture pointedly declares that we are justified apart from good works or the law (Rom. 3:21–26). God's declaration of our righteous standing before him is similar to a legal act of a Supreme Court judge giving a final verdict. The case has been decided. We are innocent and righteous based on Christ's righteousness. No further appeals or actions can be taken by the prosecution.

It must not be thought, however, that our faith is what actually *causes* our justification. Faith is not a good work that earns justification. It is merely a channel through which justification comes to the sinner.

Often the soulwinner presents the gospel as though some special kind or amount of faith is required for salvation. Satan often comes to the newborn child of God and brings doubts as to whether he has had enough faith or has believed in the right way. As far as the Scripture is concerned, God simply requires removal of trust in self and redirection of trust to Christ. It is true that a person must be sincere when trusting Christ, but it must always be remembered that Christ saves, not one's faith. Man's reception of God's great gift of salvation adds nothing to the completed work of Christ. So it is not Christ's substitutionary atonement plus faith in Christ that provides the basis for acceptance with God. Christ's work alone saves; but unless his person and work are received by faith, no benefit comes to the individual sinner. Man's faith must have a proper object if justification is to result. . . . It is always faith in God's Son as the divine substitute for sin's penalty that results in God bringing life to the spiritually dead sinner. . . . The work of Calvary means that God has done everything and man makes no contribution whatsoever to the finished work of Christ or to his own salvation. Paul indicated that the offense of the cross was the absence of human work from God's way of salvation (Gal. 5:11).[31]

A good illustration of how faith is involved in justification can be seen each Christmas. Every year gifts are bought for friends and family. Those gifts belong to the recipients even before they are received. They are paid for, wrapped, and under the tree waiting to bring joy. The recipient need only receive the gift to benefit from it. In a similar way, sinners need only receive the gift of salvation to enjoy its glorious blessings. Just as we open our hands to receive a Christmas gift, so a sinner receives salvation and justification by faith. Faith is an attitude on which God acts. By faith a sinner is merely saying, "Yes, I believe you have a gift for me. I accept it." God, in turn, gives us the gift he purchased for us with his own blood (Eph. 1:7–8).

A Death Signifying Little

The doctrine of the atonement, like many other Christian beliefs, is either obscured or totally eradicated by cults. The Unification Church, for instance, takes an especially mundane view of Jesus' death. To Reverend Moon and his followers, the crucifixion of Christ was a tragic failure because Jesus did not really come to die on the cross[32] but "had to die a reluctant death due to the disbelief of the people."[33] Jesus' death allegedly was "not an essential part of God's plan for redeeming sinful man."[34] Unification church members admit that "Unification thought diametrically contradicts the Fundamentalist view that Jesus' sole mission was to atone for the sins of mankind by dying on the cross."[35]

If Moon's teaching diametrically contradicts the view that Jesus' sole mission was to atone for the sins of mankind by dying, then Moon diametrically contradicts the Bible. Jesus explicitly declared that his purpose for coming was to first preach the gospel of God's kingdom (Mark 1:38; Luke 4:43) and then die (John 12:27) so that he could draw all men to himself (John 3:14; 12:32). Furthermore, the crucifixion was part of God's sovereign plan since before creation (Eph. 3:11; 1 Peter 1:20). Through dying, Jesus took away people's sins (1 John 3:5) and destroyed the works of the devil (v. 8).

Jehovah's Witnesses take an equally gloomy view of the atonement. Although they hold that Christ's death was indeed a part of God's plan and that it was necessary for our salvation, they deny that Jesus paid the price for each person's individual sins. The Watchtower contends that Jesus' death only paid for the sin of Adam:

> [God] could not set aside the judgment that he had entered against
> Adam. He could, however, be consistent . . . by permitting another to
> pay the debt of Adam and thereby to open the way for Adam and his
> offspring to be released from sin and death. . . . To redeem or ransom
> man from the grave means that God will provide a means of satisfac-
> tion of the judgment against Adam.[36]

Basically, the Witnesses are claiming that Christ was not completely successful in overcoming our sins by his death. He only opened
the way for us to be released from death and sin. We must augment
Christ's work with personal works of righteousness. In the world of
the cults, it is commonly taught that salvation is ultimately brought
about by good works rather than Christ's atoning death. But Scripture teaches that sinless Jesus (1 Peter 1:19) did indeed die in our
place for our sins (1 Cor. 15:3; Gal. 1:4; Heb. 9:28; 1 Peter 2:24; 3:18).

Atonement in Gethsemane?

Some cults put an especially imaginative twist on the doctrine of
the atonement. Mormons, for example, teach that Jesus did indeed
die for everyone. But this was not for the purpose of cleansing us
from our personal sins. Mormons believe that Jesus died so that all
of us could be resurrected from the grave. They call this "redemption from death" and it is applicable to *everyone*, believer and unbe-
liever alike.[37]

Latter-day Saint apostle Bruce McConkie writes that if there had
been no atonement, "temporal death would have remained forever,
and there never would have been a resurrection. The body would
have remained forever in the grave."[38] Like the Jehovah's Witnesses,
Mormons also maintain that Jesus' death merely opened a way for us
to procure our own salvation through works of righteousness.

> The Individual Effect of the Atonement makes it possible for any and
> every soul to obtain absolution from the effect of personal sins, through
> the mediation of Christ; but such saving intercession is to be invoked
> by individual effort as manifested through faith, repentance, and con-
> tinued works of righteousness. . . . [T]he blessing of redemption from

individual sins, while open for all to attain, is nevertheless conditioned on individual effort.[39]

To further complicate their erroneous view of the atonement, Mormons teach that Jesus *completed* the act of atonement in the Garden of Gethsemane where he toiled in prayer on the night of his betrayal:

> In one of his books, *Come Unto Christ,* President Benson wrote: "There [in Gethsemane] He suffered the pains of all men. . . . It was in Gethsemane that Jesus took on Himself the sins of the world. . . . His pain was equivalent to the cumulative burden of all men.[40]

In actuality, Jesus bore the sins of the world while on the cross (1 Peter 2:24; Col. 1:20), not while in Gethsemane. Furthermore, everyone is not blessed through Christ's crucifixion. Only those who accept his sacrifice and surrender their life to him will receive the benefit of Jesus' death and resurrection (Rom. 10:9), which is forgiveness of sins (Acts 10:43) and salvation (Rom. 3:24). Eternal life in Christ, rather than eternal existence through resurrection, is the free gift offered by God to humanity (Rom. 6:23). This gift is obtainable only by grace through faith (Eph. 2:8–10).

9

Death's Defeat

"He is Risen!" was the victorious cry of the early Christians. Unless we accept what the Scriptures teach about the Resurrection, the entire Christian message virtually disintegrates. The whole preaching thrust of the apostolic age was based upon the fact that one quiet morning in an obscure garden, man had vanquished his most feared enemy, the vaunted dark angel of death.

Dr. Walter Martin (1928–89)
Christian apologist and cult expert[1]

Christ's dramatic death would have counted for very little if it had not been for something that occurred three days after his crucifixion—the resurrection. This wondrous event confirmed Jesus' authority over death (Acts 2:24; 1 Cor. 15:55–57), proved his divinity in the eyes of witnesses (Acts 2:32; Rom. 1:4), fulfilled Old Testament prophecies concerning the Messiah (Ps. 16:10; Acts 26:22–23), and made possible our justification (Rom. 4:25). Christ's resurrection also serves as a guarantee that believers too will be raised from death to life everlasting (1 Cor. 15:20–23).

The apostle Paul cited both the death *and* resurrection of Jesus as being central to his gospel message (1 Cor. 15:1–4). He also declared that acceptance of Jesus' resurrection was an indispensable condition of salvation (Rom. 10:9). Distinguished Bible teacher J. Dwight Pentecost aptly summarizes the meaningfulness of the Easter miracle.

133

Since Jesus Christ is raised from the dead, we who have received Him as Saviour have the assurance that sins have been forgiven and that the next step in the program is resurrection into His glory—not resurrection to eternal damnation and judgment. So there is victory through the resurrection of Christ—victory over sin, victory over defeat, victory over despair, victory over fear— because Christ hath been raised and He said, "If I live, ye shall live also." This is the message of certainty and hope that we have, for the Word of God predicted Christ's resurrection, promised us our resurrection, and it explains to us God's program of resurrection. . . . [S]hould death be our experience, we rest in hope, for death has been robbed of its venom because Christ has been raised from the dead.[2]

Perhaps the most revealing proclamation concerning Jesus' power over death comes from Jesus himself. Just prior to raising his friend Lazarus from the dead, our Lord spoke a promise filled with uplifting truth: "I am the resurrection and the life; he who believes in Me will live even if he dies, and everyone who lives and believes in Me will never die" (John 11:25–26).

Every aspect of Christianity rests on the reality of the resurrection. Moreover, it is Jesus' resurrection that separates Christianity from all other religions. Thomas Oden, systematic theology professor at Drew University, writes: "There is no direct parallel in the history of religions of a founder whose bodily resurrection from the dead confirms and ratifies his life and teachings and enables followers to enter eternal life."[3]

Death Has No Sting

Does it really matter whether or not Jesus rose from the dead? Not according to some people. Ronald Gregor Smith, author of *Secular Christianity*, writes: "We may freely say that the bones of Jesus lie somewhere in Palestine. Christian faith is not destroyed by this admission."[4] Scripture, however, tells us that the reality of Jesus' resurrection is vital to the entire Christian belief system (1 Cor. 15:17). The resurrection also relates directly to the trustworthiness of Jesus' character. He explicitly prophesied that he would be resurrected three days after dying (Matt. 16:21; 17:22–23; 20:19; Mark 8:31; 9:31; 10:34; Luke 9:22; 18:33; John 2:19–22). If Jesus did not rise from the grave, then he was either a false prophet or a liar.

Furthermore, the veracity of Christ's resurrection has eschatological significance. Assurance of humanity's final judgment is supplied through the visible power that was manifested by God in Jesus' resurrection (Acts 17:31). Moreover, Christ is called the "the first fruits of those who are asleep" (1 Cor. 15:20) and the "firstborn from the dead" (Col. 1:18; Rev. 1:5), which shows that his resurrection is a foreshadowing of what will happen to believers: "It symbolized what was destined to happen to the members of Christ's mystical body in their justification, spiritual birth, and future blessed resurrection, Rom. 6:4, 5, 9; 8:11; 1 Cor. 6:14; 15:20–22; 2 Cor. 4:10, 11, 14; Col. 2:12; 1 Thess. 4:14."[5]

Unfortunately many individuals either deny or distort the resurrection. One of the most common cultic views rejects the materiality of Christ's body after his resurrection and asserts that Jesus came forth from the grave as a mere spirit. A number of other erroneous theories concerning the resurrection are present not only in the world of the cults but also in religious circles that are theologically liberal. While liberal critics of the resurrection are not cultic, per se, some of the doctrinal distortions they voice may occasionally surface in cultic groups. It is, therefore, wise to be aware of what these non-Christian scholars teach concerning this doctrinal issue.

Many liberal theologians, for example, allege that the accounts of Christ's post-crucifixion appearances are nothing but fictitious additions to the Gospels that were authored long after the fact in order to politically legitimize the spread of Christianity. Others say that Jesus did indeed come out of the grave but was "revived" from a fainting spell (i.e., he never really died). A few liberals maintain that Jesus attempted to fake his death but *accidentally* died, at which time he was replaced by an impostor. As we will now see, these positions do not accurately reflect the biblical records or the historical data.

Examining the Evidence

How do we know Jesus really rose from the dead? As with many historical events of long ago, the resurrection cannot be conclusively proven. No one living today can say, "I was there in A.D. 33 and saw Jesus alive after he died." Nevertheless, there exist numerous pieces of evidence which, when objectively considered, provide over-whelming support for concluding that Jesus did indeed rise from the dead. In fact, the historical arguments for the resurrection are so sub-stantial that they have "persuaded many skeptics who started to exam-ine the evidence for the purpose of disproving the resurrection."[6]

According to E. M. Blaiklock, historian and professor of classics at Auckland University, "The evidence for the life, the death, and the resurrection of Christ is better authenticated than most of the facts of ancient history."[7] Professor Thomas Arnold, who was appointed chair of modern history at Oxford, has made a similar statement: "I know of no one fact in the history of mankind which is proved by better and fuller evidence of every sort, to the understanding of a fair inquirer, than the great sign which God hath given us that Christ died and rose again from the dead."[8]

An Empty Tomb

The empty tomb in which Jesus' body was placed is the first piece of evidence that, at the very least, suggests Jesus rose from the dead. The Jewish leaders who conspired to kill him knew that an empty tomb would be a powerful sign to his followers, since he had predicted he would rise again. Consequently, the chief priests and Pharisees asked that Roman guards be placed at the tomb to prevent Jesus' dis-ciples from stealing his body and making it seem as if he had risen (Matt. 27:62–66).

Despite these precautions, the tomb was found empty three days after Jesus was buried. Witnesses to the empty tomb included Mary Magdalene (Matt. 28:1); the mother of James, also known as "the other Mary" (Matt. 28:1; Mark 16:1); a woman named Salome (Mark 16:1); Joanna (Luke 24:10); an unspecified number of "other women" (Luke 24:10); and Peter and John (John 20:2–9).

It has been argued by some non-Christians that the empty tomb discovered by the aforementioned individuals was not Jesus' tomb. Twentieth-century liberal theologian Kirsopp Lake, for instance, maintains "that in their grief the women lost their way, went to an empty tomb in the same general area where Jesus was buried, and jumped to the conclusion that Jesus had risen from the dead."[9] This theory is patently absurd.

First, Jesus' body was laid in the tomb of Joseph of Arimathea, a prominent member of the Sanhedrin. Joseph himself, along with the Pharisee Nicodemus, took Jesus' body to the grave site (Matt. 27:57–60; John 19:38–42). If any questions regarding the location of the tomb had been voiced, they easily could have been answered by either Joseph or Nicodemus. Second, the women who discovered the empty tomb knew exactly where it was located. They had, in fact, watched Joseph and Nicodemus place Jesus in it (Matt. 27:61; Mark 15:47; Luke 23:55).

Of course, an empty tomb is not by itself a significant enough piece of data on which a person could justifiably conclude that Jesus rose from the dead. But its importance is greatly enlarged by a second set of evidences: the post-resurrection appearances of Christ. These eye-witness accounts are extremely impressive.

Eyewitnesses

Scripture mentions a substantial number of people who observed, spoke to, and even ate with the resurrected Christ (Acts 10:40–42): Mary Magdalene (John 20:14–18); several women (Matt. 28:9–10); two disciples on the road to Emmaus (Luke 24:13–32); the disciples (minus Thomas) and many others in an upper room (John 20:19–25; Luke 26:36–43); the disciples including Thomas (John 20:26–31); seven disciples fishing at the sea of Galilee (John 21:1–25); all eleven disciples on a mountain in Galilee (Matt. 28:16–20); the disciples in Jerusalem (Luke 24:44–49; compare Acts 1:3–8); more than five hundred brethren (1 Cor. 15:6); James, Jesus' half-brother (1 Cor. 15:7); and the disciples present when the Lord ascended into heaven (Acts 1:3–8).[10]

Those who dismiss these accounts claim that using biblical testimony in such a manner is circular reasoning, since the Bible is being used to prove the Bible. But the New Testament is not one book written by one author. It is a *collection* of twenty-seven books written by several authors. The witnesses to whom Christ appeared are mentioned in five different books, penned by four different writers.[11] Consequently, using the biblical texts to support the reality of the resurrection is not circular reasoning. Precedent for validating historical events through texts similar to those found in the New Testament is discussed by R. L. Purtill in his insightful work *Thinking about Religion*.

> Many events which are regarded as firmly established historically have (1) far less documentary evidence than many biblical events, (2) and the documents on which historians rely for much secular history are written much longer after the event than many records of biblical events, (3) Furthermore, we have many more copies of biblical narratives than of secular histories, and (4) the surviving copies are much earlier than those on which our evidence for secular history is based. If the biblical narratives did not contain accounts of miraculous events . . . biblical history would probably be regarded as much more firmly established than most of the history of, say, classical Greece and Rome.[12]

Realistic Reports

Another form of evidence pointing to the likelihood of Jesus' resurrection involves the complementary way that the event is recorded by the Gospel writers. It is interesting that these evidences *for* the resurrection are often cited in arguments *against* the resurrection by critics of Christianity who fail to realize that the Gospels are not contradictory but complementary.

Various cults, liberal theologians, and secularists often argue that the resurrection accounts "are so full of inconsistencies that it is easy to deride them. . . . [They are] an almost hopeless jumble of confusion."[13] John Shelby Spong—controversial Episcopal Bishop of Newark, New Jersey—condemns the resurrection stories as "significantly confused, contradictory, and, in some instances, mutually exclusive."[14]

At first glance, the biblical passages relating to Jesus' return from the grave do indeed seem to be at odds with one another in various places. Consider the apparent contradiction between John 20:1, which says that Mary Magdalene went to the tomb "while it was still dark" and Matthew 28:1, which states that Mary Magdalene and "the other Mary" went to Jesus' grave "as it began to dawn."

Critics of the resurrection usually point out with great relish that there are two mistakes here. Did Mary Magdalene come alone, or was she accompanied by another woman? Did she go to the tomb while it was still dark, or did she go to the tomb when it was beginning to dawn? These questions, which seem problematic on the surface, can actually be answered with relative ease.

John does not say that Mary traveled to the tomb alone. He merely states a fact from his perspective—that Mary went to the tomb. This is what John wanted to communicate. Matthew, however, gives us more information, *complementary* information that tells us Mary was not alone. In fact, Mark informs us that a woman named Salome also was present (Mark 16:1), and Luke reveals that a fourth woman named Joanna went along as well (Luke 24:10). These are not contradictory accounts but complementary narratives based on four different perspectives.

Regarding the time of day, the Greek words used in all four Gospels, when taken together, establish a realistic passage of time covering the women's trip from Jerusalem to the tomb. Bible scholar Gleason Archer explains:

> They apparently started their journey from the house in Jerusalem while it was still dark (*skotias eti ouses*), even though it was already morning (*proi*) [John 20:1]. . . . But by the time they arrived, dawn was glimmering in the east (*te epiphoskouse*) that Sunday morning (*eis mian sabbaton*) [Matt. 28:1]. . . . Mark 16:2 adds that the tip of the sun had actually appeared above the horizon (*anateilantos tou heliou*—aorist participle; the Beza Codex uses the present participle, *anatellontos*, implying "while the sun was rising").[15]

Another alleged discrepancy relates to whether Mary encountered one angel at the tomb (Matt. 28:5) or two (John 20:12).[16] Again, these are not contradictory accounts. In their indispensable work *When Critics Ask*, Bible scholars Norman Geisler and Thomas Howe

note that, when it comes to such passages, the real difficulty lies somewhere other than in Scripture.

> Matthew does not say there was *only* one angel. . . . The critic has to
> add the word "only" to Matthew's account in order to make it con-
> tradictory. But in this case the problem is not with what the Bible
> actually says, but with what the critic adds to it. Matthew probably
> focuses on the one [angel] who spoke and "said to the women, 'Do not
> be afraid.'" (Matt. 28:5). John referred to how many angels they *saw*;
> "and she saw two angels" (John 20:12).[17]

Persons who doubt the reliability of the resurrection accounts fail
to see that the differences between the accounts provide an added
dimension of believability. If the stories were not true, then one
might expect either a myriad of unsolvable contradictions or a perfect duplication of text with a uniformity so rigid that it betrays the
accounts as having been deliberately concocted. Alister McGrath,
research lecturer in theology at Oxford University and systematic
theology professor at Regent College in Vancouver, British Columbia, makes a number of keen observations regarding the complementary nature of the resurrection accounts and how this lends them
credibility.

> Variation on minor points of detail is a characteristic feature of eye-
> witness reports. If you ever listen to witnesses in a courtroom, you will
> very often be amazed by the different way in which they describe the
> same event. They may all be able to agree on what happened, and
> when. But on minor points of detail (for example, what happened
> immediately before or after that event), they very often differ. An
> event is experienced differently by various people. Major agreement
> is accompanied by minor disagreement. Look at the way in which the
> same events are reported by different news networks on television, for
> example. Minor discrepancies in details of eyewitness reports actually
> point to their authenticity, not their inauthenticity. If the gospel
> accounts of the resurrection were based upon an invention, we would
> have expected their minor disagreements to have been removed before
> publication! . . . Critics of the New Testament resurrection accounts
> often seem to apply one set of standards to the New Testament, and
> a totally different set to their everyday existence. For example, if the

Washington Post and *New York Times* reported the same story in slightly different terms, hardly anyone (except a New Testament critic who applied his standards consistently!) would dream of suggesting that one had copied the other. . . . Let's suppose that all four gospels reported exactly the same pattern of events on that first Easter Day perhaps down to using the same words. Would that make them more credible to a critic? Certainly not! He would immediately argue that they were fabrications. They were cooked up. He would suggest that the accounts had been "doctored" to bring them into line with each other! He would dismiss them as crude forgeries. On the other hand, if they differed wildly from each other, the same critic could dismiss them with equally great ease but for different reasons. He would argue that they weren't talking about the same thing. He would suggest that it was impossible to gain any impression of what had really happened. He would dismiss them as having no importance in assessing the claim that Jesus Christ had been raised from the dead. So, totally different or totally identical accounts would be dismissed by such a critic. What, then, would such a critic accept as reliable? The answer can only be accounts which vary on minor points, but are agreed upon the central point of importance—which is exactly what we find in the gospel accounts of the discovery of the empty tomb![18]

Apologists Josh McDowell and Don Stewart observe that belief in the resurrection is not only reasonable because of the defense that can be made for it but also because of "the lack of evidence for an alternative explanation."[19] Nevertheless, countless theories and wild tales have been spun by opponents of Christianity to explain away the empty tomb left behind by Christ. Three of the more popular explanations are known as the "swoon theory," "conspiracy theory," and "Passover plot theory."

Jesus Never Died

Recently a rising number of people have promoted the "swoon theory," which contends that Jesus didn't die but instead fainted on the cross. His loss of consciousness then prompted onlookers to mistakenly believe he had expired. This led those individuals present to remove Christ from the cross and prematurely place him in a grave.

There, the spices that anointed his body and the cool air of the tomb revived Jesus. Three days later he was able to roll back the stone and emerge refreshed.

This hypothesis is riddled with improbabilities and groundless speculations. In their *Handbook of Christian Apologetics*, Peter Kreeft and Ronald K. Tacelli demonstrate just how many logical flaws are inherent in the swoon theory.

- Jesus could not have survived crucifixion. Roman procedures were very careful to eliminate that possibility. Roman law even laid the death penalty on any soldier who let a capital prisoner escape in any way, including bungling a crucifixion.
- The fact that the Roman soldier did not break Jesus' legs, as he did to the other two crucified criminals (John 19:31–33), means that the soldier was sure Jesus was dead. Breaking the legs hastened the death so that the corpse could be taken down before the Sabbath (v. 31).
- John, an eyewitness, certified that he saw blood and water come from Jesus' pierced heart (John 19:34–35). This shows that Jesus' lungs had collapsed and he had died of asphyxiation. Any medical expert can vouch for this.
- The post-resurrection appearances convinced the disciples, even "doubting Thomas," that Jesus was gloriously alive (John 20:19–29). It is psychologically impossible for the disciples to have been so transformed and confident if Jesus had merely struggled out of a swoon, badly in need of a doctor. A half-dead, staggering sick man who has just had a narrow escape is not worshiped fearlessly as divine lord and conqueror of death (John 20:28).
- How were the Roman guards at the tomb overpowered by a swooning corpse? Or by unarmed disciples?
- How could a swooning half-dead man have moved the great stone at the door of the tomb? Who moved the stone if not an angel? No one has ever answered that question. Neither the Jews nor the Romans would move it, for it was in both their interests to keep the tomb sealed; the Jews had the stone put there in the first place, and the Roman guards would be killed if they let the body "escape."[20]

Even liberal scholars from the last century voiced skepticism about the swoon theory. David Strauss, for example, a German theologian who did his best to cast doubt on the Gospels, wrote an uncharacteristically orthodox commentary in his *New Life of Jesus* (1865) regarding the implausibility of Jesus' resuscitation from a swoon.

It is impossible that a being who had been stolen half-dead out of the sepulchre, who crept about weak and ill, wanting medical treatment, who required bandaging, strengthening and indulgence, and who still at last yielded his sufferings, could have given to his disciples the impressions that he was a conqueror over death, the prince of life, an impression which lay at the bottom of their ministry. Such a resuscitation could only have weakened the impression which he had made upon them in life and in death, at most could only have given it an elegiac [a lamenting or sorrowful] voice, but could by no possibility have changed their sorrow into enthusiasm, have elevated their reverence into worship.[21]

Modern medicine also discounts the swoon theory. A March 21, 1986, article in *The Journal of the American Medical Society* concluded the following:

Clearly, the weight of historical and medical evidence indicates that Jesus was dead before the wound to his side was inflicted and supports the traditional view that the spear, thrust between his right ribs, probably perforated not only the right lung but also the pericardium and heart and thereby ensured his death. Accordingly, interpretations based on the assumption that Jesus did not die on the cross appear to be at odds with modern medical knowledge.[22]

It's a Conspiracy

According to the resurrection conspiracy theory, the disciples "practiced deliberate deception by stealing the body from the grave and then declaring the Lord had risen."[23] This theory can be traced to the original story spread by Jewish authorities soon after it was discovered that Jesus had risen from the dead (Matt. 28:11–15). A problematic question immediately comes to mind: What would the disciples have gained by perpetrating such a falsehood? History reveals that Jesus' followers lost everything, including their lives. It is highly improbable that the disciples would have allowed themselves and their families to suffer excruciating torment and death to perpetrate a known lie.

Advocates of the conspiracy theory, like promoters of the swoon theory, run into yet another logistical problem with their view—the Roman guards who were ordered to watch over the tomb. How could a ragtag band of fishermen have gotten past Roman soldiers to steal a corpse? It is doubtful that the soldiers would have fallen asleep on the job. If they had, they would have been killed. If they did fall asleep, "the crowd and the effort and the noise it would have taken to move an enormous boulder would have wakened them."[24] Even if Jesus' disciples had somehow gotten past the guards, they certainly would not have been able to do so without being seen or without having to kill the guards, which in turn would have ruined the illusion.

Finally, throughout early church history, no Christian ever confessed "freely or under pressure, bribe or even torture, that the whole story of the resurrection was a fake, a lie, a deliberate deception."[25] Even when people denied their faith under torture and worshiped Caesar, they never said that the resurrection was a conspiracy. It is only reasonable to assume that out of the thousands of souls tortured for Christ, at least one person would have revealed that the whole resurrection story was a lie if that was indeed the case. But this never happened.

The Passover Plot

Another theory that is similar to, yet slightly different from, the swoon and conspiracy theories is commonly known as the Passover plot theory. Its scenario is even more improbable because it impugns the character of Christ himself. The theory was originally advanced in the 1965 book *The Passover Plot* by Hugh J. Schonfield.

According to Schonfield, Joseph of Arimathea, Lazarus, and a mysterious "young man" conspired with Jesus to fool the disciples into thinking that Jesus was the Messiah. The plan called for Jesus to take a drug that would enable him to fake his death. Afterward, he would be revived in the tomb and emerge as the "Messiah." Unfortunately, says Schonfield, the crucifixion wounds—including the gash in Jesus' side that was made by a Roman soldier's spear—proved fatal. But the remaining plotters salvaged their plan by stealing Jesus' body and subsequently having the "young man" appear throughout Galilee as Christ. All of the encounters "Jesus" had with eyewitnesses to his resurrection were actually cases of mistaken identity.[26] We are faced with several difficulties in this theory.

First, a dishonest plot does not coincide with the character and personality that Jesus consistently displayed throughout his life. Second, no person(s) could have orchestrated the number of Old Testament prophecies fulfilled in Jesus' life including: when, where, how, from what tribe, and during which dynasty Christ would come (Dan. 9:24–26a; Micah 5:2; Isa. 7:14; 2 Sam. 7:8–16).[27] Third, too many people who were intimately acquainted with Jesus saw him after the resurrection (close friends, followers, family, etc.). It would have been virtually impossible for all of these encounters to have been cases of mistaken identity. As with all unbiblical explanations of the resurrection, the Passover plot theory fails to tarnish the bold testimony that Jesus' followers have been declaring for two thousand years: "He is risen!"

Raised a Spirit?

In the world of the cults, one of the most widespread heresies concerning Christ involves the nature of his resurrection body. Several groups allege that Jesus did not rise bodily from the grave but was raised a spirit being. In other words, the body that went into the tomb was *not* the body that emerged three days later. Unification Church leader Rev. Sun Myung Moon has openly declared that Jesus was resurrected from the dead as a spirit.[28] The Jehovah's Witnesses promote a similar view:

> The fleshly body is the body in which Jesus humbled himself, like a servant, and is not the body of his glorification, not the body in which he was resurrected.[29]

Christ Jesus was put to death in the flesh and was resurrected an invisible spirit creature. . . . This firstborn one from the dead was not raised out of the grave a human creature, but he was raised a spirit.[30]

Scripture, however, indicates that the body that hung on the cross and went into the grave was the same body that was resurrected and came out of the grave. Jesus was touched and handled (Matt. 28:9; John 20:17, 27; 1 John 1:1). He ate food to prove that he was physically present (Luke 24:30, 42–43; John 21:12–13; Acts 10:41). Our Lord himself said that he had flesh and bones (Luke 24:39).

Some cults dismiss these biblical references to Jesus' fleshly body by stating that he temporarily "materialized or took on a fleshly body, as angels had done in the past."[31] Jesus even manufactured wounds in this fake body to convince the disciples of his identity.[32] But this creates a dilemma involving the moral character of Christ, since he indicated to his disciples that the body he was showing them was the *very same* body that went from the cross to the grave: "See My hands and My feet, that it is I Myself; touch Me and see, for a spirit does not have flesh and bones as you see that I have" (Luke 24:39). Was Jesus telling the truth or not?

In John 2:19 Jesus makes yet another significant comment while in a conversation with hostile Jews: "Destroy this temple, and in three days I will raise it up." The Jews failed to grasp the meaning behind Jesus' words. John tells us in subsequent verses exactly what Jesus meant. "But He was speaking of the temple of His body. So when He was raised from the dead, His disciples remembered that He said this; and they believed the Scripture, and the word which Jesus had spoken" (vv. 21–22).

Notice that Jesus said destroy "*this* temple [meaning the body he then had] and . . . I will raise *it* [the same body] up." He did not say, "Destroy this temple and in three days I will raise up another spiritual, non-fleshly body in its place." Either Jesus did what he said he would do or he did not. Moreover, the Greek word used by John to clarify Christ's comment about his "body" (*soma*, v. 21) indicates that a fleshly body would be raised from the dead. The noun *soma* is always used in the New Testament for the physical body. Another powerful passage supporting the bodily resurrection of Jesus is Colossians 2:9, which declares that in Jesus all the fullness of deity dwells (present tense) *bodily*. If Jesus was raised a spirit, how can the fullness of deity currently dwell in his body?

Despite the Bible's clear teachings, cults and new religious movements actually seek to justify the spiritual, non-fleshly resurrection of Christ through Scripture. First Peter 3:18, which states that Jesus was "put to death in the flesh, but made alive in the spirit," is regularly cited by cults to support their position. But "being put to death in the flesh" and "made alive in the spirit" does not require that Jesus Christ be raised a spirit. The phrase "in the spirit" means under the influence of the Holy Spirit.

For example, John was "in the Spirit on the Lord's day" when he received the vision transcribed in the Book of Revelation (Rev. 1:10). David was "in the Spirit" when he wrote Psalm 110 (compare Matt. 22:43). Were John and David "spirit creatures"? Of course not. Nor was Jesus when he was made alive "in the Spirit." Furthermore, 1 Peter 3:18 can only be translated "in" or "by" the Spirit. To support the contention that Jesus was raised as a spirit, the verse would have to be translatable as "as a" spirit. This cannot legitimately be done given the Greek wording of the passage.

Luke 24:37 is also used by cults, because it states that when Jesus appeared to the disciples they "thought that they were seeing a spirit." Notice that the passage says they *thought* they were seeing a spirit. It does not say they *did* see a spirit. It is also significant that, in the passage, Jesus subsequently testified that he was, in fact, *not* a spirit at all but flesh and bone (vv. 38–39).

Jesus' appearance to two disciples on the road to Emmaus (Mark 16:12) is a third verse commonly used by cults in an attempt to prove that Jesus rose in a spirit form: "He appeared in a different form to two of them while they were walking along on their way to the country." Cultists reason that since Jesus appeared in another form, he must not have had a physical body. But is the verse really saying that Jesus appeared in another form because he actually *had* another form? No, because the parallel passage in Luke 24:13–32 reveals that Jesus appeared in another form because the eyes of the disciples were made to perceive him in an unrecognizable state. After Jesus explained the Scriptures to them, "their eyes were opened," and they instantly recognized him.

He Is Risen!

Dr. Norman Geisler states that "the overwhelming evidence is that
Jesus physically died on the cross. Likewise, there is equally good testimony that He rose from the grave in that same physical body. The
classic attempts to avoid this conclusion are without foundation."[33]
A brief look at a few comments from the theological wells of church
history confirms that Christians have always maintained Jesus' bodily resurrection. Even the earliest church fathers "consistently affirmed
that Jesus rose in the same body of flesh in which He was crucified."[34]

- Irenaeus (c. 175–95): "The Church . . . [believes] in one God
  . . . and the resurrection from the dead, and ascension into
  heaven *in the flesh* of the beloved Christ Jesus, our Lord" (emphasis mine).[35]
- Justin Martyr (c. 100–65): "Why did he [Jesus] rise *in the flesh*
  in which He suffered, unless to show the resurrection of the
  flesh?" (emphasis mine).[36]
- Epiphanius (c. 315–403): "The Word became *flesh.* . . . The
  same suffered *in the flesh;* and rose again; and went up into
  heaven in *the same body* . . . is coming in *the same body* in glory"
  (emphasis mine).[37]
- Augustine (354–430): "It is indubitable that the resurrection
  of Christ, and His ascension into heaven with *the flesh in which
  He rose,* is already preached and believed in the whole world"
  (emphasis mine).[38]
- Thomas Aquinas (1224–74): "They have not believed in the
  resurrection of the body, and have strained to twist the words
  of Holy Scripture to mean a spiritual resurrection. . . . That
  St. Paul believed in a *bodily resurrection* is clear . . . *to affirm a
  purely spiritual resurrection is against the Christian Faith*" (emphasis mine).[39]

This is not to say that the post-resurrection body of Jesus did not
gain certain additional qualities. For example, he could "appear and
disappear out of sight quite suddenly (Luke 24:31, 36; John 20:19,
26)."[40] The important fact to realize, however, is that Jesus physically

rose from the dead. The body that had died was brought back to life in a glorified state that serves as a sign of our inheritance as Christians. Because of Christ's triumph over death, believers today can confidently echo the invitation extended to the world two thousand years ago by Paul the apostle:

> "God is now declaring to men that all people everywhere should repent, because He has fixed a day in which He will judge the world in righteousness through a Man whom He has appointed, having furnished proof to all men by raising Him from the dead" (Acts 17:30–31).

Part 4

He shall come again, with glory, to judge both the quick [living] and the dead; whose kingdom shall have no end. . . . I look for the resurrection of the dead, and the life of the world to come. Amen.

Niceno-Constantinopolitan Creed

He ascended into heaven, he sitteth on the right hand of the Father God [God the Father] Almighty. From whence [there] he shall come to judge the quick and the dead. At whose coming all men shall rise again with their bodies; And shall give account for their own works. And they that have done good shall go into life everlasting: and they that have done evil, into everlasting fire.

Athanasian Creed

From Here to Eternity

10

The Other Side

The chief problem about death, incidentally, is the fear that there may be no afterlife—a depressing thought, particularly for those who have bothered to shave. Also, there is the fear that there is an afterlife, but no one will know where it's being held.

Woody Allen

As we have seen, the creeds cover numerous Christian doctrines: the nature of God, the deity and humanity of Christ, the virgin birth, Jesus' bodily resurrection, and salvation by grace alone through faith. These beliefs, often called the *essentials* of the faith, are of primary importance because adherence to them is what makes someone a Christian. But the creeds also touch on theological concepts that are considered *nonessentials* of the faith. Although meaningful, these doctrines are nonessential because believers can disagree about the Bible's teachings on them and still be Christian.

Although many beliefs fall into the nonessential category, some of them have caused more controversy than others. Among the most hotly debated topics are thanatology (the study of death, dying, and the afterlife) and eschatology (the study of last things [see chapter 11]).[1] This chapter covers the afterlife and related questions: Do we continue to exist consciously after death? Does *everyone* live eternally, or are some people annihilated out of existence? Will everyone ultimately be saved? Is there a hell?

153

Thanatology, which is by no means an exclusively Christian term, is an ancient subject dating back to the dawn of time. Archaeology confirms that the belief in life after death was an integral part of ancient civilizations, including the Chinese (c. 4365 B.C.), Sumerians (c. 3200 B.C.), Egyptians (c. 2615–1991 B.C.), Babylonians (c. 1830–1025 B.C.), Assyrians (c. 1356–609 B.C.), and Greeks (469–347 B.C.).[2]

Afterlife beliefs now permeate nearly every culture. According to historian Mircea Eliade, "[A] belief that human beings will continue to exist in some form after the experience we term death is a universal phenomenon. . . . While death is everywhere recognized as inevitable, it is seldom accepted as an absolute termination of human existence."[3]

Life after Death

Scripture teaches that even before physically dying, we are *spiritually* dead (Eph. 2:1). This fallen state was transmitted to us through Adam and Eve's disobedience (Rom. 5:12, 17; 1 Cor. 15:21–22). *Physical* death, which is the culmination of the sin nature at work within us, occurs when that part of us traditionally called the spirit/soul leaves the body (Gen. 35:18). This definition of death is echoed in both the New Testament and the Greek culture in which the New Testament was written.

The *Expository Dictionary of Bible Words* explains that the Greek word for *dead* (*nekros*) "conveyed the idea that the dead become mere matter. Whatever it was that had made the corpse a person and animated the body was gone."[4] Many biblical verses confirm that there is indeed something within us (soul/spirit) that not only animates the body but makes us who we are (1 Sam. 18:1; 2 Kings 4:27; Job 30:16; Ps. 42:4; Zech. 12:1). When this "something" is gone, *we* are gone.

The Greek word *psyche*—typically rendered "soul" in the New Testament—can also be translated "life." *Psyche*, which originally referred to the unconscious, "came to stand for the basis of life and consciousness. It is often equated to the inner person or personality."[5] Simply stated, an individual dies when this inner person or personality leaves the body. The body no longer has life: "It came about as her soul [Rachel's] was departing (for she died), that she named him Ben-oni" (Gen. 35:18). Psalm 146:4 provides further confirmation that departure of the spirit from the body is what signals death. God's Word additionally reveals that spiritual existence apart from one's body is an unnatural condition that will be rectified at the final resurrection (Rom. 6:5; 8:11; 1 Cor. 15:42–54; 1 John 3:2).

It is also important to recognize that physical death (separation of the spirit from the body) is meant to occur only once. Hebrews 9:27 says it is appointed for us "to die once and after this comes judgment." Persons who do not know Jesus as their Lord and Savior will immediately go to an intermediate state of punishment where they will await a *final* judgment (Job 21:30–34; Isa. 14:9–11; 2 Peter 2:9). At that judgment, they will be told to depart from God's presence (Matt. 7:23; Rev. 20:10–15).

Thankfully, the Lord has provided a way of escape from the consequences of our sins: Jesus Christ. He willingly tasted death for everyone (Heb. 2:9), the just for the unjust, that we might be brought to God (1 Peter 3:18). Through faith in Christ (Rom. 5:2; 10:9; Eph. 2:1–10) we appropriate his work on the cross and receive the gift God offers: eternal life in his presence (John 3:16; Rom. 6:23). Those who accept this gift will find themselves with God immediately after dying (2 Cor. 5:8; Phil. 1:21–23). Then, at the resurrection, each person's spirit will be reunited with his or her body in a glorified state (1 Cor. 15:51–52; 1 Thess. 4:14–18). In this condition, Christians will dwell with God "forever and ever" (Rev. 22:5).

"Soul Sleep"

One of the most common erroneous views of the afterlife held by cultists is the doctrine of "soul sleep," which alleges that people no longer continue to exist in a conscious state after they die. They "sleep" until the resurrection. With regard to this particular doctrine, it should be understood that although it contradicts the historical creeds of Christendom, holding such a view does not automatically place a person or group outside Christianity. Seventh-Day Adventists, for example, promote this belief even though they unwaveringly affirm all of the essential doctrines of Christianity.[6]

Other groups, however, not only affirm the idea of "soul sleep" but reject the essential beliefs of Christianity as well. Cults such as The Way International and the Jehovah's Witnesses fall into this latter class of religious groups. They summarize "soul sleep" the following way:

> Most Christians hold the belief that upon death those who belong to Christ are immediately received up into glory, commonly called Heaven or paradise, to appear before the Father. There they are alive and conscious and have a joyous existence with Him and their loved ones. Such a belief is contrary to the teachings in the Word of God.[7]

> The Word of God shows that new life to the dead comes with the return of Christ. Before Christ's coming, all those who have died remain in the grave in corruption and unconsciousness.[8]

> The dead are shown to be "conscious of nothing at all" and the death state to be one of complete inactivity (Ec 9:5, 10; Ps 146:4). . . . In both the Hebrew and the Greek Scriptures, death is likened to sleep, a fitting comparison not only because of the unconscious condition of the dead but also because of the hope of an awakening through the resurrection.[9]

> When a person is dead he is completely out of existence. He is not conscious of anything.[10]

There is nothing in Scripture that suggests a soul *cannot* exist apart from the body, nor do any passages declare that a Christian's soul ceases to exist until the resurrection at the end of the age. In fact, several passages of Scripture support the very opposite conclusion (Phil. 1:21–23; 2 Cor. 5:8). The Bible reveals with equal clarity that when unbelievers die they will go into an intermediate state of punishment where, in a conscious state, they are to await final judgment (Job 21:30–34; Isa. 14:9–11; 2 Peter 2:9).

With regard to Ecclesiastes 9:5, the context of the passage is life on earth (Eccles. 1:3, 9). Consequently, when the verse speaks of the dead not knowing anything, it is referring to the dead not having a working knowledge of day-to-day affairs on earth, or as Ecclesiastes calls it, life "under the sun." Likewise, Psalm 146:4 discusses a person's awareness of and participation in earthly events. Neither verse is pleading a case for lack of consciousness in the realm of the dead.

Another passage indicative of our conscious existence after death is Matthew 17:3, where Moses and Elijah appear and speak with Jesus. They, of course, had long since died and yet were able to converse with the Lord. Revelation 6:10 must also be considered. It mentions the conscious existence in heaven of souls who had been slain because of the Word of God.

In response to such biblical passages, cults often resort to misrepresenting the historical development of the Christian view: "How, then, did this belief about an immortal soul find its way into the teachings of Christendom's churches? Today it is frankly acknowledged that this has come about through the influence of pagan Grecian philosophy."[11]

This statement is utterly false. Belief in a soul that is separate from the body was embraced by the Jews hundreds of years before Greek philosophy could have influenced Christian thought. Genesis 35:18 speaks of Rachel's soul departing, and 1 Kings 17:21 recounts how Elijah asked God to let the soul of a child return to him. Psalms 42:4–5; 43:5; and Habakkuk 2:4 describe the soul as being *within* a person. There are similar descriptions in the New Testament (Matt. 10:28; Acts 20:10).

Despite such passages, cults and new religious movements find clever ways of altering biblical verses so that they appear to support their false position. Note the following comments made by The Way International's founder Victor Paul Wierwille regarding Jesus' promise to the thief on the cross in Luke 23:43:

> Verily I say unto thee, Today shalt thou be with me in paradise. . . . The King James puts the comma before "today." . . . Why? Because one group teaches that the moment one dies, he goes to heaven. . . . If a man is going to heaven today, heaven must be available. . . . [H]eaven is not available. . . . [T]his verse talks about paradise—and paradise is not heaven. . . . Paradise is present in Genesis chapters 1 and 2. . . . Paradise is always a place upon earth. . . . Since paradise was non-existent on the day of the crucifixion, Jesus had to say to the malefactor that sometime in the future he would be with Him, not in

heaven, but in paradise. Let us read the sentence with literal accuracy.
. . . Verily, I say to you today, thou shalt [the day is coming in the future
when you are going to] be with me in paradise.[12]

Renowned British evangelist John Blanchard has referred to plac-
ing the comma in Luke 23:43 *after* the word "today" as "a desperate
bid" and "a novel form of punctuation."[13] Did Christ really have to
tell the thief hanging on a cross next to him that he was speaking
to him on that day? Jesus "could hardly have spoken them to him
the previous day . . . or the following day. . . . The attempt to twist
the meaning of Christ's promise owes more to ingenuity than to
integrity."[14]

Moreover, the term *paradise* was not used by Jews exclusively as a
reference to the earthly location spoken of in Genesis 1 and 2. It also
was used by first-century rabbis for "the resting place for spirits of the
righteous who had died."[15] In fact, two other New Testament passages
use the Greek word for paradise *(paradeisos)* to describe heaven (2 Cor.
12:4; Rev. 2:7). In the Greek translation of the Old Testament (the
Septuagint), *paradeisos* refers to a heavenly place of blessedness "in
the presence of God" (Ezek. 28:13; 31:8–9).[16]

The Truth That Hurts

Jesus described hell as "outer darkness" (Matt. 8:11–12) and a "fur-
nace of fire" (Matt. 13:42, 50). He warned that it would provoke
"weeping and gnashing of teeth" in those who rejected God and who
would be condemned to dwell there forever (Luke 13:24–28). Christian scholars Gary Habermas and J. P. Mooreland provide a few
thought-provoking descriptions of hell in their book *Immortality: The
Other Side of Death.*

- "[Hell is] the end of a road away from God, love, and anything
  of real value."
- "[It] is also a place of shame, sorrow, regret and anguish."
- "[In hell] the pain suffered will be due to the shame and sorrow
  resulting from the punishment of final, ultimate, unending ban-

ishment from God, his kingdom, and the good life for which
we were created in the first place."
- "Hell's occupants will deeply and tragically regret all they lost."[17]

Well-known theologian R. C. Sproul admits that "there is no biblical concept more grim or terror-evoking than the idea of hell." He
goes on to state that "no matter how we analyze the concept of hell
it often sounds to us as a place of cruel and unusual punishment."[18]
Nevertheless, hell represents a side of God's character that must not
be discounted. God is loving but he is also just. His holiness demands
that unrighteousness be punished. Human courts, as imperfect and
tainted with inequity as they are, hand down punishments every
day for crimes committed against the laws of the land. Should we
expect any less from God, who is perfectly just and fair? According
to Sproul, we can at least take comfort in knowing that God is not
cruel.

> It is impossible for God to be cruel. Cruelty involves inflicting pun-
> ishment that is more severe or harsh than a crime. Cruelty in this sense
> is unjust. God is incapable of inflicting an unjust punishment. The
> judge of all the earth will surely do what is right. No innocent person
> will ever suffer at His hand.[19]

The reality of God's justice can be seen in the teaching that there
will actually be degrees of punishment in hell for unbelievers (Luke
12:45–48), just as there will be degrees of reward in heaven for believers (2 Cor. 5:10). Christ said that it would be more tolerable for some
people in the day of judgment than for others (Matt. 11:21–24). Furthermore, Hebrews 10:26–31 plainly states that some people deserve
more severe punishment than others.

Varying degrees of punishment in hell is not an improbable concept. A lustful thought during a moment of moral weakness is certainly not as offensive as actually committing adultery, although both
are sinful. Similarly, the murderous deeds of Adolf Hitler cannot be
compared to stealing a candy bar from the corner grocery store. Just
as people hand out different degrees of temporal punishments—for
example, breaking the speed limit usually results in a monetary fine,
while murder may place a perpetrator in jail for many years—so God

will hand out various levels of eternal punishment. The Bible assures us that there will be perfect equity in hell.

Nevertheless, cults denounce the doctrine of eternal conscious torment of the wicked. Consider this response from the Jehovah's Witnesses: The "fiendish concepts associated with a hell of torment slander God and originate with the chief slanderer of God, the Devil."[20] In reality, however, the doctrine of conscious punishment comes from Scripture (Matt. 25:46; Rev. 14:11; 19:20; 20:11–15). It is not fiendish, nor does it slander God's character. Furthermore, Jesus talked more about hell than heaven. Nearly all of the Bible's teaching about hell "comes from the lips of Jesus."[21]

Redefining Hell

Since the earliest days of the Christian church, believers have preached that persons who die without Christ will continue to exist in a state of eternal conscious torment (2 Thess. 1:6–10; Heb. 10:26–27). As the Athanasian Creed states: "They that have done good shall go into life everlasting: and they that have done evil, into everlasting fire." William Crockett, systematic theologian at Alliance Seminary, makes a significant observation about the historicity of the church's long-standing views on hell:

> When someone proposes to change a doctrine taught consistently since the inception of the church, it should make us wonder how everyone throughout the centuries could have been so terribly wrong. Not that an error could not have been made or that traditions are infallible. . . . The true test is how well the view conforms with the biblical data.[22]

Although cultists strenuously object to the idea of eternal conscious punishment, they cannot ignore the fact that the term *hell* does indeed appear in God's Word. Therefore, they conveniently redefine "hell." Sun Myung Moon's Unification Church, a group that does not fall within orthodox Christian boundaries, redefines it as the present state of earth.

[M]an lost his original value and became human trash. Hell is like
God's human trash can. . . . Kingdom of Hell—Paradise Lost. . . . The
master of this world, indeed, is not God, but Satan. . . . God is going
to restore the Kingdom of hell to the Kingdom of Heaven.[23]

But Scripture does not depict the earth as hell. Hell is specifically
designated as the state of being that is encountered by unbelievers
after death (Matt. 5:22, 29–30; 10:28; 18:9; Luke 16:19–31). Hell is
never described as part of this present life. Moreover, 2 Peter 2:4 mentions demons that are currently awaiting judgment in hell.

A word must be said at this point about the nature of hell itself. Is
there real fire there, or is fire a symbol of something else? Is there real
darkness there, or is darkness used symbolically? If such descriptions
are read literally, textual problems arise. For example, God himself is
called a "consuming fire" (Heb. 12:29). God, of course, is not a giant
flame. Obviously some biblical sayings are meant to be taken figuratively. We must, therefore, interpret descriptions of hell in ways that
make sense and are biblically sound. Flames, for instance, are used in
other biblical texts in reference to divine judgment (2 Thess. 1:7).
Darkness is used figuratively to describe agonizing separation and isolation, as in the parable of Matthew 22:13, where a man is cast away
from a brightly lit and joyful banquet.

From these passages, it is reasonable to conclude that the pain and
sufferings of hell will probably be the emotional, spiritual, and mental
misery that results from having full knowledge of Jesus' lordship after
having rejected him (Rom. 14:11). Several well-respected Christian
leaders and theologians (such as J. I. Packer and Billy Graham) embrace
this position, which is known as the metaphorical view of hell.

The New Testament depicts hell as a state of conscious pain, compa-
rable to that of burning, in which condemned persons realize (1) how
repulsive and guilty in their Maker's eyes was the way they lived on
earth; (2) how right was God's penal exclusion of them from his presence and joy; (3) how completely they have now lost all gladness and
pleasure; and (4) how unchangeable is their condition.[24]

Eternal torment in hell will also include having to endure God's
wrath while separated from his love, his people, and all that is of value.

It will consist of "a total absence of the favor of God" as well as "an endless disturbance of life as a result of the complete domination of sin."[25] Unbelievers will feel unending pangs of guilt, despair, regret, bitterness, anger, sorrow, frustration, fear, hopelessness, hatred, and longing. Given the nature of hell, it is not surprising that the prophet Isaiah would declare: "How lovely on the mountains Are the feet of him who brings good news, Who announces peace And brings good news of happiness, Who announces salvation" (52:7).

The Annihilationists

Some cults do not reject or redefine hell. Instead, they simply limit the length of time hell will exist and teach that eventually all of the wicked who are placed there will be annihilated. The Lord will put them out of their misery, so to speak. They will cease to exist. A "merciful oblivion" supposedly awaits these unbelievers.[26] To David Berg, founder of The Family, even the devil and his angels would be annihilated.

> I DON'T BELIEVE IN THIS ETERNAL TORTURE DOC-
> TRINE . . . . I think it would be more merciful if they were just anni-
> hilated. . . . I DON'T KNOW WHETHER YOU COULD EVER
> REHABILITATE OR CONVERT SOME OF THOSE GUYS, like
> the Devil & the Antichrist . . . & some of the worst characters in his-
> tory & the cruelest tyrants & whatnot. . . . They can be thankful they're
> just going to be annihilated.[27]

Unfortunately, increasing numbers of evangelicals are beginning to take a similar position.[28] Christian annihilationists, as well as their cultic counterparts, usually support their views by equating "death" with "annihilation" and "eternal life" with "living forever." The following explanation of annihilationism has been adopted by the Seventh-Day Adventist Church (SDA), a Christian denomination:

> God promises eternal life only to the righteous. The wages of sin is
> death, not eternal life in hell (Rom. 6:23). . . . When Christ spoke of
> "everlasting punishment" (Matt. 25:46) He did not mean everlasting

punishing. He meant that as the "eternal life" [the righteous will enjoy] will continue throughout the ceaseless ages of eternity; and the punishment [the wicked suffer] will also be eternal—not eternal duration of conscious suffering, however, but punishment that is complete and final. . . . This death will be eternal, from which there will not, and cannot, be any resurrection. The death the wicked die will be final and everlasting. . . . [T]he Bible makes it very clear that the *punishment,* not the *punishing,* is everlasting.[29]

A majority of evangelical Christians strongly disagree with such arguments because they are not well supported either contextually or linguistically in Scripture. More than a few biblical passages indicate that it is the actual *punishing* of the wicked that lasts forever, not merely the punishment sentence. Revelation 14:11 describes the smoke of the *torment* of the wicked rising "forever and ever." This picture is painted again in Revelation 20:10, which speaks of the devil, the beast, and the false prophet being *tormented* "day and night forever and ever."

Annihilationists make yet another argument for a complete destruction of the wicked based on Matthew 10:28: "Do not fear those who kill the body but are unable to kill the soul; but rather fear Him who is able to destroy both soul and body in hell." It is claimed that the Greek word used here for *destroy (apollumi)* literally means to put out of existence or annihilate. But *apollumi* can and should be taken another way:

We speak of the alcoholic who has destroyed his life. That does not mean he ceases to exist. It means that his alcoholism has deprived him of those things about life that are good and beautiful. This is the type of thing the destruction of judgment does to those who are condemned. It destroys from their existence everything that is good and beautiful. Nothing remains that is worthy of the word "life." Also, the particular word for "destroy" *(apollumi)* that the annihilationists appeal to is used sometimes with the meaning of "lose." Jesus warned us to "be afraid of the one who can destroy *(apolesai)* both soul and body in hell" (Matt. 10:28). Here is a use of the word "destroy" in the context of punishment. But earlier in the same discourse this same Greek word is used with the meaning of "lose." Jesus tells his disciples in Matthew 10:6, "Go rather to the lost *(apololota)* sheep of Israel." In the parables of the lost sheep, the lost coin, and the lost son, the word used for "lost" is this same word, *apollumi* (Luke 15:4, 6, 8, 9, 24, 32). These objects of affection were not annihilated—they were lost. We conclude that when the word "destroy" is used in connection with judgment, it takes meanings other than the cessation of existence. This is buttressed by the fact that the same authors who use the idea of destroy to describe judgment also describe judgment in ways that must be understood as meaning conscious suffering, as we have shown earlier.[30]

Contemporary day-to-day living provides a number of illustrations that can be used to further explain the concept of destruction without annihilation. A 1987 *Christianity Today* article by Roger Nicole points out that we often speak of an automobile being completely destroyed, ruined, or "totaled," yet this is not to say that the car's materials no longer exist. The terms are used when the vehicle's parts "have been so damaged and twisted that the car has become completely unserviceable."[31] In his *Systematic Theology*, Charles Hodge gives his own insightful illustration.

> To destroy is to ruin. . . . A thing is ruined when it is rendered unfit for use; when it is in such a state that it can no longer answer the end for which it was designed. A ship at sea, dismasted, rudderless, with its sides battered in, is ruined, but not annihilated. It is a ship still. A man destroys himself when he ruins his health, squanders his property, debases his character, and renders himself unfit to act his part in life. A soul is utterly and forever destroyed when it is reprobated, alienated from God, rendered a fit companion only for the devil and his angels. This is a destruction a thousandfold more fearful than annihilation. The earnestness with which the doctrine of the unending punishment of the wicked is denounced by those who reject it, should convince them that its truth is the only rational solution of the fact that Christ and his Apostles did not condemn it.[32]

The Bible also employs figures of speech to communicate the eternality of hell. It is described as a place where punishing fires are unquenchable (Matt. 3:12; Mark 9:43) and where "their worm will not die" (Isa. 66:24). Both expressions suggest a type of judgment that lasts forever. Additionally, Scripture draws parallels between everlasting *life* and everlasting *torment* (Dan. 12:2; Matt. 25:41, 46). These passages seem to say in the strongest terms that the "final states of the just and unjust are exactly analogous—both are conscious continuous modes of living—except for their respective destinations. If heavenly bliss is endless, so is hellish agony."[33]

The prospect of eventual annihilation, or the state of nonexistence, effectively cancels out the dread unbelievers should feel toward death. The following sentiments were expressed by Mark Twain in his autobiography:

> Annihilation has no terrors for me, because I have already tried it before I was born—[for] a hundred million years—and I have suffered more in an hour, in this life, than I remember to have suffered in the whole hundred million years put together. There was a peace, a serenity, an absence of all sense of responsibility, an absence of worry, an absence of care, grief, perplexity; and the presence of a deep content and unbroken satisfaction in that hundred million years of holiday which I look back upon with a tender longing and with a grateful desire to resume, when the opportunity comes.[34]

Standing against Twain's doomed hopes are the Bible and two thousand years of church history. Throughout the centuries millions of sinners have looked to Christ as their sole lifeline away from an eternity filled with anguish. Hell has provided considerable motivation for some people to look into the claims of Christianity. The importance of hell was impressed on me not too long ago when an atheist sincerely asked me an understandable question regarding my faith. "Richard," he said, "what are you being *saved* from?" I responded with as much honesty as possible: "Hell." I then proceeded to share with him the good news of Christ. As theologian J. I. Packer has observed, "When the badness of the bad news about Hell is unmuffled . . . the goodness of the good news about Christ and eternal life shines brighter."[35]

The Second Chance Myth

Many cults that find eternal conscious punishment of the wicked too distasteful to accept still recognize the need for a hell. These groups usually teach that there will be a second chance for salvation after death. According to Mormon apostle Bruce McConkie, the wicked and ungodly "will suffer the vengeance of eternal fire in hell until they finally obey Christ, repent of their sins, and gain forgiveness therefrom."[36] Mormonism is but one cult that teaches that people in hell will actually be taught the gospel and be allowed at that point to choose Jesus as their savior:

> [T]he whole spirit world (including both paradise and hell) is a *spirit prison*. . . . In a more particular sense, however, the *spirit prison* is hell, that portion of the spirit world where the wicked dwell. . . . Before Christ bridged the gulf between paradise and hell—so that the righteous could mingle with the wicked and preach them the gospel—the wicked in hell were confined to locations which precluded them from contact with the righteous in paradise. . . . [Now] the righteous spirits in paradise have been commissioned to carry the message of salvation to the wicked spirits in hell. . . . Repentance opens the prison doors to the spirits in hell; it enables those bound with the chains of hell to free themselves from darkness, unbelief, ignorance, and sin. As rapidly as they can overcome these obstacles—gain light, believe truth, acquire intelligence, cast off sin, and break the chains of hell—they can leave the hell that imprisons them and dwell with the righteous in the peace of paradise.[37]

Hebrews 9:27, however, states that it is appointed for us to die once, after which will come the judgment. There is no door left open for people to hear the gospel preached to them in some kind of spirit prison. Is this fair? Some say no. But it must be remembered that we are created beings with an extremely limited perspective, which is itself filtered through a multitude of sin-tainted thoughts and feelings. What seems "fair" to us may not line up with objective reality. God, on the other hand, is not encumbered by sin. He is holy and without limitation of insight. He is righteous and full of truth (Ps. 19:9). Consequently, we can rest assured that he will judge fairly (Ps. 96:12–13). Our job is to obediently preach the gospel: "How then will they call on Him in whom they have not believed? How will they believe in Him whom they have not heard? And how will they hear without a preacher?" (Rom. 10:14).

Although the second-chance myth may be a comforting doctrine for people who cannot bear the thought of eternal torment for the wicked, it provides individuals with a spiritually fatal excuse for not coming to Christ: They can accept him later. Persons advocating salvation after death would do well to consider the words of Paul in 2 Corinthians 6:2. His declaration serves as both a terrible warning and a blessed promise: "Now is the day of salvation."

A Universalist's Universe

Universalism, a thanatological theory similar to the second chance myth, dismisses eternal conscious punishment for the wicked as well as annihilationism. Its premise is fairly simple—eventual salvation for *everyone* "after a proper period of chastening for their sins."[38] The Unification Church declares: "God's will that all people be restored to Him is predestined absolutely, and He had elected all people to salvation."[39]

Jesus taught a very different message. He said in Matthew 7:13 that "the way is broad that leads to destruction, and there are many who enter through it. . . . The way is narrow that leads to life, and there are *few* who find it" (emphasis mine). Our Lord also declared that on the day of judgment many will be told to depart from his presence into *everlasting* torment (Matt. 7:23; 25:41–46). These scenes are even described for us prophetically through John's vision of the end of the ages (Revelation 14 and 20).

Universalists are notorious for taking Scriptures out of context in an effort to prove their presuppositions about the afterlife. For example, Romans 14:11 is cited as proof that everyone will eventually be saved: "As I live, says the Lord, every knee shall bow to Me, And every tongue shall give praise to God." This verse, however, is merely stating that, at some point in the future, every person will bow in humble acknowledgment of God's sovereignty and give account of themselves to him (v. 12). It is a picture of the great judgment, where some will be told to enter into heaven, while others are instructed to depart into everlasting torment (Matt. 7:19–23; 25:31–46).

Like the second-chance myth, universalism attempts to do two things: (1) make more emotionally palatable the final destiny of those who reject Christ in this life; and (2) make God fit human concepts of justice, holiness, and mercy. Influential countercult minister Dr. Walter Martin made the following observation in *Essential Christianity*:

> Merely because universal reconciliationists cannot conceive of God punishing eternally the infinite sin of rejecting His Son, they have sought to draw from Scripture what neither scholarship nor common sense can possibly allow. Since they cannot conceive of God so punishing the unregenerate soul, they have set up their own standard of how God *must* act based on what *they* believe is justice.[40]

Recent surveys measuring the religious beliefs of Americans show that universalism has great appeal and is increasing in popularity. A 1994 poll found that only 39 percent of U.S. citizens feel that "people who do not consciously accept Jesus Christ as their savior will be condemned to hell." It was also discovered that 46 percent of Americans—up from 40 percent in 1992—believe that all "good people," whether they accept Jesus as their Savior or not, will go to heaven.[41]

Another 1994 survey found that very few Americans ages fifteen to thirty-five could name even one of the Bible's Ten Commandments.[42] Nevertheless, as far back as 1988, 76 percent of Americans believed that they had a good to excellent chance of getting into heaven.[43] Two years later, this percentage had risen to 78 percent![44] In response to such statistics, Ajith Fernando—director of Youth for Christ in Sri Lanka—bluntly states: "Such is the confidence of this godless generation."[45]

Our Promised Land

There is, of course, the bright side of the afterlife: heaven. As early as the first century, Christians were looking forward to a new home in the loving presence of God. In a letter dated A.D. 125, Aristides describes the new religion called Christianity: "If any righteous man among the Christians passes from this world, they rejoice, and offer thanks to God; and escort the body with songs of thanksgiving, as if he were setting out from one place to another nearby."[46]

One of the most complete and complex descriptions of the eternal state for Christians is found in Revelation 21 and 22. Unfortunately, these highly symbolic chapters describing heaven ("the New Jerusalem") have produced some confusion. Many individuals either forget or neglect to distinguish the biblical imagery in Revelation from the reality such imagery represents. Some non-Christians have subsequently ended up rejecting God altogether because they look at the symbolism, fail to properly understand it, and discount the reality behind the imagery.

Christians, on the other hand, because they accept the Bible as true, end up with an entirely different interpretive misconception from failing to grasp the nature of symbolism: a thoroughly fictitious concept of heaven as a cubed city with pearly white gates, streets of shiny gold, and walls inlaid with precious gems. Theologian Donald Guthrie points out that these terms must not be taken literally.

> The whole vision is clearly symbolic of a perfect state of existence. . . . [The city image] is better able to portray the corporate character of the redeemed community. . . . It is radiant as a rare jewel. . . . It is in the form of a cube, which represents its perfection. Even its foundation is bejeweled, while its streets are of gold (21:18–21). . . . The overall impression is that redeemed man in communion with God has a glorious future in store for him. The details may be presented in a symbolic way, but the truth is unmistakable.[47]

Scripture also tells us that many things will *not* be in heaven, including death and mourning (Rev. 21:4a). There will be no more pain, for "the first things will have passed away" (v. 4b). Suffering from disease, broken relationships, unfulfilled dreams, and aged bodies will be no more. Famine will be eradicated and, with it, the pangs of hunger and thirst (7:16). Finally, all tears—"those arising from our own sin and failure, or from sorrow and bereavement, or those caused by others"[48]—will be a thing of the past (21:4).

The spiritual domain that Christians envision as their future home is a place far more beautiful than the most exquisite place on earth and filled with joy unparalleled. In his *Heaven: Better by Far* (1993), eighty-nine-year-old stalwart of the faith J. Oswald Sanders listed what he considered to be some of heaven's most blessed benefits.

- All that diminishes the quality of life on earth will be banished from heaven.
- The heights of joy we have experienced on earth will be eclipsed in heaven.
- We will be "saved to sin no more." Failure and its consequences will be a thing of the past.
- No more will we be subject to temptations from the world, the flesh, and the devil.
- Knowledge will no longer be limited.
- Limitations of the body will hamper us no more.
- Everything that would enrich our lives will be available.
- Reunion with loved ones and the formation of new relationships will make heaven a wonderful place of fellowship.
- Heaven's music will far surpass earth's finest achievements in that realm.
- There will be full satisfaction for every holy and wholesome longing and aspiration.[49]

As glorious as these aspects of heaven may be, even more wonderful is the fact that heaven is the abode of the triune God (John 14:2–3), the place where all Christians will forever dwell in holy communion with the Creator. In Matthew 10:32–33, Jesus gave a matter-of-fact promise that for believers is of the greatest comfort but for unbelievers is nothing short of a warning: "Therefore everyone who confesses Me before men, I will also confess him before My Father who is in heaven. But whoever denies Me before men, I will also deny him before My Father who is in heaven."

In light of the biblical teachings on heaven and hell, the most loving thing a Christian can do is obey the command given in Jude 22–23, which instructs all believers to "have mercy on some, who are doubting; [but] save others, snatching them out of the fire; and on some have mercy with fear, hating even the garment polluted by the flesh." In response to this admonition, systematic theologian Robert A. Peterson of Drew University writes: "May God stir us to be faithful to him and to our fellow human beings who need to know him who died to redeem sinners from hell. To God be the glory!"[50]

But just how long do Christians have to evangelize the world? Some individuals believe that Jesus will not return for possibly tens of thou-

sands of years. Others proclaim with dogmatic certainty that the conclusion of human history as we know it lies just around the corner of
the year 2000. The next chapter explores the history, current trends,
and cultic applications of various eschatological ideas. Each one is
inextricably linked to Christ's promise that one day the world would
meet its catastrophic end: "A time is coming when all who are in
their graves will hear his voice and come out—those who have done
good will rise to live, and those who have done evil will rise to be
condemned" (John 5:28–29 NIV).

11

Apocalypse Now

Whenever history takes one of its unexpected turns, the doom-sayers end up with prophetic egg on their faces. But when their schemes don't fit any more, you never see these folks owning up to it.

Tim Weber
church historian
Denver Theological Seminary[1]

Shortly before Christmas 1996, I found myself standing transfixed in the checkout line of a nearby supermarket. My attention had been grabbed by the dramatic headline emblazoned across the front page of *The Weekly World News*, a tabloid newspaper prominently displayed above the store's holiday-decorated candy racks: "Star over Bethlehem Signals the End of the World."

In subsequent weeks, this same publication featured equally alarming news flashes, complete with sensationalistic pictures and illustrations: "4 Horsemen of the Apocalypse Photographed in Arizona—Just Days to Go"; "1997: Beginning of the End of the World—World's Religions All Agree the Apocalypse Is Near!" The latter article informed me that "Planet Earth will undergo swift cataclysmic changes beginning in 1997 followed by the end of the world on January 6, 2000."

Doomsday stories are not unique to our era. In A.D. 198, for instance, panic struck as word spread throughout the land "that many witnesses had actually seen a walled city [i.e., the New Jerusalem] in the sky over

Judea" (compare Rev. 21:2).[2] For almost twenty centuries, Western society has been obsessed with Jesus' triumphant return from heaven and the catastrophic event with which it is set to coincide—the end of the world. Even a partial listing of the prophesied dates for Earth's destruction clearly shows that nearly every generation since Jesus' departure has thought that it was the last generation: 500, 1000, 1100, 1200, 1245, 1260, 1300, 1420, 1533, 1606, 1694, 1734, 1844, 1914, 1934, 1970, 1975, 1979, 1980, 1981, 1988, 1989, 1992, 1994, 2000.[3]

Historically, such end-time forecasts have usually come from theological cults and their leaders. But in this century, especially since the 1970s, several evangelical, charismatic, and Pentecostal leaders have gained widespread notoriety as America's most popular and influential prophetic date-setters. In their zeal to preach about Jesus' second coming, these well-meaning Christians have promoted a variety of end-time scenarios that are rife with sloppy scholarship, paranoia, unsubstantiated rumor, and a confused and convoluted matrix of "biblical" time calculations that, in reality, exist nowhere in Scripture.

The results have been grim, to say the least. Countless believers have suffered heartbreaking disappointment and now live in spiritual ruin due to the many false prognostications that have come from various church leaders in recent years. Furthermore, failed predictions by notable Christian leaders have seriously marred the credibility of evangelists and the validity of the gospel in the eyes of the secular world.[4]

Followers of Christ *must* start thinking more circumspectly when it comes to eschatology. God's promises concerning the last days are certainly worth in-depth study. Moreover, we are also commanded to "examine everything carefully; hold fast to that which is good" (1 Thess. 5:21). This chapter, therefore, will not only explore what the Bible says about the future but also what many cultists *and* some overzealous Christians are saying. Our exploration into these matters begins with what may be the most thought-provoking, difficult-to-understand, and yet encouraging book of the Bible—Revelation.

Just the Facts

The text of Revelation is named after the Greek word *apokalypsis*, which appears in the book's first verse: "The Revelation [*apokalypsis*] of Jesus Christ, which God gave Him to show to His bond-servants, the things which must soon take place; and He sent and communicated it by His angel to His bond-servant John." According to W. E. Vine's *Expository Dictionary of New Testament Words*, the term *apokalypsis* simply means an "uncovering." It is used throughout Scripture with numerous applications.

In Luke 2:32 *apokalypsis* describes "the drawing away by Christ of the veil of darkness covering the Gentiles." In Romans 16:25 it refers to the disclosure of God's "mystery" of the ages (his redemptive plan for both Jew and Gentile). In Ephesians 1:17 *apokalypsis* expresses what happens when knowledge about God is imparted to the soul.[5] The most familiar usage of the term, of course, is found in Revelation, where it relates to the visible manifestation of Jesus Christ at his second coming (compare 1 Cor. 1:7; 1 Peter 1:7, 13).

Paul the apostle describes this glorious day as a blessed event that all Christians should look forward to with great anticipation and joyous expectation (Titus 2:13). It will mark Jesus' return to earth (Col. 3:4; 2 Thess. 2:1–2; 1 Peter 5:4; 1 John 2:28; 3:2), the resurrection of the dead (John 5:28–29; 11:24; 1 Cor. 15:20–24), the glorification of all Christians (1 Cor. 15:50–53), the final judgment on the just and the unjust (John 5:29; Col. 3:6; Rev. 6:16), the establishment of a "new heaven and a new earth" (Rev. 21; 22:1–5), and the distribution of heavenly rewards (Rev. 22:12–13).

We can be confident that Jesus will indeed come again because he promised his followers that he would return: "In My Father's house are many dwelling places . . . I go to prepare a place for you. If I go and prepare a place for you, I will come again and receive you to Myself; that where I am, there you may be also" (John 14:2–3).

We can also know that at the *apokalypsis* both Christians and non-Christians will confess that Jesus is Lord (Phil. 2:9–11). The outcome of that confession, however, will not be the same for everyone. Those who during their lifetime rejected God's free gift of salvation through Christ will be told to depart from God's presence into everlasting torment (Matt. 7:21–23; 25:46; Rev. 14:11). Those of us remaining will receive different instructions: "Come, you who are blessed of My Father, inherit the kingdom prepared for you from the foundation of the world" (Matt. 25:34).

Obviously, Jesus' second coming is going to be an event of unparalleled magnitude. In fact, Scripture indicates that his return will cause reality as we know it to disintegrate before our eyes. The apostle Peter tells us that the heavens will pass away "with a roar" and that "the elements will be destroyed with intense heat, and the earth and its works will be burned up." He goes on to say that "the heavens will be destroyed by burning, and the elements will melt with intense heat!" (2 Peter 3:10–13).

Exactly when will all of these things take place? No one knows. The Bible gives no indications as to the date of the world's demise. God's Word only says that the Lord's second coming will be like a thief in the night; in other words, when it is *least* expected (1 Thess. 5:1–2; 2 Peter 3:10).

I Predict

Countless pseudo-Christian cults and new religious movements have made one false prophecy after another regarding the date of either Jesus' return or the end of the world. Some individuals have declared that God himself revealed the date. Others never specifically claimed that their date was revealed by God but still spoke with self-proclaimed prophetic authority. As a result, their prediction ended up being received by followers just as if it had indeed come directly from God.

Religious Group	Date Predicted	False Prediction and Year Delivered
Jehovah's Witnesses	1874	1897: "Our Lord, the appointed King, is now present, since October 1874, A.D., according to the testimony of the prophets, to those who have ears to hear it."[6]
	1914	1894: "The date of the close of that 'battle' [of Armageddon] is definitely marked in Scripture as October, 1914. It is already in progress, its beginning dating from October, 1874" (1892). "We see no reason for changing the figures. . . . They are, we believe, God's dates, not ours. But bear in mind that the end of 1914 is not the date for the *beginning*, but for the *end* of the time of trouble."[7]

RELIGIOUS GROUP	DATE PREDICTED	FALSE PREDICTION AND YEAR DELIVERED
JEHOVAH'S WITNESSES	1925	1920: "[W]e may confidently expect that 1925 will mark the return of Abraham, Isaac, Jacob and the faithful prophets of old. . . . 1925 shall mark the resurrection of the faithful worthies of old. . . . Millions now living will never die."[8]
JOSEPH SMITH (MORMONISM)	1891	1835: "President Smith then stated . . . it was the will of God that those who went to Zion . . . should be ordained to the ministry, and go forth to prune the vineyard for the last time, or the coming of the Lord, which was nigh—even fifty-six years should wind up the scene."[9]
LOUIS FARRAKHAN (NATION OF ISLAM)	1991	1991: "This war [Gulf War], should it start in a few days, will be that which the scriptures refer to as the War of Armageddon which is the final war . . . it will engulf the entire planet" (January 14, 1991).[10]
DAVID BERG (THE FAMILY)	1992–93	1972: "The Lord had given us a certain time prophecy in the Summer of 1970. . . . The total 'days of my years' were to be a total of 70, divided into two periods—the first, of 49 years, which evidently ended in 1968 . . . to be followed by a period of more than 21 years of my life, ending in the year 1989. . . . The End will come after the end of that 70 year period, or sometime after the year 1989. . . . This would coincide with other prophecies which we have received, indicating specifically that Maria would outlive me to the year 1993 or thereabouts. . . . This could mean that I will die at about the beginning of the Tribulation [1989], and that Maria will live on to the Coming of the Lord, approximately three and one-half years later, because I definitely saw her in vision witnessing the Second Coming" [emphasis in original].[11]
SUN MYUNG MOON (UNIFICATION CHURCH)	1977–78	January 1972: "I think 1977 and 1978 will be the culmination of the fight between the two powers [God and Satan]."
	1980	December 1972: "The satanic power is doomed to decline, and by the year 1980 we are sure to see that the satanic sovereignty will have fallen."
	1981	July 1973: "God plans to make the twenty years between 1960 and 1980 a period of total advancement for the heavenly dispensation. . . . These three seven-year periods will end in 1981. . . . By these twenty-one years, we are restoring the entire fallen history."

(continued)

RELIGIOUS GROUP	DATE PREDICTED	FALSE PREDICTION AND YEAR DELIVERED
SUN MYUNG MOON (UNIFICATION CHURCH)	2000	February 1977: "As of today, all the dispensational history of restoration has ended, has been completed. We will win God's territory back, inch by inch, until the year 2000."[12]

It is not surprising that every attempt to pinpoint doomsday has met with failure. The primary purpose of Scripture is to lead us to eternal life (John 20:30–31), not to tell us when the end of the world will come. The biblical information about the last days is primarily designed to let us know that our Lord is returning so that we can have hope in that future event. But nowhere are we given specific dates. The biblical prophets of old did not even know such end-time details (Eccles. 3:11; Dan. 12:8–9; Matt. 24:36).[13]

Despite centuries of failed speculations about "the end," Christians and non-Christians alike continue to dogmatically assert that doomsday is at hand. Their confidence is often tied to an erroneous assumption that the nearness of Jesus' return can be discerned by current events, especially "wars and rumors of wars . . . famines and earthquakes" (Matt. 24:6–7). But to assert that "the last days" have only recently begun because the present generation is witnessing never-before-seen tragedies is to believe what is historically untrue and biblically unsound, as we shall now see.

How Close Are We?

Many people think that today's natural disasters, man-made catastrophes, social/political unrest, and devastating diseases are unique to this era. Hence, we *must* be living in "the last days" before Jesus' return. Nothing could be further from the truth. Scripture tells us that "the last days" actually began when Jesus first came to earth (1 Cor. 7:26; Phil. 4:5; Heb. 1:2; 1 Peter 1:20). The apostle John goes so far as to describe the era in which he was writing as "the last hour" (1 John 2:18).

Concerning Matthew 24 (which mentions famines, wars, rumors of wars, etc.), this is an extremely complex passage of Scripture that has been the source of unending debate. Applying it to Christ's return is only *one* orthodox interpretation. A significant number of respected theologians and conservative Bible scholars see the coming of the Son of Man in Matthew as figurative language prophetically refer‑ring to God's judgment on Israel in A.D. 70, the year Jerusalem was destroyed. Old Testament passages lending support to such an inter‑pretation would be those that speak of God "coming" in judgment (Zech. 14:5).

Also, those who desire to properly study prophecy should bear in mind that earthquakes, famines, pestilence, and bad weather condi‑tions are not taking place at this present time with any more frequency or intensity than in past centuries. Likewise, wars and rumors of wars are no more prevalent today than they were hundreds of years ago. Consider the following facts taken from reliable and verifiable sources.

Earthquakes

According to seismological experts, the *apparent* rise in earthquakes over the last several years is just that—apparent. Scientist Charles F. Richter—inventor of the Richter Scale, which measures earthquake intensity—explains that today's sensitive seismographs can record minor earthquakes that only a few years ago would have gone entirely unnoticed. Consequently, the number of quakes worldwide has not really increased. We merely have the capability to detect more of them, which in turn makes it appear as if more quakes are taking place than ever before.[14]

Recent data concerning the world's most powerful quakes reveals that between 1897 and 1987 the number of major tremors (7.0 mag‑nitude or greater) *decreased* worldwide. The number of great tremors (8.0 magnitude and greater) decreased as well. The following chart that illustrates this fact appeared in Steven A. Austin's 1989 article "Earthquakes in These Last Days," which is currently available from the Institute for Creation Research.

Earthquake-related casualties have also decreased with time. For example, "More people died between 1715 and 1783 from earthquakes (1,373,845) than between 1915 and 1983 (1,210,597)."[15] History's worst earthquake, which killed more than 830,000 people, took place in China all the way back in 1556.[16] Surprisingly, historical records

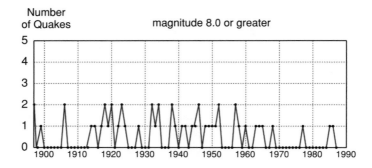

indicate that it was the first century that had record numbers of severe earthquakes. Consider the words of Roman philosopher Seneca in A.D. 65:

> How often have cities in Asia, how often in Achaia, been laid low by a single shock of earthquake! How many towns in Syria, how many in Macedonia, have been swallowed up! How often has this kind of devastation laid Cyprus in ruins! How often has Paphos collapsed! Not infrequently are tidings brought to us of the utter destruction of entire cities.[17]

End-time prophets continue to dogmatically assert that *this* generation is seeing a unique display of tectonic disasters.[18] Documentation, however, is rarely provided. The same can be said for how today's date-setters find "proof" for the imminent destruction of the world through news stories about pestilence and famine, two of the worst sources of wide-scale suffering known to humanity. Both have been around for thousands of years. But according to modern-day prophecy "experts," the worst is yet to come and, in fact, may already be here.

Sickness and Starvation

Some of today's date-setters feel that AIDS is no doubt God's end-time judgment on humanity. One prophecy pundit predicted that by 1991 everyone would know someone with AIDS.[19] Another popular Bible teacher called AIDS "the worst plague in history."[20] Still another said that by 2020 the last human being "could be expiring on this earth, killed by AIDS."[21] In reality, although the spread of AIDS is of major concern, such sensationalistic statements go far beyond what is known about the disease. Furthermore, as disastrous as AIDS is to the modern world, it is by no means the worst plague ever to strike society. That distinction belongs to the Black Death.[22]

Between 1347 and 1351, the Black Plague raced through Western Europe, killing an estimated 25 to 75 million people (roughly one-fourth to one-third of the entire population).[23] Historians have labeled it the "most lethal disaster of recorded history."[24] It struck without warning and, unlike AIDS, could be spread to persons who hardly had any contact with those unfortunate enough to be infected. All of the historians of that era chronicled the plague's horrific nature:

> The disease appeared as carbuncles [severe boils] under the armpits or in the groin, sometimes as big as an egg, and was accompanied with devouring fever and vomiting blood. It also involved a gangrenous inflammation of the lungs and throat and a fetid odor of the breath.... One sick person was sufficient to infect the whole world. The patient lingered at most a day or two.[25]

The speed and severity of the disease had never been seen before, nor has it been seen since. The city of Venice lost 100,000 residents. In Marseilles, 57,000 died in a single month. Bologna lost two-thirds of its population; Florence, three-fifths. In England, "it is estimated that one-half of the population, or 2,500,000 people, fell victim to the dread disease."[26] Clearly, the virulence of the AIDS epidemic now infecting the world pales in comparison to the ravaging power of the Black Death.

Famines have been more devastating in centuries past as well. One of the worst food shortages occurred in Ireland in the 1840s and came to be known as the Great Potato Famine. More than 1.5 million people died. In history's worst famines, which took place in China and India between 1876 and 1879, approximately 12 to 17 million people perished.[27] Famine, like pestilence, has been wreaking havoc on various cultures since before Christ. Twentieth century famines are no different, nor do they have any eschatological significance.[28]

MAJOR FAMINES	
EGYPT (c. 3500 B.C.)	The earliest written reference to a famine.
ROME (436 B.C.)	Thousands of starving people threw themselves into the Tiber River.

MAJOR FAMINES	
BRITISH ISLES (A.D. 310)	Famine kills 40,000 people.
KASHMIR, INDIA (A.D. 917)	Historical records state that the water in Jhelum River was covered by bodies. "The land became densely covered with bones in all directions, until it was like one great burial-ground, causing terror to all beings."
ENGLAND (1235)	Famine caused 20,000 deaths in London. People resorted to eating the bark of trees and grass in order to survive.
CHINA (1333–37)	Four million were reported dead in one region alone; perhaps the source of Europe's Black Death.
RUSSIA (1600)	Five hundred thousand died from both famine and plague.
INDIA (1630)	This famine began when floods followed a severe drought. Parents apparently sold their children in exchange for food. In the city of Surat, 30,000 inhabitants died.
FRANCE (1769)	This second famine in France within seventy-five years of the country's first great famine (1693) killed perhaps 5 percent of the population.
INDIA (1899–1900)	Despite relief efforts, at least 250,000 starved. The estimated death toll from famine and subsequent disease is 3.25 million.
U.S.S.R. (1921–22)	Between 250,000 and 5 million died.
ETHIOPIA (1973)	This drought-induced famine killed 100,000.
SOMALIA (1991–92)	Hundreds of thousands died, including one-fourth of all Somali children under age five. People ate their own clothes in an effort to survive.

Wars and Rumors of Wars

There have been very few years in recorded history when a war was not taking place somewhere on the planet. Many individuals, however, believe that World War I and World War II were different. "So many lives were lost and so many countries were involved," they argue. "Surely these two conflicts signal the beginning of the end, don't they?" Again, history reveals that proponents of today's "we're in the last of the last days" mentality are mistaken.

The Thirty Years' War (1618–1648) involved ten nations and claimed the lives of 30 to 40 percent of the total German population—7 to 8 million people. Germany did not suffer such losses after World War I. Furthermore, the Manchu-Chinese War of 1644 left 25 million dead, "about twice as many as were killed militarily in World War I."[29] The Napoleonic Wars (1792–1815) took 5 to 6 million lives, and the Taiping Rebellion (1850–64), "the most destructive war of the entire 19th century," resulted in the deaths of approximately 30 million![30]

According to one study of the history of warfare, humanity has waged more than fourteen thousand wars that left approximately 3.6 billion people dead.[31] In other words, the battles that have been fought within the last hundred years are little more than the tail end of a long and bloody road paved by sin. The signs of these times *really* point to only one thing: People need Jesus. This is the intended purpose of prophecy. Jesus said, "I am telling you before it comes to pass, so that when it does occur, you may believe that I am He" (John 13:19).

In other words, most of the prophecies in Scripture were given so that after the events were fulfilled people could look back on the prophecy and draw comfort and encouragement from seeing that God knew what was coming, fulfilled all of his plans, and is in control. As professor D. Brent Sandy of Liberty University states, "Much of the detail in biblical prophecy . . . is not intended to reveal the future as much as it is intended to confirm and explicate the past, or illumine the present."[32] New Testament scholar F. F. Bruce agrees in terms that are crystal clear: "Holy Writ does not provide us with the means of plotting the course of future events."[33] Sadly, this truth has been replaced by a growing cacophony of sensationalistic pronouncements that the end is near—again.

Prophets among Us

Over the last several years the national and international news media have expended most of their energy investigating the now infamous apocalyptic cults we discussed in chapter 2. Consequently, some of the less spectacular prophetic personalities, their followers, and the events associated with them have not received widespread attention. It is to these obscure, and certainly less violent, examples of "last days madness" that we now turn our attention, if for no other reason than because many of them involve Christian leaders and their failed predictions.

Before examining these eschatologically embarrassing episodes, it must be pointed out that nearly all of today's most notable end-time date-setters hold to premillennialism, which is currently the most popular Christian eschatology. Pivotal to this last days scenario is the idea that just before the world's end a final period of unparalleled turmoil—the tribulation—will occur under a satanic, world dictator: the Antichrist. There are several different kinds of premillennialism, the two most popular types being *pretribulational-dispensationalism* and *historic*.

According to pretribulational-dispensational premillennialism, the tribulation will follow "the rapture," an event wherein Christians are miraculously transformed into glorified physical beings and transported to heaven. Then, after the seven years of the tribulation, all Christians will return to earth with Jesus in order to overthrow the Antichrist and set up the "Millennial kingdom," a thousand-year era during which Jesus will rule from Jerusalem.[34] When that golden age of peace expires, Jesus will judge humanity and establish eternity.

Historic premillennialism takes a slightly different view of the end. Like pretribulational-dispensationalists, historic premillennialists believe that during the tribulation the Antichrist (sometimes called the Beast) will halt all normal means of purchasing food, acquiring housing, and obtaining employment. Only by receiving the dreaded mark of the Beast (666) will anyone be able to function normally in society (Rev. 13:15–18).[35] But unlike pretribulational-dispensational premillennialists, historic premillennialists believe Christians will *not* be rescued from the tribulation. They will instead be forced to endure the Antichrist's reign.

This latter mind-set has given rise to many survivalist sects and militia-like extremist groups in America. Large numbers of so-called Christian patriots—many of whom are actually white supremacists belonging to the theologically cultic Christian Identity Movement— have responded to the looming threat of the Antichrist by retreating to isolated regions of America with large quantities of food and weapons. Their hope is to live as quietly as possible during the seven-year reign of the Antichrist, who will supposedly rule the earth through a one-world government.[36] This period will culminate in the battle of Armageddon, which in turn will usher in the second coming of Christ.

This is not to say that all premillennialists are obsessed with the endtimes or make irresponsible pronouncements about doomsday. On the contrary, many well-respected theologians and scholars who shun date-setting are premillennial. Unfortunately there seems to be an equal number of leaders within the Christian community who insist on claiming that the end of the world is near. Some of them have even made a lucrative career of selling doomsday dates.

Edgar Whisenant: 1988 . . . , 1989 . . . , 1990 . . .

For many years, retired NASA engineer Edgar C. Whisenant was just an average, hard-working American citizen who enjoyed going to church. Then in 1988 he wrote two books that catapulted him to prophetic stardom: 88 Reasons Why the Rapture Could Be in 1988 and On Borrowed Time. Although both volumes presented a mind-boggling assortment of interlocking date and number calculations, the basic thrust of Whisenant's message came through loud and clear: Sometime between September 11 and September 13, 1988— the Jewish Feast of Trumpets, or Rosh Hashanah—Jesus was going to return and "rapture" his church out of the world. It would be the beginning of the tribulation, the beginning of the end![37]

Whisenant had no doubts about his position: "Only if the Bible is in error am I wrong, and I say that unequivocally. There is no way Biblically that I can be wrong; and I say that to every preacher in town."[38] Some Christians dismissed this prognostication as ludicrous. But others, especially prophecy buffs, stood behind Whisenant 100 percent. For example, Hart Armstrong, president of Christian Communications of Witchita, Kansas, repeatedly pinpointed the Feast of Trumpets 1988 "or September 29, 30, 1989, as possible times for His coming." Armstrong even issued a "Rapture Alert."[39]

Equally supportive of Whisenant were Trinity Broadcasting Network (TBN) founders Jan and Paul Crouch. They actually altered their regular programming for September 11–13. Instead of airing their nightly Praise the Lord television talk show, they ran videotapes of prerecorded shows dealing with the rapture. For unbelievers who might be watching, the revised programming included specific instructions on what to do in case Christian family members or friends suddenly disappeared and the world was thrust into the tribulation.[40]

Despite warnings by more theologically sound church leaders, Christians nationwide flocked to local bookstores to get copies of Whisenant's works. In fact Christian booksellers had a hard time keeping his volumes in stock. Eventually more than 4.5 million copies of 88 Reasons had been printed, approximately 300,000 of which had been sent out *free* to ministers around the country.

But Rosh Hashanah 1988 came and went uneventfully. This, however, did not deter Whisenant in the least. Immediately after the scheduled time of Christ's return, the *Atlanta Journal and Constitution* reported that the Arkansas prophet had "revised his prediction, saying that the Rapture could possibly occur by 10:55 a.m. Wednesday [September 15]."[41] As September drew to a close, Whisenant still had not lost confidence. He revised his date again—to October 3. Even when that date passed, Whisenant remained undaunted: "The evidence is all over the place that it is going to be in a few weeks anyway," he told *Christianity Today*.[42]

After his "few weeks" had gone by, Whisenant finally saw the error of his ways. He claimed that he had made a slight miscalculation of one year because of a fluke in the Gregorian calendar. Jesus was actually going to return during Rosh Hashanah of 1989! Whisenant published his discovery in *The Final Shout—Rapture Report 1989*, which has since been retitled yearly as *The Final Shout—Rapture Report 1990, 1991, 1992, 1993*, and so on.[43] He continues to revise his date annually.

John Hinkle: TBN-ite

According to John Hinkle—Pastor of Christ Church, Los Angeles—God spoke to him in "the most awesome voice" he had ever heard. But the sound of the Lord's voice was nothing compared to the prophecy it brought forth: "On Thursday, June 9, [1994] I Will Rip the Evil out of This World." Hinkle shared this astounding bit of information on the January 25, 1994, *Praise the Lord* television talk show, hosted by Paul and Jan Crouch. In front of millions of viewers,

Hinkle declared, "The most cataclysmic experience that the world has ever known since the Resurrection . . . is going to happen."[44]

In subsequent weeks, Paul Crouch assured his worldwide audience that Hinkle would be his guest on June 9, 1994, to assess the eschatological situation, providing that all Christians had "not already been lifted to meet the Lord in the air!"[45] In a financial appeal letter to his supporters, Crouch gave assurances that Hinkle's prophecy was legitimate. The voice, said Crouch, was "so *loud* and *clear* that it sounded like a great bell being rung by his ear."[46]

But when June 9, 1994, arrived, Hinkle was absent from the TBN television talk show on which he had promised to appear. Paul Crouch said nothing, and his nightly *Praise the Lord* program aired as if nothing spectacular had ever been planned for that evening. Whatever happened to Hinkle? Although he never explained himself to TBN viewers, he did send his congregation the following communiqué: "At first myself and others were very disappointed it did not take place the way we expected. It did begin, and is continuing to take place, but it happened in the spiritual realm first."[47]

Hinkle had resorted to an old cult technique for getting out of false prophecies: Change the location of the prophecy's fulfillment to the invisible realm, where it cannot be tested or disproven. This same route had been taken more than one hundred years earlier by Jehovah's Witnesses (known at that time as Second Adventists), who expected Jesus to return in 1873–74. When Christ's second advent failed to materialize, they maintained that they had been right about the *date* of his return but had been wrong about the *manner* of his return. They deduced that he must have returned *invisibly,* even though Scripture clearly teaches that Jesus will return visibly for everyone to see (Acts 1:9–11; Rev. 1:7).

Looking back to 1871, we see that many of our company were what are known as Second Adventists, and the light they held briefly stated, was that there would be a second advent of Jesus. . . . This they claimed would occur in 1873. . . . Well, 1873 came . . . and yet no burning of the world. . . . But prophecies were found which pointed positively to 1874 as the time when Jesus was due to be present. . . . The autumn of 1874, anxiously expected, finally came, but the earth rolled on as ever. . . . Then the prophetic arguments were carefully re-examined.

Was an error found? No, they stood the test of all investigation. . . .
Dark indeed seemed the outlook; all were discouraged. . . . Just at this
time Bro. Keith (one of our contributors), was used of the Lord to
throw another beam of *light* on the subject which brought order out
of confusion, and caused all of the former "light" to shine with ten-
fold brightness. . . . [A] new idea of *a presence* unseen, except by the
eye of faith. . . . [W]e realized that when Jesus should come, it would
be as unobserved by human eyes as though an angel had come. . . . Here
was a new thought: Could it be that the *time prophecies* . . . were really
meant to indicate when the Lord would be *invisibly present* to set up
his kingdom? . . . [T]he evidences satisfied me.[48]

Harold Camping: Man of the Year

Both Edgar Whisenant and John Hinkle were relatively obscure
individuals until they made their false prophecies. The year 1992,
however, saw well-known Christian radio personality Harold Camping, founder of Family Radio and Open Forum, making his own end-
time predictions. In his best-selling book *1994?* he wrote: "When
September 6, 1994, arrives, no one else can become saved, the end
has come."[49] Camping made sure that readers clearly understood him:
"No book ever written is as audacious or bold as one that claims to
predict the timing of the end of the world, and that is precisely what
this book presumes to do."[50] A year later he released *Are You Ready?*,
which was yet another volume pointing to 1994.

A *New York Times* article quoted Camping as stating, "I keep checking and checking and listening to everyone that wants to speak to the
issue. Is there anything I've missed? Is there anything I've overlooked?
Is there anything that [my debate opponents] could offer that I've
missed? . . . Frankly, I didn't hear [any good rebuttals]."[51] In another
interview he declared, "Sometimes, I've thought, 'Wow, I wish September was not the month. But I doubt it. I doubt it. I doubt it. I'm
more convinced than I've ever been the world is about to end.'"[52]

What made Camping so sure? In a 1993 interview with the *Christian Research Journal*, he revealed the reason for his confidence: "I'm
methodical. And when I began studying the Bible over 30 years ago,
I started seeing things others had missed. I discovered that God had
a timeline running from Genesis to Revelation, and with precise calculation the end of the world can accurately be determined."[53] Many

people seemed to agree with Camping, whose books quickly became huge successes. In fact *1994?* rose almost immediately to the number four spot on the Christian Bookseller Association's best-selling prophecy book chart.[54]

On September 7 Camping acknowledged that he had made an ever-so-slight miscalculation and revised his date to the middle of the month. A few weeks later he pinpointed September 29. Then he named October 2. He subsequently made several guesses about the end arriving somewhere between Christmas and December 31. This was followed by yet another date: March 31, 1995, which Camping claimed still counted as 1994 *per the Jewish calendar.*

Camping, of course, was wrong—and it could not have turned out any other way. No one will ever know the timing of Jesus' second coming, the rapture, or Armageddon. Every specific date or approximate time that is given will eventually go down in history as just another false prediction. God's Word plainly teaches that no one will ever know when, or even *about* when, the apocalypse will occur (Matt. 24:44; 25:13; Mark 13:35–37; Luke 12:40, 46; 1 Thess. 5:2–3; 2 Peter 3:9–10; Rev. 3:3).

Numerous predictions like those voiced by Whisenant, Hinkle, and Camping have been made throughout recent years. In his 1987 book *I Predict 2000 A.D.*, Pentecostal preacher Lester Sumrall unabashedly proclaimed, "I predict the absolute fullness of man's operation on planet Earth by the year 2000 A.D. Then Jesus shall reign from Jerusalem for 1000 years."[55] In 1979, North Carolina prophecy teacher Colin Deal stated that "Christ will return bodily to the earth or in the air for the church by 1988."[56] Some prophecy pundits get on an eschatological roll they cannot stop. Charles Taylor, for instance, can be credited with a long list of predicted rapture dates: 1975, 1976, 1980, 1981, 1982, 1983, 1985, 1986, 1987, 1988, 1989, 1992, 1994.[57] But not all Christian prophecy pundits are willing to be as bold.

America's *Almost* False Prophets

Recently a new method of date-setting has become popular. It is perhaps best described as date-*suggesting* rather than date-*setting.* By

enclosing their predictions within vague time frames—"near," "close
to," "just beyond," "not long after," "possibly by," "according to the
best calculations," and "as far as I can see"—many church leaders
have built a sort of eschatological safety net for themselves. In so
doing, they protect themselves from being condemned as false
prophets under the biblical indictment of Deuteronomy 18:21–22,
which targets only individuals who attribute their predictions *directly*
to God. It says nothing about persons who make predictions based
on feelings, time calculations, or faulty biblical interpretations.

One of today's most well-known date-suggesters is televangelist
Jack Van Impe. He has been churning out nonstop doomsday dates
ever since publishing an April 1, 1975, newsletter that read, "Messiah 1975? The Tribulation 1976?"[58] Van Impe adamantly declares
that we cannot know the *exact* day or hour of Christ's second coming.[59] But like all date-suggesters, he then goes on to predict the year,
or years, of Jesus' "possible," "likely," or "almost certain" return.

Van Impe implied a 1988 date for the rapture, which would be followed by the tribulation until 1996.[60] However, a subsequent time calculation seemed to zero in on 1992 for the rapture and 1999 for the
end of the world.[61] This particular schedule was used with tragic consequences by the Korean *Hyoo-go* movement (see chapter 2).[62] Next,
the year 2000 became Van Impe's imminent date for the possible termination of human history.[63] He has since moved on to "the year 2000,
and perhaps as far ahead as the year 2012."[64] His new video *2001:
Countdown to Eternity* is allegedly a "powerful" film that will prepare
viewers "for the end of the age—and the beginning of eternity."
According to a 1995 advertisement, this $24.95 video shows "how a
Millenial Kingdom is predicted to begin shortly after A.D. 2000."[65]

Such careless teachings have terrified some Christians into pack-
ing their bags and fleeing civilization, leaving their friends and relatives dumbfounded. Consider the words of David and Michele, who
wrote a letter to the Christian Research Institute of Southern California, a ministry dedicated to providing information to the public
about cults, the occult, and aberrant Christian sects. The Christian
couple asked for advice on how to help some distraught acquaintances
who had taken to heart the information in Van Impe's 1990 video
A.D. 2000: The End?: "Our friend and several of her friends are now
trying to liquidate their assets and buy land in the country, to live on

and grow food on, in the event of a crisis (a form of 'Millennial Madness,' if you will)."[66]

Unfortunately, Van Impe is only one of many date-suggesters. Some
of these "soothsayers of the second advent"[67] are surprisingly well-
known and respected members of the evangelical, charismatic, and
Pentecostal communities. Their books have sold millions of copies,
and many of them pastor large churches. A few of them even host
their own shows on Christian television. None of them, however, has
ever said that God *told* them the world was going to end on this date
or that date. Nevertheless, each one regularly gives the distinct
impression that we may confidently expect Jesus' return at any
moment due to alleged "signs" of the end, the most notable sign being
the reestablishment of Israel as a nation in 1948.

The popularity of interpreting recent events in such a manner,
especially Israel's restoration, can be traced to the publication of Hal
Lindsey's mega-best-seller *The Late Great Planet Earth* (1970). Lindsey also popularized the term "this generation" as a description of
those persons who will actually see Jesus return (i.e., most of us who
are now alive). The result has been a deluge of date-suggestions that
have come perilously close to actual date-settings. The implication
is also made that such dates do indeed come from God via a proper
understanding of his Word.

These Christian leaders may be sincere but are they being responsible? Although none of them has ever placed a "thus saith the Lord"
before their predictions, the effect is often the same for some listen-
ers due to the force with which they air their "personal" opinions,
convictions, and biblical interpretations. After all, when a well-
respected Bible teacher and pastor states all his plans are predicated
on a certain date for the Lord's return, trusting followers will likely
do the same thing. They may forego school, postpone marriages, or
give all of their money away only to never see the "near," "soon," and
"any moment" return of Jesus materialize.

Historian Mark Noll gives a timely warning that church leaders
should take to heart:

> The verdict of history seems clear. Great spiritual gain comes from liv-
> ing under the expectation of Christ's return. But wisdom and restraint
> are also in order. At the very least, it would be well for those in our

age who predict details and dates for the End to remember how many before them have misread the signs of the times.[68]

A well-known children's story is particularly relevant to the issues of date-setting and date-suggesting.

> [A] Shepherd Boy tended a flock of sheep. . . . One day, just to cause some excitement, the Shepherd Boy ran down from the hills shouting, "Wolf! Wolf!" The townsfolk came running with sticks to chase the Wolf away. All they found was the Shepherd Boy, who laughed at them. . . . The Shepherd Boy tried it again the next day. Again he ran down from the hills shouting, "Wolf!" Again the townsfolk ran to his aid in vain. But the day after, it happened that a Wolf really came. The Shepherd Boy, now truly alarmed, shouted, "Help! Come and help me! The Wolf is killing the sheep!" But this time the townsfolk said, "He won't fool us again with that trick!" They paid no attention to his cries, and the Wolf destroyed the entire flock.[69]

Prophecy Guidelines

Within Christianity there exists more than one biblically viable view of the endtimes. Unlike some of the other doctrines covered in this book, eschatology is a gray area of Scripture on which Christians may legitimately disagree. Some orthodox views do not even include a personal Antichrist, a rapture, or a seven-year tribulation. The importance of eschatology lies in the Bible's crystal clear teaching that Jesus will one day return physically and visibly (John 14:2–4; Titus 2:13; Rev. 1:7). Until then, at least five basic facts should be remembered to avoid the emotional pain experienced by those who have put too much confidence in the date speculations of either cultic false prophets or sincere Bible-believing date-suggesters.

> 1. *The Bible gives no specific date for Jesus' second advent.* Any teaching that goes beyond Scripture and assigns a never-before-known time calculation to the rapture or Christ's second advent is suspect. Even current events such as the 1948 reestablishment of Israel as a state cannot be used to calculate the nearness of Jesus' return.

Nowhere does Scripture explicitly mention the year 1948 or any other date in such a context.

2. *Only by guesswork and preconceived notions can any date for the end of the world be obtained.* Human beings are not meant to know the time—hour, day, week, month, season, or year—of Christ's return (compare Matt. 24:44; Mark 13:35–37; Luke 12:40). In Acts 1:7 Jesus reveals that future events, including significant prophetic times and ages, are not for us to know. God has sovereignly declared that such knowledge is off-limits to everyone.

3. *This era is not witnessing an increase in natural disasters and man-made catastrophes.* Earthquakes, famines, storms, outbreaks of disease, and wars have been an integral part of humankind's history since before the time of Christ.

4. *Prophecies are often meant figuratively.* Prophetic passages of Scripture must be read within their historical and cultural setting. Biblical prophecies often point to a specific time period, place, and people within the Bible narrative itself, rather than to some contemporary event. Consequently, many verses that are being applied to today's daily occurrences have already had their fulfillment through events of the past. Be careful about pulling prophecies out of context.

5. *Apocalyptic verses cannot be dogmatically interpreted.* No human being has all the answers about the end. Various prophetic passages in the Bible are understood by orthodox Christians in various ways and can be applied to events past, present, or future. Everyone—whether they admit it or not—is using some degree of personal speculation and assumption in coming to a view of how Scripture paints the future.

There is nothing wrong with looking forward to the return of our Lord and Savior. The apostles John and Paul both prayed for Jesus to come back (1 Cor. 16:22; Rev. 22:20). I, too, long for the *apokalypsis*. In fact our Lord's return is the Christian's future hope that Scripture tells us can be embraced with full confidence (2 Tim. 4:8; Titus 1:2). Christ will definitely come back to rescue us from this world of suffering, but only God knows when that will occur. It may be today, tomorrow, next year, or ten thousand years from now.

Until the second advent, all of us must remember that the *time* of Jesus' return is not nearly as important as the *fact* of Jesus' return. As Seventh-Day Adventist pastor Ross Winkle says, the "hub of the

Christian's hope is in a Person—not in a time-table. And our focus should be on Jesus—not on wars, famines, or earthquakes."[70] In other words, we should be keeping our eyes on Jesus, the author and perfecter of our faith (Heb. 12:2), not on intangible and ever-changing speculations about his return.

12

Onward Christian Soldiers

I think people are searching for a sense of security in a world
that's gone pretty mad, and they have the feeling that there must
be more to life than this craziness.

Hedda Lark
New Age publisher[1]

According to a December 22, 1996, *Los Angeles Times* article, God
and spirituality "are proving to be the rage of the late 1990s."[2] Signs
confirming this assertion are numerous. For example, 1996 saw several television specials on religion, including the ten-part PBS series
Genesis: A Living Conversation (hosted by Bill Moyers), HBO's *How
Do You Spell God?*, and journalist Hugh Hewitt's four-part PBS special *Searching for God in America*.

The publishing industry presents additional evidence of a great
religious awakening. Ingram Book Company—one of the largest book
distributors in the U.S.—found that "demand for religious and spiritual titles jumped more than 300 percent from June 1993 to June
1995."[3] Not surprisingly, 25 percent of the titles on the December
1994 *New York Times* best-sellers list dealt with spiritual issues.

Many Christians believe that this recent wave of spiritual fervor
is indicative of a new outpouring of God's Holy Spirit; a precursor, so
to speak, of worldwide Christian revival. But results from a December 1994 Roper survey show that churchgoing has actually *declined*

among all age groups. Only 38 percent of Americans between ages thirty and forty-four had attended church during the week prior to December 9, 1994, "down from 42 percent in 1976." Churchgoing among younger adults, ages eighteen to twenty-nine, had fallen as well, "from 35 percent in 1976 to 27 percent in 1994."[4]

If today's spiritually starved individuals are not turning to Christianity, then where are they going? A December 1994 *Psychology Today* piece titled "Desperately Seeking Spirituality" notes that Transcendental Meditation and other Eastern philosophies have become "permanently embedded in the American scene," as have shamanistic practices from various cultures.[5] Instructional courses on occultic practices like out-of-body travel are also being widely accepted now.[6]

Apparently, a majority of modern truth-seekers are flocking to alternative forms of religious expression. This may account for why the last decade has seen a dramatic increase in the popularity of non-Christan authors (e.g., James Redfield, M. Scott Peck, Marianne Williamson, Betty Eadie, John Bradshaw) and a rise in the number of best-sellers that promote non-Christian spirituality (*Chicken Soup for the Soul, A Return to Love, Embraced by the Light, Further Along the Road Less Traveled*).

In our fast-paced, information-overloaded world of nontraditional religious groups, cults, self-proclaimed gurus of "light," and counterfeit Christian organizations, how can a follower of Jesus effectively share the gospel? How can a Christian guard himself or herself from the dangers—physical, emotional, intellectual, and spiritual—that are consistent with cultic involvement? How can a believer in Christ protect friends and family from false belief systems? Scripture has the answers.

Sharing the Gospel

It is not always easy to share the gospel, especially with a non-Christian who has comfortably settled into another religious belief system that he or she thinks *is* Christian. Nevertheless, we are commanded by Scripture to "preach the word; be ready in season and out of season [all the time]" (2 Tim. 4:2). This same exhortation is found in 1 Peter 3:15: "Sanctify Christ as Lord in your hearts, always being ready to make a defense to everyone who asks you to give an account for the hope that is in you."

Unfortunately there seems to be some confusion about the attitude with which we are to witness. Peter says it should be done with gentleness and reverence (v. 15). Paul the apostle admonishes us that spreading the Good News involves having great patience with a view toward instructing (2 Tim. 4:2) rather than browbeating. In 2 Timothy 2:24–26, Paul further teaches that every witnessing encounter is to be permeated with gentleness and kindness:

> The Lord's bond-servant must not be quarrelsome, but be kind to all, able to teach, patient when wronged, with gentleness correcting those who are in opposition, if perhaps God may grant them repentance leading to the knowledge of the truth, and they may come to their senses and escape from the snare of the devil, having been held captive by him to do his will.

Sharing one's faith in such a manner not only demonstrates obedience to God but provides one of the most powerful and irrefutable proofs of Christianity—God's love. Jesus said that our Christian identity and the proper presentation of it to society are inextricably linked to how we show love (John 13:35). Ephesians 4:15 plainly instructs us to speak the truth *in love*. Of course, it can be difficult to show the fruit of the Holy Spirit (Gal. 5:22–23) when witnessing, especially if cultists become hostile when their misrepresentations of God and the Bible are exposed. Fortunately there are a number of ways to counteract the natural frustrations, fears, and insecurities that invariably plague a Christian who is just beginning to share his or her faith.

Show Respect

Cultists, like everyone else, deserve respect. Their belief systems should never be mocked. They have invested a great deal of time and energy in the cult to which they belong. Their entire life is usually wrapped up in their faith. The quickest way to destroy communication with a cultist is to make them feel foolish about their beliefs.

They will automatically raise emotional walls in an effort to preserve their dignity.

Rather than ridiculing a cultist, *respond* to them with thoughtful answers that are prefaced by words of kindness, which show you respect their viewpoint. For example, before correcting a misinterpretation of Scripture, try saying: "That's a pretty good point, but have you thought of this?" or "I can certainly understand why you might see it that way, but I think there's something you're missing," or "That's certainly possible, but I see a problem with looking at it like that."

When exposing someone's unbiblical doctrines, try to put yourself in their place. Imagine how you would feel if someone began showing you that orthodox Christianity was a sham and that your spiritual leader (pastor) was teaching false doctrines. This would be quite painful. Such is the case when cultists begin to see the deceptive nature of their belief system. At the forefront of your mind should be Jesus' command to treat others as you would want them to treat you (Luke 6:31).

Know Your Enemy

There is a vast difference between the *deceivers* in a cult and the *deceived*. The latter are usually rank-and-file members who only believe what they believe because they have trusted the words of their leaders (the deceivers). Many of the cultists with whom I have spoken are sincere individuals who simply do not have enough information to choose the correct path. Cultists are not enemies to be theologically conquered. They are victims to be helped, captives to be freed. They need to be shown that although they may be sincere, they are sincerely wrong.

Our true enemies are spiritual forces of darkness. God's Word warns believers that with the progression of time there will appear many deceitful spirits and doctrines of demons to draw people away from God (1 Tim. 4:1). We are additionally told that people are blinded to the gospel by Satan (2 Cor. 4:3–4), who is the ultimate originator and propagator of false beliefs.

The battle waged in the world of the cults is actually a spiritual battle. Our struggle is not against flesh and blood but against spiritual entities (Eph. 6:12). Consequently, the weapons of our warfare cannot be carnal but must be spiritual weapons of righteousness that include God's Word, the fruit of the Holy Spirit, and, above all, prayer (Luke 22:32; 2 Cor. 6:7; 10:4; Eph. 6:18; Heb. 4:12; James 5:16).

Be Humble

No one can know everything about a cult's doctrines. This means that at some point a cultist will probably bring up a biblical or theological issue with which you are unfamiliar. When this happens, do not panic. Let them know that you are not prepared to deal with that particular subject; then ask if it would be agreeable to discuss another relevant topic. You might even want to suggest one. A cultist will more than likely agree to this because he or she will not want to lose a potential convert.

It also should be recognized that cultists have a number of highly complex and seemingly good arguments for some of their positions. If a scriptural argument they offer does indeed seem to support the view and you have no answer for it, *don't make up an answer!* Simply admit that you will have to take a closer look at that particular verse and do some more research on it. Most cultists will readily accept this response, appreciate your honesty and humility, and end up being even more comfortable with you, which in turn will make them more inclined to hear your opinions.

It's God's Job, Not Yours

Perhaps the number one mistake made by Christians when witnessing to cultists is to forget about God. This sounds unbelievable, but it is true. A Christian need not try to do it all alone. Room must be left for the Holy Spirit to work. One of the best ways to accomplish this is by backing off when you see that your point has been made. Do not always demand that a cultist agree with you before moving on to another topic. Once a concept has been presented and understood by the cultist, allow that truth to sink into the cultist's soul where the Lord can use it to its maximum effectiveness.

Closely associated with this aspect of witnessing is the tendency Christians have to assess a particular encounter as either successful or unsuccessful. We often look for either an on-the-spot conversion or at least an admission of error by the cultist. Both *rarely* happen, because the major effects of witnessing occur by the working of the Holy Spirit in a place that cannot be seen, inside the cultist's heart. Generally speaking, any move by a cultist toward Christianity often takes many meetings with different Christians over the course of several years. Each encounter with truth slowly moves that person closer to God. Unrealistic expectations can cause a lot of frustration for a Christian who wants to be effective.

Our responsibility is simply to share the truth of the gospel and leave the rest up to God. Conversion is *his* work, not ours. The simplest words spoken from a pulpit—"Jesus loves you, and you can be forgiven right now for your sins"—have resulted in dozens of people repenting and accepting Christ. What we say and how we say it are certainly important, but even more important is God, who is working through what we say and how we say it. God's Word will do exactly what he wants it to do (Isa. 55:11). There will *always* be an effect when truth is presented. As Sir Winston Churchill noted, "Truth is incontrovertible. Panic may resent it; ignorance may deride it; malice may distort it, but there it is."[7]

It is crucial for Christians to realize that they are merely sound devices that God uses to spread the Good News of salvation. As the apostle Paul said, one person waters and another plants, but it is God who gives the increase (1 Cor. 3:5–9). All evangelistic successes are because of God's work in the heart of the converted. Ultimately, we have little to do with the eventual outcome of a witnessing encounter. Knowing this protects us from two destructive emotional traps—pride and discouragement.

Christians who forget God's part in "making converts" often grow prideful if a cultist eventually becomes a Christian. These same individuals, however, can fall into discouragement if a cultist does not accept Christ. Both mind-sets are spiritually harmful and stem from a distorted view of how important their role is in evangelism.

When one understands that it is ultimately God who is in charge, all of the praise for conversions is given to him alone, which cancels out pride. At the same time, possible guilt over not being able to bring someone to the Lord is alleviated as a Christian remembers God is in control. Simple obedience is what makes *every* witnessing encounter successful, no matter what happens.

Guarding Your Own Soul

As concerned as we should be for cultists, we must make sure that we ourselves do not become ensnared in a spiritually dangerous group. One of the best ways to protect ourselves is to know our Bible and check against God's Word everything we hear or experience in a religious setting: "All Scripture is inspired by God and profitable for teaching, for reproof, for correction, for training in righteousness; so that the man of God may be adequate, equipped for every good work" (2 Tim. 3:16–17).

Furthermore, any church, Bible study, pastor, evangelist, or religious organization that attempts to discourage questioning of its teachings should immediately be viewed with an eye of suspicion. In Acts 17:11 we find the citizens of Berea actually being commended for comparing the doctrines of Paul and Silas to Scripture. God is not against a little skepticism and an inquiring mind. Only cults and cultists discourage rigorous testing of their doctrines.

It is also common for cults to trivialize clear thinking and rational discourse. Members are told to "just believe" or "just trust" the words of a particular leader. There is often an emphasis on following certain doctrines because they just "feel" right. The basic premise is that the mind is incapable of correctly analyzing a situation or teaching. Feelings are said to be the *true* source of spiritual wisdom. But this contradicts Jesus, who taught us to love God with all of our heart, soul, and *mind* (Matt. 22:37).

Protecting Others

Given the fact that there are millions of cultists throughout the world, the chances are quite good that you will at some point in your life have a family member or friend approached by a theological cult. Some of your acquaintances may even become involved in a cult.

You may eventually be their only contact with the domain of truth. Keeping a few witnessing tips in mind could make interaction with them much easier.

First, seek godly advice from a knowledgeable cult counselor at either your church or a countercult ministry (see appendix). By contacting a pastor, former cult member, or trained cult specialist, you will immediately have access to helpful information. Such individuals can also offer prayer support, which is imperative in cult-related situations.

Second, take time to get your facts straight regarding the group's doctrines. Criticize what you *know* they believe, not what you *think* they believe. Much of your credibility will depend on how fair and unbiased you can be. A sincere desire to understand a group's beliefs will add more weight to any criticisms and concerns you may eventually voice. After all, no one likes to be judged without getting a fair hearing. To learn more about the specific cult in which your family member or friend is involved, you might want to read a good countercult or theology book that discusses that particular group.

Third, remember that, in order for a person to choose Scripture over error, they must be thinking clearly. Blind acceptance of any group's teachings leads to problems. As Adolf Hitler remarked, "What luck for the rulers that men do not think."[8] To help facilitate analytical thought, ask probing questions that get your friend or family member to think about the teachings they are beginning to embrace. Try to get them to see for themselves that there are problems with the group in which they have become involved. Point out apparent doctrinal contradictions with the Bible, and gently ask for an explanation. Also bring up any inconsistencies within the overall doctrinal system. If the organization has a history of false prophecies or scandals, these, too, can be brought up as issues that cause you concern.

Fourth, realize that your friend or family member is probably experiencing some kind of emotional draw to the cult. Try to find out *why* they are so interested in the group. Do they have doctrinal questions that only the cult seems able to answer? Are they in a period of personal crisis and receiving emotional support from the cult? Have they become disillusioned with orthodox Christianity because of bad experiences at a church? Are they lonely and in need of companionship?

Finding out this information is crucial, because a person can sometimes be rescued from cultic involvement more easily if their emotional issues as well as their theological issues are addressed.

Fifth, make sure you always come across as caring rather than condemning. Even if a family member or friend chooses to ignore your warnings, let them know that you still love and accept them. Stress to them that you want to remain in contact with them and that you are always open to looking at any information they may have to show you, as long as you can share with them how you feel about that information. Stay in touch with them as long as they will allow it.

Some Closing Thoughts

There have always been cults, and there probably always will be. Why? We cannot know for sure. It is clear that God is displeased with false doctrines that deceive people (Deuteronomy 13), yet we cannot deny that he allows this form of evil to continue. Perhaps God, in his infinite wisdom, chooses to use cults as a means of demonstrating his power in the lives of those who are eventually rescued from such groups. The Bible teaches that God will allow suffering so that his power can be displayed through it (John 9:3).

Cults might also exist as a means of God's judgment. On more than one occasion, I have seen cultists realize that their position was wrong and yet refuse to repent. For example, one Mormon woman with whom I spoke admitted to me that she had come to a point where the Bible did not matter. Even after seeing that Scripture contradicts Mormonism, she proclaimed to me that she would always remain a Mormon simply because she "liked" the Mormon God. For such individuals, a cult serves as a vehicle through which they have consciously chosen their eternal destination.

Fortunately God promises that those who *truly* seek after him will eventually find him (Deut. 4:29). We can also rest assured that if cultists accept Christ as their personal Lord and Savior, even their cult-related experiences will eventually work toward an ultimate good in either their life or someone else's life. Many former cultists, for instance, end up starting countercult ministries so that they comfort others with the comfort they received from God (2 Cor. 1:4). The Bible specifically tells us that God can use for good those things humans intended for evil (Gen. 50:20; Rom. 8:28).

Our acceptance of God's sovereignty makes it possible for us to confidently reach out to those who are spiritually lost and dying in the confusing world of cults, new religious movements, and various other forms of counterfeit Christianity. Because we know that God is in control, we can be "steadfast, immovable, always abounding in the work of the Lord, knowing that [our] toil is not in vain in the Lord" (1 Cor. 15:58).

Appendix

Recommended Ministries

General Cults

Religious Information Center
President/Founder—Richard Abanes
P.O. Box 80961
Rancho Santa Margarita, CA 92688
714-858-8936 (phone/fax)
raric@aol.com
http://www.geocities.com/Athens/
Delphi/1419

Watchman Fellowship
National Director—James Walker
P.O. Box 13340
Arlington, TX 76094
817-277-0023 / 817-277-8098 (fax)
http://www.watchman.org

Answers In Action
Founders/Directors—Bob and
Gretchen Passantino
P.O. Box 2067
Costa Mesa, CA 92628
714-646-9024
http://answers.org

Christian Research Institute
President—Hank Hanegraaff
30162 Tomas
Rancho Santa Margarita, CA 92688
714-858-6100
http://www.equip.org

American Family Foundation
Executive Director—Michael D.
Langone
P.O. Box 2265
Bonita Springs, FL 33959
212-533-5420
http://www.csj.org

Personal Freedom Outreach
President—Kurt Goedelman
P.O. Box 26062
Saint Louis, MO 63136
314-388-2648

Jude 3 Missions
Founder/Director—Kurt Van Gorden
P.O. Box 1901
Orange, CA 92668
714-247-1850

Gospel Truths Ministries
Executive Director—Luke Wilson
1340 Monroe Ave. N. W.
Grand Rapids, MI 49505
616-451-4562 / 616-451-8907 (fax)

Centers for Apologetic Research
Director—Paul Carden
26300 Via Escolar
San Juan Capistrano, CA 92675
714-364-1191 / 714-364-7266 (fax)

205

Reasoning from the Scriptures
   Ministries
Founder/Director—Ron Rhodes
P.O. Box 80087
Rancho Santa Margarita, CA 92688
714-888-8848

Jehovah's Witnesses

Comments from the Friends
Founder/Director—David Reed
Box 819
Assonet, MA 02702
508-763-8050
http://www.ultranet.com/~comments

Free Minds, Inc.
Founder/Director—Randall Watters
P.O. Box 3818
Manhattan Beach, CA 90266
310-545-7831 / 310-545-0068 (fax)
http://www.freeminds.org/rwatters.htm

Witness, Inc.
National Director—Duane Magnani
P.O. Box 597
Clayton, CA 94517
510-672-5979

Equippers, Inc.
Director—Peter Barnes
4621 Soria Dr.
San Diego, CA 92115
619-270-2991

Mormonism

Utah Lighthouse Ministry
Founders/Directors—Jerald and Sandra
   Tanner
P.O. Box 1884
Salt Lake City, UT 84110
801-485-8894 / 801-485-0312 (fax)
http://www.alphamin.org/catalog.html

Mormonism Researched
Founder/Director—Bill McKeever
P.O. Box 20705
El Cajon, CA 92021
619-447-3873 (phone/fax)
http://www.mrm.org

Utah Missions, Inc.
Director—John L. Smith
P.O. Box 348
Marlow, OK 73055
405-658-5631
800-654-3992 (orders)

Notes

Introduction

1. Karen Hall, "Would Jesus Belong to the Christian Coalition?" *Cosmopolitan*, September 1996, 40.

2. Philip Schaff, *The Greek and Latin Creeds*, vol. 2 of *The Creeds of Christendom*, (Grand Rapids: Baker, 1996), 45–71.

3. Walter Martin, *The Kingdom of the Cults* (1965; reprint, Minneapolis: Bethany, 1985), 18.

4. Joseph Smith, *History of the Church*, vol. 6 (1950; reprint, Salt Lake City: Church of Jesus Christ of Latter-day Saints, 1980), 303; Bruce McConkie, *Mormon Doctrine* (1958; reprint, Salt Lake City: Bookcraft, 1977), 516; Milton R. Hunter, *The Gospel through the Ages* (1945; reprint, Salt Lake City: Deseret, 1958), 12–15, 21.

5. Martin, *The Kingdom of the Cults*, 20.

6. In reference to David Koresh's Branch Davidians, James D. Tabor—Religious Studies Department professor at the University of North Carolina—erroneously states: "They are warm, intelligent and dear people who love God and the Bible" (*Bible Review* [February 1994]: 60). In the *Encyclopedia of American Religions*, religion scholar J. Gordon Melton refers to The Family—an infamous cult with a history of officially sanctioned sexual excesses that include prostitution, child pornography, and adultery—as a "Christian" commune and church (*Encyclopedia of American Religions*, 5th ed. [Detroit: Gale Research, 1996], 607, 941).

7. Larry B. Stammer, "Gospel Based on Jewish Stories, Not Literal Truth, Bishop Says," *Los Angeles Times*, 26 October 1996, sec. B, pp. 8–9. Peter Steinfels, "Female Concept of God Is Shaking Protestants," *New York Times*, 14 May 1994, p. 8.

8. "Survey Finds Born-Again Christians Are Often Ignorant about Their Faith," *EP News Service*, 29 March 1996, pp. 1–2.

Chapter 1:
A Clear and Present Danger

1. George Santayana, *Life of Reason*, vol. 1 of *Reason in Common Sense*, quoted in Robert Andrews, *The Columbia Dictionary of Quotations* (New York: Columbia University, 1993), 409.

2. David Holley, "Secretive Japanese Cult Linked to Germ Weapons Plan," *Los Angeles Times*, 28 March 1995, sec. A, p. 3; Robert Davis and Juan J. Walte, "Swiss Cult's Bizarre Last Act Leaves 'Wax Museum' of Death," *USA Today*, 6 October 1994, sec. A, p. 6; Mark Potok and J. Michael Kennedy, "4 Federal Agents Killed in Shootout with Cult in Texas," *Los Angeles Times*, 1 March 1993, sec. A, p. 1.

3. *EP News Service*, 9 October 1992, quoted in B. J. Oropeza, *99 Reasons Why No One Knows When Christ Will Return* (Downers Grove, Ill.: InterVarsity Press, 1994), 11.

4. Oropeza, *99 Reasons*, 168.

5. Taberah World Missions, *Rapture!* (Los Angeles: 1992), 3–4.

6. *The Last Plan of God* (Seoul, Korea: Taberah World Missions, 1992), 94–96, quoted in Oropeza, *99 Reasons*, 37.

7. *EP News Service*, 6 November 1992, p. 5.

8. Ibid.

9. Reuters, "Korean Sect Stunned as 'Rapture' Doesn't Come," *Orange County Register*, 29 October 1992, sec. A, p. 21.

10. *EP News Service*, 6 November 1992, p. 5.

11. Russell Chandler, *Doomsday* (Ann Arbor, Mich.: Servant Publications, 1993), 261.

12. "Expert Says Cult Had Illegal Arms," *New York Times*, 15 January 1994, sec. A, p. 10; Gordon Witkin, "Raking Up the Ashes," *U.S. News and World Report*, 24 July 1995, 30; Ken Carter, "Branch Davidian Firearms," *Machine Gun News* (March 1994), 5. Texas Rangers found a total of forty-eight illegal machine guns and four illegal hand grenades in the ruins of the Branch Davidian compound.

13. Stephen Labaton, "Report on Assault on Waco Cult Contradicts Reno's Explanations," *New York Times*, 9 October 1993, sec. A, p. 1.

14. Douglas Frantz, "Justice Department Report Absolves FBI, Blames Koresh for 75 Waco Deaths," *Los Angeles Times*, 9 October 1993, sec. A, p. 17; compare Dean M. Kelley, "Waco: A Massacre and Its Aftermath," *First Things*, May 1995, 25.

15. Richard Lacayo, "In the Reign of Fire," *Time*, 17 October 1994, 59.

16. Tom Post, "Mystery of the Solar Temple," *Newsweek*, 17 October 1994, 42.

17. Thomas E. Hitchings, ed., "53 Cultists Found Dead in Switzerland and Canada," *Facts on File Yearbook 1994* (New York: Facts on File, 1995), 748.

18. Michael S. Serrill, "Remains of the Day," *Time*, 24 October 1994, 42.

19. Lacayo, "In the Reign of Fire," 59.

20. "53 Cultists Found Dead," 748.

21. Ibid.

22. Post, "Mystery of the Solar Temple," 44.

23. *Transit pour le Futur*, as reprinted in Ted Daniels, Ph.D., "Solar Temple Letters 3: Transit pour le Future," *Millenial Prophecy Report* 3, no. 5 (1994), internet edition at http://www.channel1.com/mpr/transit.htm.

24. "53 Cultists Found Dead," 748.

25. Luc Jouret, taped message, quoted in Post, "Mystery of the Solar Temple," 43.

26. Davis and Walte, "Swiss Cult's Bizarre Last Act," sec. A, p. 6.

27. Scott Kraft, "Cult Ritual Suspected in Deaths," *Los Angeles Times*, 24 December 1995, sec. A, p. 3.

28. James Walsh, "The Sunburst Sacrifices," *Time*, 8 January 1996.

29. Kraft, "Cult Ritual Suspected in Deaths," sec. A, p. 3.

30. AP, "French Police End Cult Probe," 11 November 1996, America Online.

31. Katherine Wilton, "Police Probe Rumor of Third Solar Temple Suicide," *The Gazzette* (Montreal, Canada), 4 April 1996, sec. A, p. 3.

32. Walsh, "The Sunburst Sacrifices," 45.

33. Patrick Vuarnet, letter to Alain Vuarnet, quoted in Walsh, "The Sunburst Sacrifices," 45.

34. Fred Guterl, "Nerve Gas in the Subway," *Discover* (January 1996), 73.

35. "Japanese Cult Leader Arrested, Charged with Subway Nerve-Gas Attacks," *Facts on File*, 1995, 353.

36. David E. Kaplan and Andrew Marshall, *The Cult at the End of the World* (New York: Crown, 1996), 16; cf. Michelle Magee, "Cult Leader's Case Expected to Take Years," *San Francisco Chronicle*, 7 June 1995, sec. C, p. 1. Asahara called himself "Christ" in his 1992 manifesto *Declaring Myself the Christ*.

37. Teresa Watanabe, "Japanese Police Seek Sect Chief in Wider Probe," *Los Angeles Times*, 24 March 1995, sec. A, p. 10.

38. Anthony Spaeth, "Engineer of Doom," *Time*, 12 June 1995, 57.

39. Shoko Asahara, quoted in Edward W. Desmond, "Under Arrest—Finally," *Time*, 9 May 1995, 43.

40. Peter Landers, "Cult Leader's Life Story Is Nothing If Not Bizarre," *San Francisco Chronicle*, 24 March 1995, sec. A, p. 10.

41. Shoko Asahara, quoted in *Twilight Zone*, cited in David Holley, "Japan Guru—Young Bully's Power Quest," *Los Angeles Times*, 27 March 1995, sec. A, p. 6.

42. Holley, "Japan Guru," sec. A, p. 7.

43. David E. Kaplan and Andrew Marshall, The Cult at the End of the World (New York: Crown, 1996), quoted in John Burnham Schwartz, "Terror in Tokyo," *Newsday*, 7 July 1996, sec. C, p. 35, internet edition at http://www.elibrary.com:80/getdoc.cgi?id=54648250x0y370&Form=EN&Button=MEM.

44. Steven Strasser, "Tokyo Grabs the Doomsday Guru," *Newsweek*, 29 May 1995, 48.

45. Senator Sam Nunn, "The New Terror: Nutcakes with Nukes," *New Perspectives Quarterly*, 13 (January 1, 1996): 32, internet edition at http://www.elibrary.com:80/getdoc.cgi?id=54648250x0y370&OIDS=0Q004D018&Form=RL.

46. Strasser, "Tokyo Grabs the Doomsday Guru," 48.

47. Teresa Watanabe and Carol J. Williams, "Japan Sect Uses Pain to Impel Faith," *Los Angeles Times*, 25 March 1995, sec. A, p. 13.

48. Ibid., sec. A, p. 12.

49. Focus, 1995, quoted in David Holley, "Cult Attracted Many Followers and Notoriety," *Los Angeles Times*, 23 March, 1995, sec. A, p. 19.

50. Teresa Watanabe, "Police Seize Toxic Chemicals in Raid on Japanese Sect," *Los Angeles Times*, 23 March 1995, sec. A, pp. 1, 18.

51. Watanabe and Williams, "Japan Sect Uses Pain," sec. A, p. 12.

52. David E. Kaplan and Andrew Marshall, "The Cult at the End of the World," *Wired* (July 1996): 178.

53. "Aum Shinrikyo's Cultic Style," *The Cult Observer* 12, no. 4 (1995): 3.

54. Kaplan and Marshall, "The Cult at the End of the World," 177.

55. David Holley, "Police Search for Bodies at Sect's Compound," *Los Angeles Times*, 29 March 1995, sec. A, p. 8.

56. Murray Sayle, "Letter from Tokyo," The New Yorker, 1 April 1996, internet edition at http://www.enews.com/magazines/new_yorker/archive/960401–001.html.

57. "Asahara and O. J.," *The Economist*, 4 May 1996, internet edition at http://www.enews.com/magazines/economist/archive/05/960504–001.html.

58. AP, "Japan Guru Ordered from Court," 8 November 1996, America Online.

59. Ibid.

60. "Asahara and O. J."; Reuters, "Japan Guru Trial Spurs Fresh Anger and Bitterness," 24 April 1996, America Online.

61. Kaplan and Marshall, "The Cult at the End of the World," 136–37, 176.

62. Strasser, "Tokyo Grabs the Doomsday Guru," 48; "The Cult's Broad Reach," *Newsweek*, 8 May 1995, 54.

63. "The Cult's Broad Reach," 54.

64. "Korean Woman Beaten to Death in Ceremony to 'Cast out Demons,'" *EP News Service*, 24 March 1995, p. 3; "Week of Beatings in Exorcism Ends in Woman's Death," *Cult Awareness Network News* (August 1995): 3.

65. "Korean Woman Beaten to Death," p. 3.

66. "Alleged Leader of D.C. Cult Accused of Kidnapping Woman," *Washington Post*, 15 June 1995, sec. D, p. 3.; compare "D.C. Police Arrest Religious Leader on Kidnapping Charge," *Cult Awareness Network News* (July 1995): 4.

67. Faith Tabernacle, *Death of Self*, quoted in Jackie Alnor, "Faith Tabernacle:

Lives Cut Short," *Christian Sentinel* (spring 1995): 8.

Chapter 2: World of the Cults

1. Ronald Enroth, *Evangelizing the Cults* (Ann Arbor, Mich.: Servant Publications, 1990), 11.

2. Churches have normally been thought of as "large denominations [e.g., Roman Catholicism, Methodism, Lutheranism] characterized by their inclusive approach to life and their identification with the prevailing culture" (J. Gordon Melton, *Encyclopedic Handbook of Cults in America* [New York: Garland Publishing, 1992], 3). Sects are generally seen as those groups that have broken away from established churches. Although they tend to retain most of the doctrines and practices of their parent church, they usually add to or subtract from the various teachings of the larger religious body from which they emerged. Sects often grow into established churches and/or religions. Christianity, for instance, began as a sect of Judaism. Protestantism started as a sect of Roman Catholicism. Sects normally make it very clear that they are no longer part of their parent church or religion.

3. Daniel G. Reid, Robert D. Linder, Bruce L. Shelley, and Harry S. Stout, *Dictionary of Christianity in America* (Downers Grove, Ill.: InterVarsity Press, 1990), 331.

4. Irving Hexham, in Walter A. Elwell, ed., *Evangelical Dictionary of Theology* (1984; reprint, Grand Rapids: Baker, 1996), 289.

5. John A. Saliba, *Understanding New Religious Movements* (Grand Rapids: Eerdmans, 1995), 144–45. The Local Church—a religious group many persons consider a cult—serves as an excellent example of how some new religious movements use lawsuits to silence critics. Since 1979 the Local Church has either sued or threatened to sue several Christian publishers and authors, including Ronald Enroth, *The Lure of the Cults* (Christian Herald Books); Jack Sparks, *The Mind Benders* (Thomas Nel-

son); Jerram Barrs, *Shepherds and Sheep* (InterVarsity Press); Bob Larson, *Larson's Book of Cults* (Tyndale House). In all of the above cases, references to the Local Church were either partially or entirely removed from the book in question. The most visible legal action taken by the Local Church involved the Berkeley, California, Spiritual Counterfeits Project (SCP), which had published Neil T. Duddy's *The God-Men*, a book extremely critical of the practices and beliefs of the Local Church. The suit ended in 1985 with an $11 million judgment against SCP. The countercult organization pleaded no contest due to lack of funds and was forced to file bankruptcy.

6. Hexham in Elwell, *Evangelical Dictionary of Theology*, 289.

7. Sociological red flags of a cult, although they may run contrary to the normal practices of society, are not always heinous or illegal. The practice of having marriages arranged entirely by an organization's leader, for instance, would qualify a group as cultic from a sociological perspective in the United States because arranged marriages are no longer the societal norm in America. Even in cultures where marriages are still arranged, such a group would probably qualify as a cult because, in those societies, marriages are usually arranged by either family members or a designated matchmaker in the community.

8. Robert T. Miller and Ronald B. Flowers, *Toward Benevolent Neutrality: Church, State, and the Supreme Court*, vol. 2, 5th ed. (Waco: Baylor University, 1996), 722–35.

9. Saliba, *Understanding New Religious Movements*, 7.

10. Ibid., 8, 107.

11. Ibid., 6.

12. There are two types of deprogramming: legal and illegal. Illegal deprogramming is a controversial practice involving the abduction of a cult member and the introduction of him or her to a "deprogrammer," who then proceeds to use forceful techniques (verbal as well as physical) to try to break the cult's psychological hold

on the cultist. Legal deprogramming does not entail infringement on anyone's civil rights. It is marked by civilized discussions between a cultist and a deprogrammer. During these meetings, the deprogrammer tries to get the cultist to rationally evaluate the teachings of the group in which he or she is involved.

13. CAN's Appeal against the Scott Judgment, 3 September 1996, "Statement of Issues," Question 6.

14. The term "anticult" is a negatively charged description sociologists use in reference to individuals and organizations that place a judgment of any kind on cults: i.e., distraught parents of cultists, organizations dedicated to disseminating information about cults, former cult members, Christians, countercult ministries such as the Christian Research Institute.

15. Priscilla Coates (CAN representative, California), author's 2 December 1996 telephone conversation with Coates.

16. CAN's Appeal against the Scott Judgment, 3 September 1996, electronic edition.

17. Dr. Ronald Enroth's works include Youth, Brainwashing, and Extremist Cults (Grand Rapids: Zondervan, 1977); The Lure of the Cults, rev. ed. (Downers Grove, Ill.: InterVarsity Press, 1987); Evangelizing the Cults (Ann Arbor, Mich.: Servant Publications, 1990); Churches That Abuse (Grand Rapids: Zondervan, 1992).

18. Enroth, The Lure of the Cults, 124.

19. Michael D. Langone, Recovery from Cults (New York: W. W. Norton and Co., 1993), 34.

20. Ibid.

21. Ibid.

22. Points 1–4 are taken from Langone, Recovery from Cults, 5, 67–68, 76–77, 89–91, 98–99. Point 5 is taken from Joan Carol Ross and Michael D. Langone, Cults: What Parents Should Know (New York: Carol Publishing Group, 1988), 122 (compare Enroth, Churches That Abuse, 157–79). Points 6–8 are taken from James and Marcia Rudin, Prison or Paradise: The New Religious Cults (Philadelphia: West-

minster Press, 1980), 26ff., as cited in J. Gordon Melton, Encyclopedic Handbook of Cults in America, 6. Points 9–16 are taken from Ronald Enroth, "Voices from the Fringe," Moody Monthly, October 1989, 94–104; Ronald Enroth, "Voices on the Fringe," Eternity, October 1986, 17–22; and Enroth, Churches That Abuse, quoted in Dr. Paul Martin, Cult-Proofing Your Kids (Grand Rapids: Zondervan, 1993), 31–32.

23. C. C. and D. F., "A Cult or Not a Cult?" Modern Maturity, June 1994, 30.

24. Ronald Enroth, Churches That Abuse, 242; compare Enroth, What Is a Cult? (Downers Grove, IL: InterVarsity Press, 1982), 12. Quoted in Paul Martin, 21.

25. Martin, The Kingdom of the Cults, 11.

26. Gordon Lewis, Confronting the Cults (Grand Rapids: Baker, 1975), 4.

27. Walter Martin, The Rise of the Cults (Grand Rapids: Zondervan, 1955), 11–12, quoted in Irvine Robertson, What the Cults Believe (1966; reprint, Chicago: Moody, 1991), 13.

28. Josh McDowell and Don Stewart, Handbook of Today's Religions (San Bernardino, Calif.: Here's Life Publishers, 1983), 17.

29. Alan W. Gomes, Unmasking the Cults (Grand Rapids: Zondervan, 1995), 7.

30. Christian Research Institute, "Cults and Aberrational Groups," Statement DC–920.

31. Douglas Groothuis, "Countering Cults: The Retailer's Responsibility," Bookstore Journal (October 1994): 61.

32. Ibid.

Chapter 3: God's Best-Seller

1. King Henry VIII, Parliamentary Speech, 24 December 1545, quoted in The MacMillan Dictionary of Quotations, rev. ed. (New York: Macmillan, 1989), 44.

2. Don Lattin, "Move Over King James," San Francisco Chronicle, 24 December 1995, sec. Z, p. 1.

3. Ibid.

4. Peter Matthews, ed., *The Guinness Book of Records 1995* (New York: Bantam, 1995), 334.

5. "Huge Share of Market, Low Share of Mind," *The Barna Report* 1, no. 4 (1996): 3–4.

6. J. I. Packer, *"Fundamentalism" and the Word of God* (Grand Rapids: Eerdmans, 1958), 85.

7. J. D. Douglas and Merrill C. Tenney, eds., *The New International Dictionary of the Bible* (Grand Rapids: Zondervan, 1987), 149.

8. Robert L. Thomas, gen. ed., *New American Standard Exhaustive Concordance of the Bible* (Nashville: Holman Bible Publishers, 1981), 1158–59.

9. Millard J. Erickson, *Christian Theology* (1983; reprint, Grand Rapids: Baker, 1989), 202.

10. Wayne Grudem, "Scripture's Self-Attestation and the Problem of Formulating a Doctrine of Scripture," in *Scripture and Truth*, ed. D. A. Carson and John D. Woodbridge (1983; reprint, Grand Rapids: Baker, 1992), 44; Norman L. Geisler and William E. Nix, *A General Introduction to the Bible*, rev. ed. (Chicago: Moody, 1986), 237.

11. Geisler and Nix, *General Introduction to the Bible*, 358, 387.

12. Josh McDowell and Don Stewart, *Answers to Tough Questions*, rev. ed. (San Bernardino, Calif.: Here's Life Publishers, 1983), 5.

13. F. F. Bruce, *The New Testament Documents: Are They Reliable?* (Grand Rapids: Eerdmans, 1977), 15.

14. Ibid.

15. Ibid., 16.

16. David L. Edwards and John Stott, *Evangelical Essentials* (Downers Grove, Ill.: InterVarsity Press, 1988), 102–3; W. E. Vine, *An Expository Dictionary of New Testament Words*, in *Vine's Complete Expository Dictionary of Old and New Testament Words*, ed. W. E. Vine, Merrill F. Unger, and William White (Nashville: Thomas Nelson, 1985), 540.

17. Martin, *Essential Christianity* (1962; reprint, Ventura, Calif.: Regal Books, 1980), 19.

18. Ibid., 19–20.

19. Michael D. Lemonick, "Are the Bible Stories True?" *Time*, 18 December 1995, 62–69.

20. Menahem Mansoor, "Scholars Speak Out," *Biblical Archeology Review* (May/June 1995): 29.

21. John Elson, "The New Testament's Unsolved Mysteries," *Time*, 18 December 1995, 70.

22. Edwin Yamauchi, quoted in H. S., *Biblical Archeology Review*, 35.

23. Bryant G. Wood, quoted in H. S., *Biblical Archeology Review*, 34.

24. Elson, "The New Testament's Unsolved Mysteries," 67; cf. Kevin Dale Miller, "The Fingerprint of Jeremiah's Scribe," *Christian Reader* (July/August 1996), 82–83.

25. William B. Ries, "Found: The Biblical City of Loaves and Fishes," *Seattle Post-Intelligencer*, 19 October 1987, sec. A, p. 2.

26. Elson, "The New Testament's Unsolved Mysteries," 70.

27. Miller, "The Fingerprint of Jeremiah's Scribe," 83–84.

28. James Talmage, *A Study of the Articles of Faith*, 26th ed. (Salt Lake City: Church of Jesus Christ of Latter-day Saints, 1948), 236.

29. Orson Pratt, "The Bible and Tradition, without Further Revelation, an Insufficient Guide," *Divine Authenticity of the Book of Mormon No. 3*, 1 December 1850, 47. Republished in *Orson Pratt's Works* (Orem, Utah: Grandin Books, 1990).

30. Ibid.

31. McConkie, *Mormon Doctrine*, 383.

32. Keith Marsten, *Missionary Pal: Reference Guide for Missionaries and Teachers*, rev. ed. (Salt Lake City: Publishers Press, 1974), 26–28.

33. Ibid., 26.

34. Mark Prophet and Elizabeth Clare Prophet, *The Lost Teachings of Jesus 1* (Liv-

ingston, Mont.: Summit University Press, 1988), front cover.

35. Ibid., 1.

36. Roy Masters, *Walter Martin Debates Roy Masters* (part 1), cassette tape C-102, n.d., available from the Christian Research Institute.

37. The following quotations represent only a small sampling of the material that documents The Family's involvement with the practices listed in the main text:

Pornography: "CAMERAMAN . . . BE NOT AFRAID OF THEIR FACES. . . . Our kids' faces are their credentials. . . . You should seldom get further away than waist-up . . . unless they've got pretty bare legs, that you want to show off & be sexy!" (David Berg, *Mugshots: DO 979,* 979:16, 18–19); ". . . BE SURE NOT TO FOOLISHLY LABEL ANY OF THE TAPES themselves inside with such curiosity-arousing investigation-inspiring & perhaps even illegal titles such as 'Love Tape' or 'So & so strips' or any other sexy titles. . . ." (David Berg, *Mugshots: DO 979,* 979:62)."

Incest: ". . . WHAT ABOUT INCEST? . . . We'll just have to tell the kids that it's not prohibited by God, but you'd better watch out. . . . IT IS THE MOST DANGEROUS FORM OF SEX & THE MOST PROHIBITED BY THE SYSTEM! [the world outside the Family]. . . . I DON'T KNOW WHAT THE HELL AGE HAS GOT TO DO WITH IT. . . ." (David Berg, *The Devil Hates Sex: DFO 999,* 999:20–21, 23).

Fornication: "I THINK THE TEENAGE YEARS WERE WHEN I NEEDED SEX THE MOST! Isn't it ridiculous though, that it's just at the age when you need sex the most that it's the most forbidden? . . . I hope all of our young kids have plenty of sex. I hope they won't have all those frustrations . . . from sex deprivation. . . . Why did the Lord make you able to have children at the age of 11, 12 & 13 if you weren't supposed to have sex then?" (David Berg, *Child Brides: DO 902,* 902:1, 5–6).

Adultery: "I'M NOT SELFISH WITH MY WIVES, I GIVE THEM AWAY RIGHT AND LEFT & share them with others who need help & need wives" (David Berg, "Sex Jewels," DO 919:37). ". . . WE BELIEVE IN SHARING . . . in coming home and sleeping with the same mate nearly every night, but often after we've been out sleeping awhile with somebody else!" (David Berg, *Nuns of Love: ML 570—DFO,* 570:50).

Adult-Child Sexual Contact: "I'M TALKING ABOUT NATURAL NORMAL GODLY LOVE AS MANIFESTED IN SEX, as far as I'm concerned for whomever!—There are no relationship restrictions or age limitations in His Law of Love" (David Berg, *The Devil Hates Sex: DFO 999,* 999:110).

Child-Child Sexual Relations: "WE WANTED TO ADD A WORD ABOUT THE CHILDREN'S SEX & LOVE LIFE TOO. We have not really interfered. . . . Rubin [age 6] & Jonas [age 8 1/2] both have their little lovers among other little sisters who visit sometimes" (David Berg, *Family News International,* no. 50, 34).

38. David Berg, *The Word—New and Old: (MT 13:52): ML 329—GP,* 329:11, 12–15.

39. *The Watchtower,* 15 December 1972, 755.

40. *Zion's Watch Tower and Herald of Christ's Presence,* 15 September 1910, 298–99, as quoted in the WTBTS's 1919 reprints, *The Watchtower,* vol. 5 (Allegheny, Pa.: Watch Tower Bible and Tract Society, 1919), 4685.

41. *The Watchtower,* 1 December 1981, 27.

42. *The Watchtower,* 1 October 1967, 587; *The Watchtower,* 15 February 1981, 19.

43. *The Watchtower,* 1 July 1973, 402; *The Watchtower,* 1 October 1967, 587.

44. *Theocratic Aid to Kingdom Publishers* (Brooklyn, N.Y.: Watch Tower Bible and Tract Society, 1945), 249–50.

45. *The Watchtower,* 1 May 1938, 143.

46. "Our Kingdom Service" (Brooklyn, N.Y.: Watch Tower Bible and Tract Society, 1981), 1.

47. *Qualified to Be Ministers* (Brooklyn, N.Y.: Watch Tower Bible and Tract Society, 1967), 156.

48. *The Watchtower*, 15 January 1983, 27.

49. Julius R. Mantey, letter from Mantey to the Watch Tower Bible and Tract Society, 11 July 1974, 2.

50. Mary Baker Eddy, *Science and Health: With Key to the Scriptures* (1875; reprint, Boston: First Church of Christ Scientist, 1971), 338.

51. Mark L. Prophet and Elizabeth Clare Prophet, *The Lost Teachings of Jesus 3* (Livingston, Mont.: Summit Lighthouse Press, 1988), 273–74.

52. David Spangler, *The Laws of Manifestation* (Forres, Scotland: Findhorn Publications, 1983), 23–24.

53. McConkie, *Mormon Doctrine*, 764–65.

54. Ibid., 764.

55. Ezra T. Benson, *Ensign* (November 1984): 7.

56. Meredith J. Sprunger, *The Origin of the Urantia Book*, 3.

Chapter 4: Lord of Israel

1. Theophilus, *Theophilus to Autolycus: Book I*, in *The Ante-Nicene Fathers*, vol. 2, ed. Alexander Roberts and James Donaldson, rev. ed. A. Cleveland Coxe (Grand Rapids: Eerdmans, 1994), 89–90.

2. Philip Schaff, *Nicene and Post-Nicene Christianity*, vol. 3 of *History of the Church* (Grand Rapids: Eerdmans, 1950), 673.

3. Millard J. Erickson, *Christian Theology* (1983; reprint, Grand Rapids: Baker, 1989), 321.

4. Everett F. Harrison, ed., *Baker's Dictionary of Theology* (1960; reprint, Grand Rapids: Baker, 1994), 531; compare Stanley J. Grenz, *Theology for the Community of God* (Nashville: Broadman and Holman, 1994), 70.

5. Louis Berkhof, *Systematic Theology* (Grand Rapids: Eerdmans, 1993), 85.

6. Elwell, ed., *Evangelical Dictionary of Theology*, 732; compare Walter A. Elwell, ed., *Baker Encyclopedia of the Bible*, vol. 2 (1988; reprint, Grand Rapids: Baker, 1995), 1485.

7. Gleason L. Archer, *Encyclopedia of Bible Difficulties* (Grand Rapids: Zondervan, 1982), 359.

8. Ibid., 359.

9. Wayne Grudem, *Systematic Theology* (Grand Rapids: Zondervan, 1994), 227. Grudem's argument is supported by many sources, including E. Kautzsch's 1910 edition of *Gesenius' Hebrew Grammar*, which, in reference to the plurality of majesty explanation, states, "The plural used by God in Genesis 1:26 . . . has been incorrectly explained in this way." E. Kautzsch, ed., *Gesenius' Hebrew Grammar* (Oxford: Clarendon Press, 1910), section 124g, n. 2.

10. Berkhof, *Systematic Theology*, 85.

11. Robert P. Lightner, *Handbook of Evangelical Theology* (Grand Rapids: Kregel, 1995), 47.

12. H. P. Mansfield, ed., *God Is One, Not Three* (West Beach, South Australia: Christadelphians, n.d.), 2.

13. J. F. Rutherford, *Reconciliation* (Brooklyn, N.Y.: Watch Tower Bible and Tract Society, 1928), 101; compare *Let God Be True*, rev. ed. (Brooklyn, N.Y.: Watch Tower Bible and Tract Society, 1952), 100–101.

14. *Let God Be True*, 100.

15. Emory H. Bancroft, *Elemental Theology*, ed. Ronald B. Mayer (1960; reprint, Grand Rapids: Kregel, 1996), 203–4.

16. *The Watchtower*, 15 September 1961, 551.

17. Charles Taze Russell, *Studies in the Scriptures*, vol. 1 of *The Plan of the Ages* (1886; reprint, Allegheny, Pa.: Watch Tower Bible and Tract Society, 1908), 81–82.

18. *Zion's Watch Tower and Herald of Christ's Presence* (October/November 1881), 10, as quoted in the WTBTS's 1919 reprints, *The Watchtower*, vol. 1 (Allegheny, Pa.: Watch Tower Bible and Tract Society, 1919), 297–98.

19. *Zion's Watchtower and Herald of Christ's Presence* (December 1881), 3, as quoted in the WTBTS's 1919 reprints, *The Watchtower,* vol. 1 (Allegheny, Pa.: Watch Tower Bible and Tract Society, 1919), 301.

20. *Listening to the Great Teacher* (Brooklyn, N.Y.: Watch Tower Bible and Tract Society, 1971), 139.

21. Joseph Smith, "Sermon by the Prophet—The Christian Godhead—Plurality of Gods," 16 June 1844, as reprinted in *History of the Church*, vol. 6 (Salt Lake City: Deseret Book Co., 1980), 476.

22. Ibid., 474; compare McConkie, *Mormon Doctrine*, 270, 317, 576.

23. Smith, "Sermon by the Prophet . . . ," 474.

24. McConkie, *Mormon Doctrine*, 576.

25. Orson Pratt, "A Discourse by Elder Orson Pratt," 18 February 1855, *Journal of Discourses*, vol. 2 (1855; reprint, London: F. D. Richards, 1966), 345.

26. Brigham Young, "Remarks by President Brigham Young," 8 October 1859, *Journal of Discourses*, vol. 7 (1860; reprint, London: Amasa Lyman, 1966), 333.

27. Spencer W. Kimball, "The Privilege of Holding the Priesthood," *Ensign* (November 1975): 80.

28. Gregory Boyd, *Oneness Pentecostals and the Trinity* (Grand Rapids: Baker, 1992), 28.

29. Elliot Miller, *A Crash Course on the New Age Movement* (Grand Rapids: Baker, 1989), 15.

30. Russell Chandler, *Understanding the New Age* (1991; reprint, Grand Rapids: Zondervan, 1993), 341.

31. Benjamin Creme, *The Reappearance of the Christ and the Masters of Wisdom* (London: Tara Press, 1980), 110–11.

32. David Bernard et al., *Meet the United Pentecostal Church* (Hazelwood, Mo.: Pentecostal Publishing House, n.d.), 58; compare *You Can Live Forever in Paradise on Earth* (Brooklyn, N.Y.: Watch Tower Bible and Tract Society, 1982), 39; and *Let God Be True*, 111.

33. Robert Bowman, *Why You Should Believe in the Trinity* (Grand Rapids: Baker, 1989), 22.

34. Victor Paul Wierwille, *Jesus Christ Is Not God* (New Knoxville, Ohio: American Christian Press, 1975), 12.

35. Hippolytus, *Against the Heresy of One Noetus*, in *The Ante-Nicene Fathers*, vol. 5, 227.

36. Wierwille, *Jesus Christ Is Not God*, 11–12.

37. *You Can Live Forever*, 40–41.

38. *Let God Be True*, 101.

39. Bowman, *Why You Should Believe in the Trinity*, 45.

40. Archer, *Encyclopedia of Bible Difficulties*, 361.

41. Mansfield, *God Is One, Not Three*, 3.

42. Grenz, *Theology for the Community of God*, 92.

43. Ibid., 99.

44. Grudem, *Systematic Theology*, 226.

45. Archer, *Encyclopedia of Bible Difficulties*, 357.

46. St. Augustine, quoted in Lightner, *Handbook of Evangelical Theology*, 47.

Chapter 5: Jesus of Nazareth

1. Justin Martyr, *The First Apology of Justin*, in *The Ante-Nicene Fathers*, vol. 1, 184.

2. *The 1995 Almanac* (Boston: Houghton Mifflin, 1995), 413.

3. Ignatius, *Epistle of Ignatius to the Ephesians*, in *The Ante-Nicene Fathers*, vol. 1, 52; compare Ignatius, *Epistle of Ignatius to the Smyrnaeans*, in *The Ante-Nicene Fathers*, vol. 1, 86.

4. Justin Martyr, *The First Apology of Justin*, in *The Ante-Nicene Fathers*, vol. 1, 184.

5. Irenaeus, *Irenaeus against Heresies: Book III*, in *The Ante-Nicene Fathers*, vol. 1, 440, 448.

6. Pliny the Younger, Epistles 10.96.7, quoted in Everett Ferguson, *Backgrounds of Early Christianity* (1987; reprint, Grand Rapids: Eerdmans, 1993), 558.

7. Nicaeno-Constantinopolitan Creed, in Schaff, *The Creeds of Christendom*, vol. 1 of *The History of Creeds* (Grand Rapids: Baker, 1996), 27–28.

8. R. C. Sproul, *Essential Truths of the Christian Faith* (Wheaton: Tyndale House, 1992), 78.

9. Chalcedon Creed, in Louis Berkhof, *The History of Christian Doctrines* (1937; reprint, Carlisle, Pa.: Banner of Truth Trust, 1991), 107.

10. Lightner, *Handbook of Evangelical Theology*, 81.

11. Erickson, *Christian Theology*, 683.

12. Ibid., 684.

13. Bowman, *Why You Should Believe in the Trinity*, 106.

14. Wierwille, *Jesus Christ Is Not God*, 79.

15. Ibid., 5.

16. *Should You Believe in the Trinity?* (Brooklyn, N.Y.: Watch Tower Bible and Tract Society, 1989), 15.

17. Peter Kreeft and Ronald K. Tacelli, *Handbook of Christian Apologetics* (Downers Grove, Ill.: InterVarsity Press, 1994), 159–60.

18. Ian Wilson, *Jesus: The Evidence* (New York: Harper and Row, 1984), 51.

19. T. B. Wakeman, quoted in John E. Remsburg, *The Christ* (1909; reprint, Amherst, N.Y.: Prometheus Books, 1994), 330–31.

20. Wilson, *Jesus: The Evidence*, 51.

21. Josephus, *Antiquities of the Jews*, in *The Life and Works of Flavius Josephus*, trans. William Whiston (New York: Holt, Rinehart and Winston, n.d.), 598.

22. Tacitus, quoted in Ferguson, *Background of Early Christianity*, 556.

23. Lucian, quoted in Ferguson, *Background of Early Christianity*, 561–62.

24. Suetonius, quoted in F. F. Bruce, *The Spreading Flame* (1958; reprint, Grand Rapids: Eerdmans, 1995), 137.

25. Michael Grant, *Jesus: An Historian's Review of the Gospels* (New York: Charles Scribner's Sons, 1977), 199.

26. Ibid., 199–200.

27. Ibid., 200.

28. Wilson, *Jesus: The Evidence*, 65.

29. Doug Groothuis, *Jesus in an Age of Controversy* (Eugene, Ore.: Harvest House, 1996), 261.

30. Max Heindel, *The Rosicrucian Philosophy in Questions and Answers* (London: N. L. Fowler, 1910), 181.

31. Prophet and Prophet, *The Lost Teachings of Jesus 1*, 79.

32. Elizabeth Clare Prophet, *Profile: Elizabeth Clare Prophet—Teachings of the Ascended Masters* (Livingston, Mont: Summit University Press, n.d), 7.

33. Ron Rhodes, "The Christ of the New Age Movement," *Christian Research Journal* 12, no. 1 (Summer 1989): 9.

34. Charles C. Ryrie, *Basic Theology* (Wheaton: Victor, 1986), 237, quoted in Ron Rhodes, *Christ before the Manger* (Grand Rapids: Baker, 1992), 35.

35. F. F. Bruce, *The Gospel of John* (London: Pickering and Inglis, 1983), 43.

36. Rhodes, *Christ before the Manger*, 40–41.

37. *Jehovah's Witnesses in the 20th Century* (1979; reprint, Brooklyn, N.Y.: Watch Tower Bible and Tract Society, 1989), 13; compare *You Can Live Forever in Paradise on Earth*, 58.

38. David Berg, *Vespers: Psalm 2:6–8: DO 2359*, 2359:14–15, 18.

39. Sproul, *Essential Truths*, 6.

40. KHEI, *Rosicrucian Fundamentals* (New York: Flame Press, 1920), 151.

41. Joseph Fielding Smith, *Doctrines of Salvation*, vol. 1 (Salt Lake City: Bookcraft, 1956), 18.

42. Young Oon Kim, *Unification Theology* (New York: The Holy Spirit Association for the Unification of World Christianity, 1980), 172, quoted in Ruth Tucker, *Another Gospel* (Grand Rapids: Zondervan, 1989), 197.

43. The following comparison summarizes Berg's teachings.

Original View

"Which was the more remarkable . . . the more intimate experience for Mary?—When Gabriel stood there merely making an announcement to her, or when the Lord Himself came in unto her, & had intercourse with her, held her in His arms & gave her such a spiritual orgasm that produced His Own Son!" (Berg, *Listen: DO 998*, 998:18).

"GOD HIMSELF HAD SEX WITH MARY TO HAVE JESUS. . . . God Himself took human form & literally f———d Mary to make her pregnant with Jesus!" (Berg, *The Devil Hates Sex: DFO 999*, 999:111).

Revised View

"Why couldn't God have used the angel Gabriel to f—k Mary. . . . Gabriel supplied the sperm, Mary supplied the egg & God supplied the Spirit. . . . 'HE CAME IN UNTO HER,' & that expression's only used in having sex throughout the Bible" (Berg, *Answers to Your Questions!—No. 8: DFO 1566*, 1566:6).

"Gabriel was a spirit, an angel of God. He is already, in a sense, a part of God, or a representation of God. . . . The angel came 'in unto her' is a term, a phrase used in the Bible only for sexual intercourse. . . . Since the wording is so specific that He did come 'in unto her'; He in other words had sexual intercourse with her. . . . It was the Angel <u>Gabriel</u> that 'came in unto' her. . . . I did that this morning with you. I came in unto you when we had sexual intercourse." (Berg, *More on TM and the Unified Field!: DO 1854*, 1854:42–43, 45, 48).

44. McDowell and Stewart, *Answers to Tough Questions*, 55–56.

Chapter 6: Spirit of Truth

1. R. A. Torrey, "Personality and Deity of the Holy Spirit," in *The Fundamentals*, vol. 2, ed. R. A. Torrey, A. C. Dixon et al. (1917; reprint, Grand Rapids: Baker, 1996), 323.

2. H. Spencer Lewis, *Rosicrucian Questions and Answers with Complete History* (1929; reprint, San Jose: Supreme Grand Lodge of AMORC, 1961), 237.

3. KHEI, *Rosicrucian Fundamentals*, 155.

4. Mary Baker Eddy, *Science and Health*, 55, 471.

5. Mansfield, *God Is One, Not Three*, 15.

6. *Holy Spirit* (Brooklyn, N.Y.: Watch Tower Bible and Tract Society, 1976), 11.

7. Victor Paul Wierwille, *Receiving the Holy Spirit Today* (New Knoxville, Ohio: American Christian Press, 1972), 4.

8. Albert Pike, *Morals and Dogma of the Ancient and Accepted Scottish Rite of Freemasonry* (1871; reprint, Richmond, Va.: L. H. Jenkins, 1921), 734.

9. *What You Need to Know about the Light and Sound of God* (Minneapolis: Eckankar, 1991), 1.

10. Prophet, *Profile: Elizabeth Clare Prophet*, 9.

11. Berkhof, *Systematic Theology*, 95.

12. Grudem, *Systematic Theology*, 249.

13. Ibid.

14. *Awake!*, 8 December 1973, 27.

15. Vine, *Expository Dictionary of New Testament Words*, 29.

16. Berg, *The Goddess of Love: DFO 723*, 723:3, 6, 11, 14.

17. Sproul, *Essential Truths*, 111–12.

18. Talmage, *A Study of the Articles of Faith*, 488.

19. Wierwille, *Jesus Christ Is Not God*, 127–28.

Chapter 7: Natural Born Sinners

1. Cornelius Plantinga Jr., *Not the Way It's Supposed to Be: A Breviary of Sin* (Grand Rapids: Eerdmans, 1995), 1–2.

2. Kevin Carter, private letter to his parents, quoted in Scott MacLeod, "The Life and Death of Kevin Carter," *Time*, 12 September 1994, 71.

3. MacLeod, "The Life and Death of Kevin Carter," 70, 73.

4. Carter, quoted in MacLeod, "The Life and Death of Kevin Carter," 73.

5. Paul Enns, *The Moody Handbook of Theology* (Chicago: Moody, 1989), 308; compare C. F. Keil and F. Delitzsch, *Biblical Commentary on the Old Testament*, vol. 1 (Grand Rapids: Eerdmans, 1968), 84–86.

6. Berkhof, *Systematic Theology*, 259.

7. Enns, *Moody Handbook of Theology*, 310.

8. J. I. Packer, *Concise Theology* (Wheaton: Tyndale House, 1993), 82.

9. Enns, *Moody Handbook of Theology*, 310.

10. Packer, *Concise Theology*, 83.

11. Laura Meyers, "Report: Children More Violent, Victimized," *Orange County Register*, 8 September 1995, news section, p. 3.

12. Mimi Hall, "Violence up in 38% of Schools," *USA Today*, 2 November 1994, sec. A, p. 1.

13. "Headline News," 7 September 1995, Channel 45 (Cox Cable).

14. *Parenting Today*, 7 September 1996, CNN.

15. John J. DiIulio Jr., quoted in David G. Savage, "Strict Florida Stand on Teen 'Thugs' Fuels Policy Debate," *Los Angeles Times*, 11 July 1996, sec. A, p. 20.

16. Paul Leavitt, "Maximum Prison Term for Teen," *USA Today*, 8 November 1994, sec. A, p. 4.

17. "Youth Sentenced," *USA Today*, 4 November 1994, sec. A, p. 3.

18. "Boy, 11, Who Cut Throat of Woman, 83, Gets Probation," *Los Angeles Times*, 9 December 1994, sec. A, p. 55.

19. Savage, "Strict Florida Stand," sec. A, pp. 3, 20.

20. Efrain Hernandez Jr. and Jose Cardenas, "Youth, 14, Held after Mother Is Shot in Head," *Los Angeles Times*, 17 August 1996, sec. A, p. 10; and Efrain Hernandez Jr., "Boy Wanted to Shoot Someone, 2 Friends Say," *Los Angeles Times*, 18 August 1996, sec. A, p. 30.

21. Associated Press, "Girl, 12, Sentenced to up to 20 Years in Fatal Beating of Child in Day Care," *Los Angeles Times*, 10 August 1996, sec. A, p. 9.

22. Rev. Thomas Whitelaw, "The Biblical Conception of Sin," in *The Fundamentals*, 13–14.

23. Mary Baker Eddy, *Miscellaneous Writings 1893–1896* (Boston: Trustees under the Will of Mary Baker G. Eddy, 1924), 27; compare Eddy, *Science and Health*, 428.

24. Eddy, *Science and Health*, 480.

25. H. Emilie Cady, *Lessons in Truth* (Kansas City, Mo.: Unity School of Christianity, 1920), 37.

26. Ibid., 38.

27. David Spangler, *Revelation: The Birth of a New Age* (San Francisco: Rainbow Bridge, 1976), 123.

28. Iris Belhayes, *Spirit Guides* (San Diego: ACS Publications, 1985), 11, quoted in Elliot Miller, *A Crash Course on the New Age Movement*, 239.

29. Jack Underhill, "New Age Quiz," *Life Times Magazine*, 6, quoted in Russell Chandler, *Understanding the New Age* (1991; reprint, Grand Rapids: Zondervan, 1993), 28.

30. McConkie, *Mormon Doctrine*, 268.

31. Smith, *Doctrines of Salvation*, 113.

32. Ibid., 114–15.

33. Boyd Packer, *Duties and Blessings of the Priesthood: PART B* (Salt Lake City: The Church of Jesus Christ of Latter-day Saints, 1980), 186, quoted in Mark J. Cares, *Speaking the Truth in Love to Mormons* (Milwaukee: Northwestern Publishing House, 1993), 27.

34. John Ankerberg and John Weldon, *The Secret Teachings of Freemasonry*, rev. ed. (Chicago: Moody, 1990), 141.

35. Raymond Lee Allen et al., *Tennessee Craftsmen or Masonic Textbook*, 14th ed. (Nashville: Tennessee Board of Custodians Members, 1963), 27, quoted in Ankerberg and Weldon, *Secret Teachings of Freemasonry*, 141.

36. Talmage, *Articles of Faith*, 476, 478–79.

37. Robert Roberts, *The Christadelphian Instructor* (Birmingham, England: The Christadelphian, 1974), 39.

38. *The Watchtower*, 15 August 1972, 492.

39. *The Watchtower*, 1 July 1947, 204.

40. *The Watchtower*, 15 February 1983, 12–13.

41. *Life Everlasting—In Freedom of the Sons of God* (Brooklyn, N.Y.: Watch Tower Bible and Tract Society, 1966), 400.

Chapter 8: At the Cross

1. Berkhof, *Systematic Theology*, 367; Harrison, *Baker's Dictionary of Theology*, 71; Erickson, *Christian Theology*, 781; Dyson Hague, "At-One-Ment by Propitiation," in *The Fundamentals*, 78.

2. William Evans, *The Great Doctrines of the Bible* (n.p., 1912), 70, quoted in Bancroft, *Elemental Theology*, 165.

3. Elwell, ed., *Baker Encyclopedia of the Bible*, vol. 1, 231.

4. Douglas and Tenney, *New International Dictionary of the Bible*, 108.

5. Ibid.

6. Ibid., 108–9.

7. Richards, *Expository Dictionary*, 82.

8. Ibid., 83.

9. Ibid.

10. Ibid., 83–84.

11. Ladd, *A Theology of the New Testament*, 469.

12. *Racovian Catechism*, trans. Thomas S. Rees (1818; reprint, Lexington: American Theological Library Association, 1962), sec. 5, ch. 8, quoted in Erickson, *Christian Theology*, 816.

13. Berkhof, *Systematic Theology*, 376.

14. Ibid.

15. Enns, *Moody Handbook of Theology*, 325.

16. Vine, *Expository Dictionary of New Testament Words*, 493.

17. Enns, *Moody Handbook of Theology*, 325.

18. John MacArthur, "John MacArthur's Response on the Blood of Christ," 1. MacArthur writes: "My teaching on the blood simply is that the *literal* blood of Christ has no magical or mystical saving power. It is not some supernaturally preserved form of the actual blood of Christ that washes believers of their sin. . . . 'The shedding of blood' in Scripture is an expression that means much more than just bleeding. It refers to violent, sacrificial death."

19. R. C. Sproul, "An Ongoing Finished Work," *Tabletalk* (August 1992): 39.

20. Ibid.

21. Richards, *Expository Dictionary*, 516.

22. Ibid.

23. Ibid.

24. Enns, *Moody Handbook of Theology*, 323.

25. Vine, *Expository Dictionary of New Testament Words*, 515.

26. Fritz Rienecker, *A Linguistic Key to the Greek New Testament* (Grand Rapids: Zondervan, 1980), 655, quoted in Enns, *Moody Handbook of Theology*, 324.

27. Vine, *Expository Dictionary of New Testament Words*, 515.

28. Charles Hodge, *Systematic Theology*, vol. 3 (reprint, Grand Rapids: Eerdmans, 1995), 118.

29. Enns, *Moody Handbook of Theology*, 326.

30. John Calvin, *Institutes of the Christian Religion*, vol. 2, trans. Henry Beveridge (1845; reprint, Grand Rapids: Eerdmans, 1964), 38 (3.11.2), quoted in R. C. Sproul, *Faith Alone* (Grand Rapids: Baker, 1995), 101.

31. Lightner, *Handbook of Evangelical Theology*, 201.

32. Sun Myung Moon, *Divine Principle* (New York: The Holy Spirit Association for the Unification of World Christianity, 1973), 178, quoted in McDowell and Stewart, *Handbook of Today's Religions*, 102.

33. Moon, *Divine Principle*, 143, 152, quoted in David J. Hesselgrave, *Dynamic Religious Movements* (Grand Rapids: Baker, 1978), 112.

34. Moon, *Divine Principle*, 143, quoted in McDowell and Stewart, *Handbook of Today's Religions*, 101.

35. Young Oon Kim, *Unification Theology* (New York: The Holy Spirit Association for the Unification of World Christianity, 1980), 132–33, 164, quoted in Tucker, *Another Gospel*, 251.

36. J. F. Rutherford, *Life* (Brooklyn, N.Y.: Watch Tower Bible and Tract Society, 1929), 199, 206.

37. McConkie, *Mormon Doctrine*, 65.

38. Ibid., 63.

39. Talmage, *Articles of Faith*, 89.

40. Ezra Taft Benson, *Teachings of Ezra Taft Benson*, quoted in "Gethsemane Was Site of 'Greatest Single Act,'" *Church News* (June 1, 1991): 14.

Chapter 9: Death's Defeat

1. Martin, *Essential Christianity*, 63.

2. J. Dwight Pentecost, *Things Which Become Sound Doctrine* (1965; reprint, Grand Rapids: Kregel, 1996), 159.

3. Thomas Oden, *The Word of Life* (San Francisco: HarperCollins, 1989), 464, quoted in Ted M. Dorman, *A Faith for All Seasons* (Nashville: Broadman and Holman, 1995), 224.

4. Ronald Gregor Smith, *Secular Christianity* (London: Collins, 1966), 103, quoted in McDowell and Stewart, *Answers to Tough Questions*, 47.

5. Berkhof, *Systematic Theology*, 346.

6. Grudem, *Systematic Theology*, 608. Two of the best-known accounts of going from skeptic to believer are Frank Morrison, *Who Moved the Stone,* (1930; reprint, Grand Rapids: Zondervan, 1958) and Simon Greenleaf, *The Testimony of the Evangelists* (Grand Rapids: Baker, 1984).

7. E. M. Blaiklock, quoted in Josh McDowell, "Evidence for the Resurrection," *Southern California Christian Times* (April 1992): 9.

8. Thomas Arnold, quoted in McDowell, "Evidence for the Resurrection," 9.

9. Dorman, *A Faith for All Seasons*, 226.

10. Robert L. Thomas and Stanley N. Gundry, eds., *A Harmony of the Gospels* (Chicago: Moody, 1978), 252–64.

11. Luke wrote not only his Gospel but also Acts.

12. R. L. Purtill, *Thinking about Religion* (New York: Prentice Hall, 1978), 84–85, quoted in Kreeft and Tacelli, *Handbook of Christian Apologetics*, 195.

13. Wilson, *Jesus: The Evidence*, 138.

14. John Shelby Spong, *Liberating the Gospels* (San Francisco: Harper San Francisco, 1996), 279.

15. Archer, *Encyclopedia of Bible Difficulties*, 347–48.

16. Wilson, *Jesus: The Evidence*, 138; Spong, *Liberating the Gospels*, 282.

17. Norman Geisler and Thomas Howe, *When Critics Ask* (Wheaton: Victor, 1992), 365.

18. Alister McGrath, *Explaining Your Faith* (1988; reprint, Grand Rapids: Baker, 1995), 72–74.

19. McDowell and Stewart, *Answers to Tough Questions*, 48.

20. Kreeft and Tacelli, *Handbook of Christian Apologetics*, 183–84.

21. David Strauss, *A New Life of Jesus*, vol. 1 (London: Williams and Norgate, 1879), 412, quoted in Geisler, *Battle for the Resurrection*, 77–78; compare Wilson, *Jesus: The Evidence*, 140.

22. *The Journal of the American Medical Society* 255, no. 11 (March 21, 1986): 1463, quoted in Geisler, *Battle for the Resurrection*, 76–77.

23. Berkhof, *Systematic Theology*, 348.

24. Kreeft and Tacelli, *Handbook of Christian Apologetics*, 183–84.

25. Ibid., 185.

26. Hugh J. Schonfield, *The Passover Plot* (New York: Bantam: 1965), 83–180.

27. Geisler, *Battle for the Resurrection*, 79.

28. Moon, *Divine Principle*, 211–12, quoted in Spiritual Counterfeits Project, "Is Divine Principle Really Divine?" (tract); compare Sun Myung Moon, *Master Speaks 4* (n.d.), 9, cited in Martin, *The Kingdom of the Cults*, 343.

29. *The Truth Shall Make You Free* (Brooklyn, N.Y.: Watch Tower Bible and Tract Society, 1943), 264.

30. *Let God Be True*, 122, 272.

31. *You Can Live Forever*, 144–45; compare *The Kingdom Is at Hand* (Brooklyn, N.Y.: Watch Tower Bible and Tract Society, 1944), 259, and Charles Taze Russell, "The Time Is at Hand," 127.

32. *You Can Live Forever*, 145.

33. Geisler, *Battle for the Resurrection*, 86.

34. Ibid., 52.

35. Irenaeus, *Irenaeus Against Heresies: Book I*, in *The Ante-Nicene Fathers*, vol. 1, 330.

36. Justin Martyr, *Justin on the Resurrection*, in *The Ante-Nicene Fathers*, vol. 1, 298.

37. Epiphanius, "Second Creed of Epiphanius," in Schaff, *The Creeds of Christendom*, vol. 2, 37.

38. Augustine, *The City of God: Book 22*, in *The Nicene Fathers*, vol. 1, ed. Philip Schaff (Grand Rapids: Eerdmans, 1993), 482.

39. Thomas Aquinas, *III Summa contra Gentiles*, 79, quoted in Thomas Gilby, *St. Thomas: Theological Texts* (Durham, N.C.: Labyrinth Press, 1982), no. 662; compare Geisler, *Battle for the Resurrection*, 59.

40. Grudem, *Systematic Theology*, 612.

Chapter 10: The Other Side

1. Technically, eschatology also includes the study of death, dying, and the afterlife. These aspects of eschatology are classified as aspects of "individual eschatology," whereas the study of future events involving all humankind (e.g., Christ's second coming, the rapture, final judgment, etc.) fall into the category of "general eschatology." For clarity, these two aspects of eschatology have been separated.

2. Richard Abanes, *Journey into the Light* (Grand Rapids: Baker, 1996), 21–26.

3. Mircea Eliade, ed., *The Encyclopedia of Religion*, vol. 1 (New York: Macmillan, 1987), 116.

4. Richards, *Expository Dictionary*, 408.

5. Ibid., 410.

6. *Seventh-Day Adventists Believe . . .* (Hagerstown, Md.: General Conference of Seventh-Day Adventists, 1988), 16–58.

7. Victor Paul Wierwille, *Are the Dead Alive Now?* (New Knoxville, Ohio: American Christian Press, n.d.), 21.

8. Karen W. Martin, foreword to Wierwille, *Are the Dead Alive Now?* 9.

9. *Insight on the Scriptures*, vol. 1 (Brooklyn, N.Y.: Watch Tower Bible and Tract Society, 1988), 597.

10. *You Can Live Forever*, 88.

11. *Is This Life All There Is?* (Brooklyn, N.Y.: The Watch Tower Bible and Tract Society, 1974), 43.

12. Victor Paul Wierwille, *Power for Abundant Living* (New Knoxville, Ohio:

American Christian Press, 1971), 133–35. The bracketed text in this quotation appeared in the original.

13. John Blanchard, *Whatever Happened to Hell?* (Wheaton: Crossway, 1995), 82.

14. Ibid.

15. Douglas Connelly, *Afterlife* (Downers Grove, Ill.: InterVarsity Press, 1995), 70.

16. Grudem, *Systematic Theology*, 593.

17. Gary Habermas and J. P. Mooreland, *Immortality: The Other Side of Death* (Nashville: Thomas Nelson, 1992), 158–59.

18. Sproul, *Essential Truths*, 285–86.

19. Ibid., 286.

20. *Reasoning from the Scriptures* (Brooklyn, N.Y.: Watch Tower Bible and Tract Society, 1985), 175.

21. Sproul, *Essential Truths*, 285.

22. William Crockett, ed., *Four Views of Hell* (Grand Rapids: Zondervan, 1992), 62–63.

23. Sun Myung Moon, 18 September 1974 speech, *Washington Post* reprint, 17 October 1974; compare Sun Myung Moon, *Divine Principle*, 111–12.

24. J. I. Packer, foreword to Ajith Fernando, *Crucial Questions about Hell* (Wheaton: Crossway, 1994), x.

25. Berkhof, *Systematic Theology*, 736.

26. H. P. Mansfield, ed., *What Your Decision for Christ Demands* (West Beach, South Australia: Eureka Press, 1979), 12.

27. David Berg, *Judah on Pearly Gate and the Doctrine of Annihilation: DO 2142*, 2142:7–10.

28. Although most Christian scholars and theologians view these individuals as being in error, they are still considered Christian as long as they hold to all of the other doctrines that directly affect one's identification of and relationship to God (e.g., the Trinity, Christ's deity, the virgin birth, salvation by grace alone through faith, Jesus' bodily resurrection).

29. *Seventh-Day Adventists Believe. . . ,* 370–71.

30. Fernando, *Crucial Questions about Hell*, 41–42.

31. Roger Nicole, "Universalism: Will Everyone Be Saved?" *Christianity Today*, 20 March 1987, 34.

32. Hodge, *Systematic Theology*, vol. 3, 874.

33. Habermas and Mooreland, *Immortality*, 170–71.

34. Mark Twain, *Autobiography*, ed. Charles Neider (1959), quoted in Robert Andrews, *The Columbia Dictionary of Quotations*, 222.

35. Packer, in Fernando, *Crucial Questions about Hell*, xi.

36. McConkie, *Mormon Doctrine*, 816.

37. Ibid., 755.

38. Martin, *Essential Christianity*, 115.

39. *Declaration of Unification Theological Affirmations at Barrytown, New York, October 14, 1976*, quoted in Frederick Sontag, *Sun Myung Moon and the Unification Church* (Nashville: Abingdon, 1977), 104.

40. Martin, *Essential Christianity*, 124.

41. George Barna, *The Index of Leading Spiritual Indicators* (Dallas: Word, 1996), 72.

42. John Leo, "Thou Shalt Not Command," *U.S. News and World Report*, 18 November 1996, 16.

43. Fernando, *Crucial Questions about Hell*, 95.

44. Robert A. Peterson, *Hell on Trial: The Case for Eternal Punishment* (Phillipsburg, N.J.: Presbyterian and Reformed Publishing, 1995), 236.

45. Fernando, *Crucial Questions about Hell*, 95.

46. J. Oswald Sanders, *Heaven: Better by Far* (Grand Rapids: Discovery House, 1993), 21.

47. Donald Guthrie, *New Testament Theology* (Downers Grove, Ill.: InterVarsity Press, 1981), 887.

48. Sanders, *Heaven: Better by Far*, 68.

49. Ibid., 22–23.

50. Peterson, *Hell on Trial*, 242.

Chapter 11: Apocalypse Now

1. Tim Weber, quoted in Steve Rabey, "Warning: The End Is Near, Again," *Gaz-ette Telegraph*, 28 December 1991, sec. D, p. 2.

2. Daniel Cohen, *Waiting for the Apocalypse* (New York: Prometheus Books, 1983), 49.

3. These prophetic dates have been discussed in several books that deal with false prophecies and their history. Among the best are: Gary DeMar, *Last Days Madness* (Atlanta: American Vision, 1994); Oropeza, *99 Reasons*; Chandler, *Doomsday*; William A. Alnor, *Soothsayers of the Second Advent* (Old Tappan, N.J.: Revell, 1989); and Carl E. Armerding and W. Ward Gasque, eds., *A Guide to Biblical Prophecy*, rev. ed. (Peabody, Mass.: Hendrickson, 1989).

4. Tim Callahan, "The Fall of the Soviet Union and the Changing Game of Biblical Prophecy," *Skeptic* 3, no. 2 (1995): 92–97; Edmund D. Cohen, "Harold Camping and the Stillborn Apocalypse," *Free Inquiry* 15, no. 1 (1994/95): 35–40.

5. Vine, Unger, and White, *Vine's Complete Expository Dictionary*, 532.

6. Charles Taze Russell, *Millenial Dawn*, vol. 4 (Allegheny, Pa.: Watch Tower Bible and Tract Society, 1897), 621; compare J. F. Rutherford, *Prophecy* (Brooklyn, N.Y.: Watch Tower Bible and Tract Society, 1929), 65. Rutherford wrote: "The Scriptural proof is that the second presence of the Lord Jesus Christ began in A.D. 1874."

7. *Zion's Watchtower and Herald of Christ's Presence*, 15 January 1892, 21–23, as reprinted in *The Watchtower's* 1919 reprints, vol. 2 (Allegheny, Pa.: Watch Tower Bible and Tract Society, 1919), 1355; *Zion's Watchtower and Herald of Christ's Presence*, 15 July 1894, 226–31, as reprinted in *The Watchtower's* 1919 reprints, vol. 2, 1677.

8. J. F. Rutherford, *Millions Now Living Will Never Die!* (Brooklyn, N.Y.: International Bible Students Association), 89–90, 97. The International Bible Students Association was a name under which early Jehovah's Witnesses gathered together for Bible studies and meetings. It eventually became the name of a British corporation

started by Charles Taze Russell, the man whose teachings eventually gave rise to the Jehovah's Witnesses. The British corporation continues to function today under the direction of the Watch Tower Bible and Tract Society.

9. Joseph Smith, *History of the Church,* vol. 2 (1948; reprint, Salt Lake City: Deseret Books, 1976), 182.

10. Louis Farrakhan, speech, 14 January 1991, cited in "So You Think," 1991, quoted in Mattias Gardell, *In the Name of Elijah Muhammad* (Durham, N.C.: Duke University Press, 1996), 162.

11. David Berg, *70-Years Prophecy: No. 156,* 1 March 1972, 156:9–12.

12. Moon, *Master Speaks,* quoted in Sontag, *Sun Myung Moon,* 120, 122, 126.

13. Oropeza, *99 Reasons,* 41–42.

14. Charles F. Richter, quoted in Cohen, *Waiting for the Apocalypse,* 197.

15. Oropeza, *99 Reasons,* 78.

16. James Cornell, *The Great International Disaster Book* (New York: Pocket Books, 1979), 131.

17. *Seneca Ad Lucilium Epistulae Morales,* trans. Richard M. Gummere, vol. 2 (London: 1920), 437, quoted in DeMar, *Last Days Madness,* 252.

18. Hal Lindsey, *The 1980s: Countdown to Armageddon* (King of Prussia, Pa.: Westgate Press, 1980), 30; compare Hal Lindsey, *Apocalypse Planet Earth* (Torrance, Calif. Jeremiah Films: 1990), video.

19. J. R. Church, *Hidden Prophecies in the Song of Moses* (Oklahoma City: Prophecy Publications, 1991), 106, cited in Oropeza, *99 Reasons,* 77.

20. Noah Hutchings (Southwest Radio Church), appeal letter, n.d., quoted in Oropeza, *99 Reasons,* 77.

21. Jack Van Impe, *The AIDS Cover-Up,* TV soundtrack, 1986, quoted in Chandler, *Doomsday,* 157.

22. Technically, the worst case of pestilence—the Plague of Justinian—occurred in A.D. 500–650 throughout the Middle East, Europe, and Asia. Although it took the lives of an estimated 100 million people, it is not considered more devastating than the Black Death because it was a *series* of bubonic plague outbreaks rather than one outbreak that continued to spread, as in the case of the Black Death.

23. Cornell, *The Great International Disaster Book,* 183–84.

24. Barbara Tuchman, *A Distant Mirror: The Calamitous 14th Century* (London, 1979), xiii, quoted in DeMar, *Last Days Madness,* 249.

25. Philip Schaff, *The Middle Ages,* vol. 4 of *History of the Christian Church* (Grand Rapids: Eerdmans, 1949), 100.

26. Ibid., 100–101.

27. Cornell, *The Great International Disaster Book,* 155.

28. Famine chart adapted from *Compton's Living Encyclopedia,* America Online.

29. DeMar, *Last Days Madness,* 253.

30. Ibid., 254.

31. Carl Olof Jonsson and Wolfgang Herbst, *The Sign of the Last Days—When?* (Atlanta: Commentary Press, 1987), 147.

32. D. Brent Sandy, "Did Daniel See Mussolini?" *Christianity Today,* 8 February 1993, 36.

33. F. F. Bruce, foreword to Armerding and Gasque, *A Guide to Biblical Prophecy,* 7.

34. J. R. Church, "Chronology of the End Time," *Prophecy in the News* (November 1994), 4, 6.

35. Terry Cook, *Satan's System: 666* (Terry Cook Productions, 1994), video.

36. Richard Abanes, *American Militias: Rebellion, Racism, and Religion* (Downers Grove, Ill.: InterVarsity, 1996).

37. Edgar Whisenant, *On Borrowed Time* (Nashville: World Bible Society, 1988); *88 Reasons Why the Rapture Could Be in 1988* (Nashville: World Bible Society, 1988).

38. Edgar Whisenant, quoted in *A Critique on the 1988 Rapture Theory* (Oklahoma City: Southwest Radio Church, 1988), 2.

39. Hart Armstrong, "Till There Is No Remedy," tract #43222 (Wichita, Kans.:

Christian Communications, 1988), 12, quoted in Alnor, 29.

40. Alnor, *Soothsayers of the Second Advent*, 28.

41. Edgar Whisenant, quoted in Joe Drape, "Ready or Not, the Rapture Didn't Come," *Atlanta Journal and Constitution*, 14 September 1988, sec. A, p. 1, quoted in DeMar, *Last Days Madness*, 48.

42. Dean C. Halverson, "88 Reasons: What Went Wrong?" *Christian Research Journal* 11, no. 2 (fall 1988): 14; compare "Rapture Seer Hedges on Latest Guess," *Christianity Today*, 21 October 1988, 43.

43. Chandler, *Doomsday*, 273.

44. John Hinkle, *Praise the Lord*, 25 January 1994, TBN.

45. Paul Crouch, "Send Us around the World," 2, quoted in Hank Hanegraaff, "D-Day Declarations," *Christian Research Journal* 18, no. 2 (fall 1995): 54.

46. Crouch, "Send Us around the World," quoted in Hanegraaff, "D-Day Declarations," 54.

47. John Hinkle, "Further Message from John J. Hinkle concerning 6/9/94," 15 June 1994, quoted in Hanegraaff, "D-Day Declarations," 54.

48. *Zion's Watchtower and Herald of Christ's Presence* (February 1881), 3, as reprinted in *The Watchtower's* 1919 reprints, vol. 1, 188; *Zion's Watchtower and Herald of Christ's Presence* (August 1883), 1, as reprinted in *The Watchtower's* 1919 reprints, vol. 1, 513; *Zion's Watchtower and Herald of Christ's Presence*, 15 July 1906, 230–31, as reprinted in *The Watchtower's* 1919 reprints, vol. 5, 3822.

49. Harold Camping, *1994?* (New York: Vantage Press, 1992), 533.

50. Camping, *1994?* xv.

51. Camping, quoted in *New York Times*, and reprinted in *Buffalo News*, 16 July 1994, cited in Barry Karr, "It's the End of the World (And I Feel Fine)," *Skeptical Briefs*, internet edition at http://www.csicop.org/sb/9409/endofworld.html.

52. Camping, quoted in David Briggs, "Broadcaster Sees World's Sign-Off," *Orange County Register*, 15 July 1994, news section, p. 6.

53. Camping, quoted in Perrucci Ferraiuolo, "Could '1994' Be the End of Family Radio?" *Christian Research Journal* 16, no. 1 (summer 1993): 6.

54. Ferraiuolo, "Could '1994' Be the End?" 5.

55. Lester Sumrall, *I Predict 2000 A.D.* (South Bend, Ind.: LeSEA Publishing Co., 1987), 74.

56. Colin Deal, *Christ Returns by 1988: 101 Reasons* (Rutherford College, N.C.: Colin Deal, 1979), 158.

57. Alnor, *Soothsayers of the Second Advent*, 135–42; DeMar, *Last Days Madness*, 18; Oropeza, *99 Reasons*, 57.

58. Jack Van Impe, "Messiah 1975? The Tribulation 1976?" *The Jack Van Impe Crusade Newsletter* (April 1975), 1, quoted in DeMar, *Last Days Madness*, 99.

59. Jack Van Impe, *A.D. 2000: The End?* (Troy, Mich.: Jack Van Impe Ministries, 1990).

60. Rabey, "Warning: The End Is Near, Again," sec. D, p. 1 compare Oropeza, *99 Reasons*, 89.

61. Oropeza, *99 Reasons*, 89.

62. *Rapture!* (Los Angeles: Tabera World Missions, n.d.), 3–4.

63. Van Impe, *A.D.. 2000: The End?*

64. Jack Van Impe, *2001: On the Edge of Eternity* (Dallas: Word, 1996), 16.

65. Advertisement for Van Impe's video *2001: Countdown to Eternity*, *Bookstore Journal* (July 1995): 40.

66. David and Michele, letter to the Christian Research Institute, 7 December 1992, quoted in Oropeza, *99 Reasons*, 32–33.

67. To borrow Alnor's book title, *Soothsayers of the Second Advent*.

68. Mark Noll, "Misreading the Signs of the Times," *Christianity Today*, 6 February 1987, 10–11.

69. DeMar, *Last Days Madness*, 21–22.

70. Ross Winkle, "Here Comes the End Again," *Signs of the Times* (October 1991): quoted in Chandler, *Doomsday*, 296.

Chapter 12:
Onward Christian Soldiers

1. Hedda Lark, quoted in Martin E. Marty, "An Old New Age in Publishing," *The Christian Century*, 18 November 1987, 1019.

2. Steve Proffitt, "Karen Armstrong," *Los Angeles Times*, 22 December 1996, sec. M, p. 3.

3. Gergen, "A Pilgrimage for Spirituality," 80.

4. "National News Shorts," *EP News Service*, 9 December 1994, p. 10.

5. Eugene Taylor, "Desperately Seeking Spirituality," *Psychology Today* (November/December 1994): 56, 64.

6. Bob Ortega, "Research Institute Shows People a Way out of Their Bodies," *Wall Street Journal*, 20 September 1994, sec. A, p. 1.

7. Winston Churchill, speech before the House of Commons, 17 May 1916. Internet text available from The Churchill Society, http://www.churchill-society-london.org.uk/enquiry.htm.

8. Adolf Hitler, quoted in Martin, *Cult-Proofing Your Kids*, 106.

Selected Bibliography

Abanes, Richard. *American Militias: Rebellion, Racism, and Religion*. Downers Grove, Ill.: InterVarsity, 1996.
———. *Embraced by the Light and the Bible*. Camp Hill, Pa: Horizon Books, 1994.
———. *Journey into the Light*. Grand Rapids: Baker, 1996.
Ankerberg, John, and John Weldon. *The Secret Teachings of Freemasonry*, 1989. Reprint, Chicago: Moody, 1990.
Archer, Gleason. *Encyclopedia of Bible Difficulties*. Grand Rapids: Zondervan, 1982.
Bancroft, Emory H. *Elemental Theology*. 1960. Reprint, edited by Ronald B. Mayer, Grand Rapids: Kregel, 1996.
Barna, George. *The Index of Leading Spiritual Indicators*. Dallas: Word, 1996.
Berkhof, Louis. *The History of Christian Doctrines*. 1937. Reprint, Carlisle, Pa.: The Banner of Truth Trust, 1991.
———. *Systematic Theology*. 1939. Reprint, Grand Rapids: Eerdmans, 1993.
Blanchard, John. *Whatever Happened to Hell?* Wheaton: Crossway, 1995.
Bowman, Robert. *Why You Should Believe in the Trinity*. Grand Rapids: Baker, 1989.
Bruce, F. F. *The Gospel of John*. London: Pickering and Inglis, 1983.
———. *The New Testament Documents: Are They Reliable?* Grand Rapids: Eerdmans, 1977.
Carson, D. A., and John D. Woodbridge, eds. *Scripture and Truth*. Grand Rapids: Baker, 1983.
Chandler, Russell. *Doomsday*. Ann Arbor, Mich.: Servant Publications, 1993.
———. *Understanding the New Age*. 1991. Reprint, Grand Rapids: Zondervan, 1993.
Connelly, Douglas. *Afterlife*. Downers Grove, Ill.: InterVarsity, 1995.
Crockett, William, ed. *Four Views of Hell*. Grand Rapids: Zondervan, 1992.
Douglas, J. D., and Merrill C. Tenney, eds. *The New International Dictionary of the Bible*. Grand Rapids: Zondervan, 1987.
Elwell, Walter A., ed. *Baker Encyclopedia of the Bible*. 2 vols. 1988. Reprint, Grand Rapids: Baker, 1995.
———. *Evangelical Dictionary of Theology*. 1984. Reprint, Grand Rapids: Baker, 1996.
Enroth, Ronald. *Churches That Abuse*. Grand Rapids: Zondervan, 1992.
———. *Evangelizing the Cults*. Ann Arbor, Mich.: Servant Publications, 1990.
———. *The Lure of the Cults*. 1979. Reprint, Chappaqua, N.Y.: Christian Herald Books, 1987.
———. *Youth, Brainwashing, and Extremist Cults*. Grand Rapids: Zondervan, 1977.
Erickson, Millard. *Christian Theology*. 1983. Reprint, Grand Rapids: Baker, 1989.

Fernando, Ajith. *Crucial Questions about Hell*. Wheaton: Crossway, 1994.
Geisler, Norman L., and William E. Nix. *A General Introduction to the Bible*. 1968. Reprint,
    Chicago: Moody, 1986.
Gomes, Alan W. *Unmasking the Cults*. Grand Rapids: Zondervan, 1995.
Grenz, Stanley J. *Theology for the Community of God*. Nashville: Broadman and Holman,
    1994.
Groothuis, Doug. *Jesus in an Age of Controversy*. Eugene, Ore.: Harvest House, 1996.
Grudem, Wayne. *Systematic Theology*. Grand Rapids: Zondervan, 1994.
Guthrie, Donald. *New Testament Theology*. Downers Grove, Ill.: InterVarsity, 1981.
Harrison, Everett F., ed. *Baker's Dictionary of Theology*, 1960. Reprint, Grand Rapids:
    Baker, 1994.
Hodge, Charles. *Systematic Theology*. 3 vols. Grand Rapids: Eerdmans, 1995.
Keil, C. F., and F. Delitzsch. *Biblical Commentary on the Old Testament*. 10 vols. Grand
    Rapids: Eerdmans, 1968.
Ladd, George Eldon. *A Theology of the New Testament*. 1974. Reprint, Grand Rapids:
    Eerdmans, 1993.
Lewis, Gordon. *Confronting the Cults*. Grand Rapids: Baker, 1975.
Lightner, Robert P. *Handbook of Evangelical Theology*. Grand Rapids: Kregel, 1995.
McDowell, Josh, and Don Stewart. *Answers to Tough Questions*. 1980. Reprint, San
    Bernardino, Calif.: Here's Life Publishers, 1983.
———. *Handbook of Today's Religions*. 1983. Reprint, San Bernardino, Calif.: Here's Life
    Publishers, 1992.
McGrath, Alister. *Explaining Your Faith*. 1988. Reprint, Grand Rapids: Baker, 1995.
Martin, Walter. *Essential Christianity*. 1962. Reprint, Ventura, Calif.: Regal, 1980.
———. *The Kingdom of the Cults*. 1965. Reprint, Minneapolis: Bethany, 1985.
———. *The Rise of the Cults*. Grand Rapids: Zondervan, 1955.
Miller, Elliot. *A Crash Course on the New Age Movement*. Grand Rapids: Baker, 1989.
Oropeza, B. J. *99 Reasons Why No One Knows When Christ Will Return*. Downers Grove,
    Ill.: InterVarsity, 1994.
Packer, J. I. *Concise Theology*. Wheaton: Tyndale House, 1993.
———. *"Fundamentalism" and the Word of God*. Grand Rapids: Eerdmans, 1958.
Pentecost, J. Dwight. *Things Which Become Sound Doctrine*. 1965. Reprint, Grand Rapids:
    Kregel, 1996.
Peterson, Robert A. *Hell On Trial: The Case for Eternal Punishment*. Phillipsburg, N.J.:
    Presbyterian and Reformed Publishing, 1995.
Plantinga, Cornelius, Jr. *Not the Way It's Supposed to Be: A Breviary of Sin*. Grand Rapids:
    Eerdmans, 1995.
Reid, Daniel G., Robert D. Linder, Bruce L. Shelley, and Harry S. Stout. *Dictionary of
    Christianity in America*. Downers Grove, Ill.: InterVarsity Press, 1990.
Rhodes, Ron. *Christ Before the Manger*. Grand Rapids: Baker, 1992.
Richards, Lawrence O. *Expository Dictionary of Bible Words*. 1985. Reprint, Grand Rapids:
    Zondervan, 1991.
Robertson, Irvine. *What the Cults Believe*. 1966. Reprint, Chicago: Moody, 1991.
Sanders, J. Oswald. *Heaven: Better by Far*. Grand Rapids: Discovery House, 1993.
Schaff, Philip. *The Creeds of Christendom*. 3 vols. Grand Rapids: Baker, 1996.
———. *History of the Christian Church*. 8 vols. Grand Rapids: Eerdmans, 1949.
Sproul, R. C. *Essential Truths of the Christian Faith*. Wheaton: Tyndale House, 1992.
———. *Faith Alone*. Grand Rapids: Baker, 1995.
Thomas, Robert L., and Stanley N. Gundry, eds. *A Harmony of the Gospels*. Chicago:
    Moody, 1978.
Torrey, R. A., A. C. Dixon et al. *The Fundamentals*. 4 vols. Grand Rapids: Baker, 1996.

Scripture Index

Subject Index

235

Richard Abanes is a nationally recognized cult researcher/specialist who has appeared on numerous radio and television talk shows across the country, including *Hard Copy, EXTRA, Rolanda,* and the Fox Television Network special "Millennium Prophecies." He has also been quoted as a cult researcher in several notable publications, including the *New York Times* and the *Chicago Tribune.* His articles have appeared in *Christianity Today, Charisma,* and the *Christian Research Journal.*

Abanes is a member of the Evangelical Press Association, Investigative Reporters and Editors, Inc., and the Society of Professional Journalists. He may be contacted by writing to: The Religious Information Center, P.O. Box 80961, Rancho Santa Margarita, CA 92688; e-mail: raric@aol.com; web site: http://www.geocities.com/Athens/Delphi/1419